THE ILLUSTRATED
CHILDREN'S
BIBLE

Written by Janice Emmerson
Illustrations by Netscribes
Printed in China

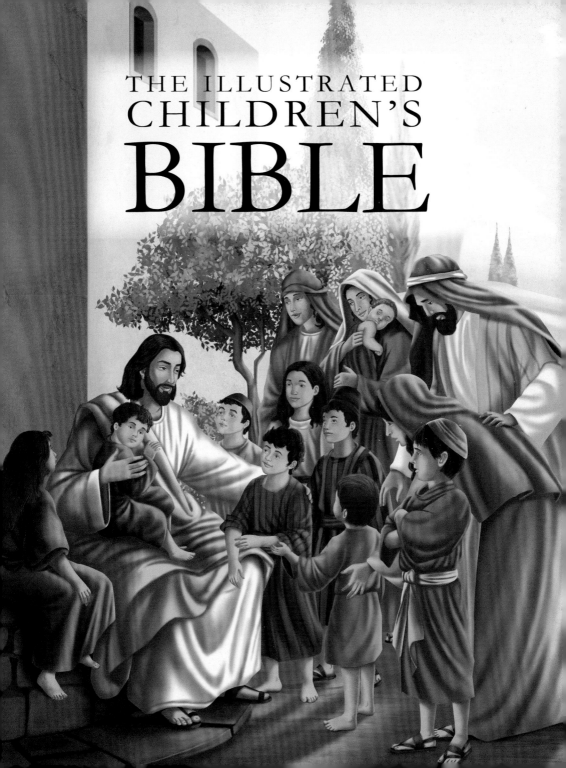

THE ILLUSTRATED
CHILDREN'S
BIBLE

CONTENTS

Old Testament

MOSES AND THE EXODUS

THE RISE OF ISRAEL

THE TIME OF THE PROPHETS

New Testament

THE EARLY CHURCH

THE OLD
TESTAMENT

Black Sea

MACEDONIA

Troy

LYDIA

HITTITES

Athens

Tarsus

CRETE

CYPRUS

PHOENICIA

The Great Sea
(Mediterranean)

Sidon

Tyre

Sea
Gali

Caesarea

ISRA

Samaria

Joppa

Jeri

Jerusalem

Dead
Sea

PHILISTIA

JUDAH

EDOM

Alexandria

THE OLD
TESTAMENT
WORLD

EGYPT

Sinai
Desert

MIDIAN

Mt Sinai

Red Sea

River Nile

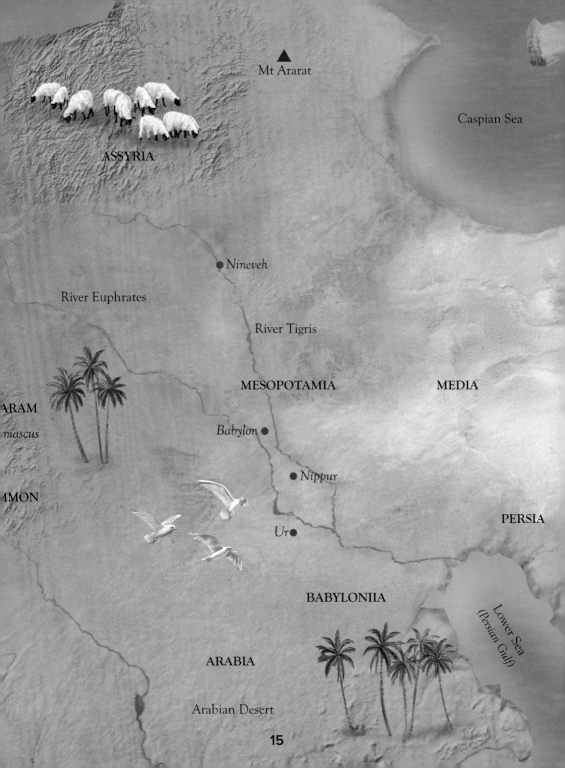

Mt Ararat

Caspian Sea

ASSYRIA

● Nineveh

River Euphrates

River Tigris

MESOPOTAMIA

MEDIA

ARAM

mascus

Babylon ●

● Nippur

MMON

PERSIA

Ur ●

BABYLONIIA

Lower Sea
(Persian Gulf)

ARABIA

Arabian Desert

15

GOD MAKES THE WORLD

Genesis 1-2

In the beginning, there was nothing at all. Then God created the heaven and the earth, but everything was still covered in darkness, so God said, "Let there be light," and there was light! God called the light day and the darkness night, and that was the first day and the first night!

In the days that followed, God separated the water from dry land, and covered the land with beautiful plants and trees. He made the sun to shine during the day and the moon and stars to light up the night sky.

Then God filled the seas with enormous whales and shiny fish, leaping dolphins and wobbly jellyfish, and he filled the skies with colourful birds. He made animals of all shapes and sizes – swift cheetahs, slow tortoises, huge elephants, and many more.

Last of all, God made man and told him to take care of this wonderful world and all the creatures.

God was pleased with all he had made and done, so on the seventh day, he rested, and made that day a special day to rest and give thanks.

THE BEAUTIFUL GARDEN
Genesis 2

God created the beautiful Garden of Eden for Adam — a marvellous paradise filled with green grass, colourful plants and wonderful trees. God told Adam that he might help himself to fruit from any of these trees except for one: the Tree of Knowledge. But there were still plenty of other wonderful things for him to eat!

God brought all the animals and birds to Adam so that he could name them. But none of the animals were like him, and Adam was lonely, so God created a woman, Eve, to be his special friend.

18

19

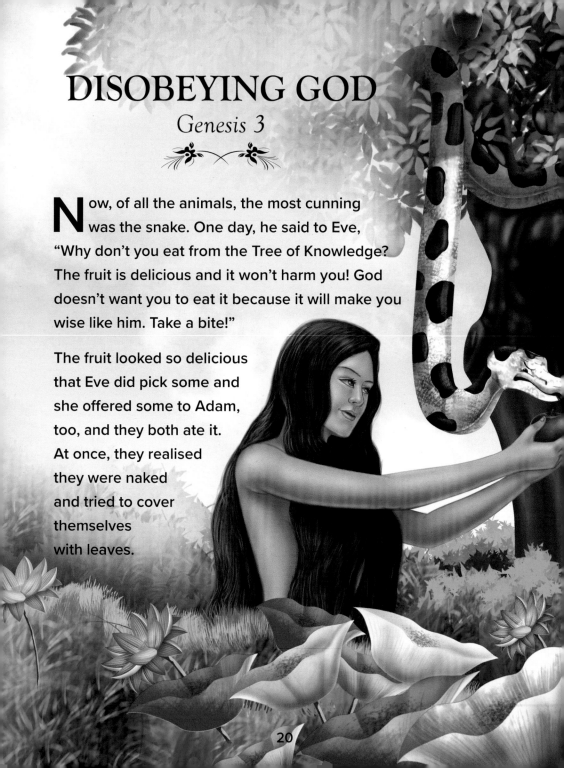

DISOBEYING GOD

Genesis 3

Now, of all the animals, the most cunning was the snake. One day, he said to Eve, "Why don't you eat from the Tree of Knowledge? The fruit is delicious and it won't harm you! God doesn't want you to eat it because it will make you wise like him. Take a bite!"

The fruit looked so delicious that Eve did pick some and she offered some to Adam, too, and they both ate it. At once, they realised they were naked and tried to cover themselves with leaves.

When God found Adam and Eve hiding behind some bushes, he knew what had happened and was very angry. He cursed the snake, and banished Adam and Eve from the Garden of Eden, telling them that from now on they would have to work hard to make their own food and clothes. Then he placed an angel with a flaming sword to stand guard at the entrance to the Garden.

CAIN AND ABEL

Genesis 4

Adam and Eve had two sons. Cain was a farmer who worked in the fields and Abel was a shepherd. One day, both Cain and Abel brought offerings to God. Abel brought the very best meat to offer to God and God was pleased, but he was not so pleased with the crops that Cain had brought.

Cain was very jealous of his brother, and in a fit of anger, he went with him into a field and killed him. When God asked him where his brother was, Cain answered him rudely, "How should I know? Am I my brother's keeper?"

But God saw Abel's blood on the ground and was angry. He punished Cain and sent him away from his home and family.

NOAH BUILDS THE ARK
Genesis 6

Many years passed, and soon there were lots of people in the world. But they were becoming more and more wicked and this made God very sad. He made up his mind to send a terrible flood to destroy everything that he had created.

But there was one good man on earth, who loved and obeyed God. His name was Noah and he had three sons. God told Noah to build an enormous boat, an ark, so that he and his family might be saved, along with two of every living creature.

People laughed at Noah for building a boat in the middle of the land, but he ignored them, for he trusted God.

THE FLOOD

Genesis 7-9

When the ark was finished, Noah loaded it with food for his family and the animals, and then God sent the animals to the ark, two by two, one male and one female of every kind of animal and bird that lived upon the earth or flew in the skies.

When they were all safely in, it began to rain. And how it rained! Water poured down from the skies and covered all the land. Every living creature was drowned. All the towns and cities were washed away. But the ark and its precious cargo floated free on a world of water.

For forty days and forty nights it rained. Then, at last, it stopped. After a while, the flood waters began to go down. Noah sent out a dove and when it returned with an olive leaf in its beak, Noah knew that the flood was over, for the trees were growing again.

Then it was time for Noah and the animals to leave the ark. Noah was filled with gratitude and God promised him that he would never again send such a dreadful flood. He put a beautiful rainbow in the sky to remind him of this promise.

THE TOWER OF BABEL

Genesis 11

To begin with, the whole world had only one language, so everyone could understand everyone else. There came a time when a group of Noah's descendants decided to settle down and build a city which would be famous throughout the land, with a tower that would reach to the heavens.

But when God saw what they were doing, he was not happy. He feared they were becoming too proud and vain – they had forgotten about God.

So God made them unable to understand one another. Soon a great babble of voices was heard all over the city, with everyone speaking in a different language. No one could understand his neighbour.

In all the confusion, building stopped. The wonderful tower was left unfinished, the people scattered far and wide, and the tower became known as the Tower of Babel.

GOD CALLS ABRAHAM

Genesis 12-13

A braham was a good man, who trusted in God. God asked Abraham to leave his home, his country and his family and go to another land. He promised to bless him and to make him the father of a great nation.

Abraham had a good home, with large flocks of sheep and cattle, but when God told him to leave, he took his wife Sarah, his nephew Lot, and his servants and set out for Canaan.

Along the way, God appeared to Abraham and told him, "I will give this land to your children." Sarah and Abraham had been unable to have children, but Abraham was overjoyed at this news and built an altar to God and praised him.

Later, Abraham took his family to Egypt, for there was a terrible famine. By the time he left Egypt to return to Canaan he had become very wealthy and owned many animals.

GOING SEPARATE WAYS

Genesis 13-14

Abraham and his nephew Lot had large flocks of cattle, sheep, and donkeys – so large that there wasn't enough grazing land for them all, and their herdsmen began to fight. Abraham decided that they would have to split up. He gave Lot the first choice of where to go, and Lot chose to leave Canaan and set off east to the fertile Jordan Valley. Abraham stayed in Canaan.

After Lot had left, God called Abraham to him. "Look as far as you can. All the land that you can

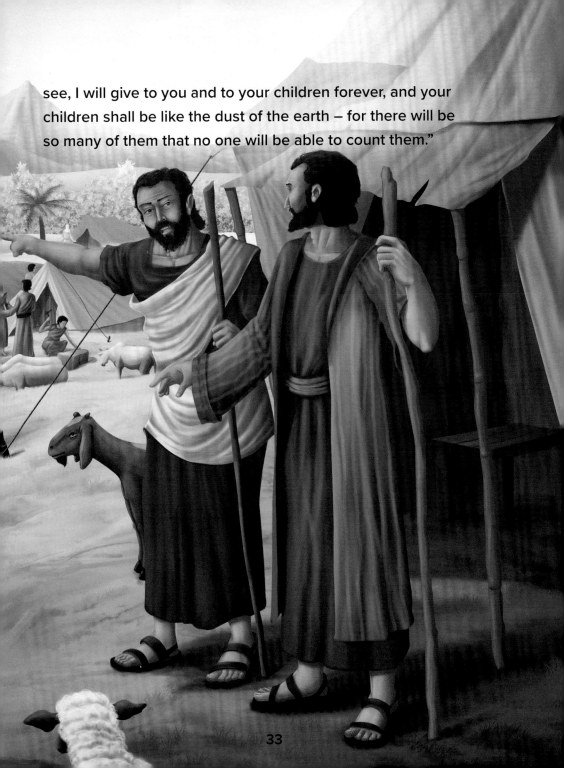

see, I will give to you and to your children forever, and your children shall be like the dust of the earth — for there will be so many of them that no one will be able to count them."

GOD'S PROMISE
Genesis 15-17

Abraham and his wife were very old and hadn't had a child, but Abraham trusted in God. God told him that he would be a father and that he would have too many descendants to count – as many as the stars in the sky – and that the land would belong to them. Then God told him to prepare a sacrifice.

That evening, God spoke to him again, telling him that his descendants would be slaves in a country not their own for four hundred years, but that they would at last be free and would return to their own land, and that those who had enslaved them would be punished.

When the sun had set and darkness had fallen, a smoking firepot with a blazing torch appeared and passed between the pieces of the sacrifice as a sign to Abraham from God.

ABRAHAM ENTERTAINS ANGELS

Genesis 18

Not long after this, Abraham saw three strangers passing by. He hurried out to meet them and offered to bring water to wash their feet, and food to eat while they rested in the shade of a nearby tree. Sarah baked some bread, while Abraham brought his choicest meat for the men to eat, and milk for them to drink.

Then one of the men, who was really God, asked Abraham where his wife was. When Abraham replied that she was inside the tent, God told him that he would come back within a year, and that Sarah would have given birth to a son.

Sarah was listening in the tent, and could not help laughing out loud, for she was far too old to have children. But God asked, "Why is Sarah laughing? Nothing is too hard for the Lord." Sure enough, nine months later Sarah gave birth to a baby boy, and named him Isaac, which means 'he laughs'!

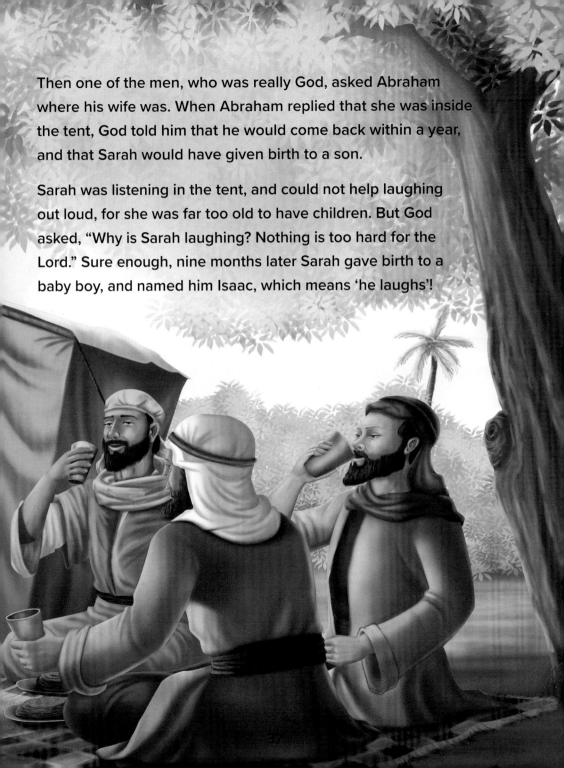

THE BAD CITIES
Genesis 18-19

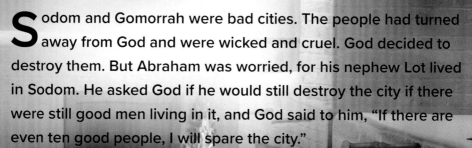

Sodom and Gomorrah were bad cities. The people had turned away from God and were wicked and cruel. God decided to destroy them. But Abraham was worried, for his nephew Lot lived in Sodom. He asked God if he would still destroy the city if there were still good men living in it, and God said to him, "If there are even ten good people, I will spare the city."

Lot was standing by the city gates when two strangers – angels in disguise – passed through. He begged them to spend the night in his house. He gave them water to wash their feet and prepared a meal for them, but an angry, violent crowd gathered, demanding that he send the strangers outside.

Lot begged them to leave the strangers alone, for they were his guests, but the mob became angry with Lot and the angels had to pull him back inside the house. Then they struck the crowd with blindness so that they could not find the door to break in.

GOD DESTROYS SODOM

Genesis 19

The angels warned Lot to leave the city with his wife and daughters that very night, as God was angry and the city would be punished. They took them by the hand and led them to safety, urging them to hurry, "Flee for your lives! Run to the mountains and don't look back!"

As Lot and his family hurried away, they could hear dreadful sounds, as a storm of burning sulphur rained down on the city. Nothing and no one survived – not one building, not one person. But Lot's wife could not help looking back, and as she did so, she was instantly turned into a pillar of stone. Lot and his daughters were the only ones to survive the destruction.

ISAAC IS BORN

Genesis 21

When Sarah was ninety years old, she gave birth to a baby boy, Isaac, just as God had promised. Abraham and Sarah were overjoyed, but Sarah believed her maidservant Hagar was making fun of her. She was so angry with her that she made Abraham send her away, along with her son, Ishmael, who was also Abraham's son.

Abraham was sad, but God told him things would work out for Ishmael, so he handed Hagar some food and water and sent her and Ishmael into the desert.

Soon all the water was gone and they began to weep. But the angel of God called to Hagar from heaven and said, "Do not be afraid, Hagar. God has heard the boy crying. Lift him up and take him by the hand, for he will be the father of a great nation."
Then God opened her eyes and she saw a well of water!

God was with the boy as he grew up. He lived in the desert and became an archer.

ABRAHAM IS TESTED
Genesis 22

Isaac grew up to be a fine young boy and his father and mother were very proud of him and thankful to God. But one day, God decided to test Abraham's faith. He told Abraham that he must offer the boy as a sacrifice!

Abraham was heartbroken, but his faith in God was absolute, and so he prepared everything, just as he had been commanded.

But as he lifted up his knife, suddenly an angel spoke to him, "Abraham, Abraham! Do not harm the boy! I know now that you love the Lord your God with all your heart, for you would be willing to give up your own son."

God sent a ram to be sacrificed in the boy's place, and the angel told Abraham that God would truly bless him and his descendants because of his faith.

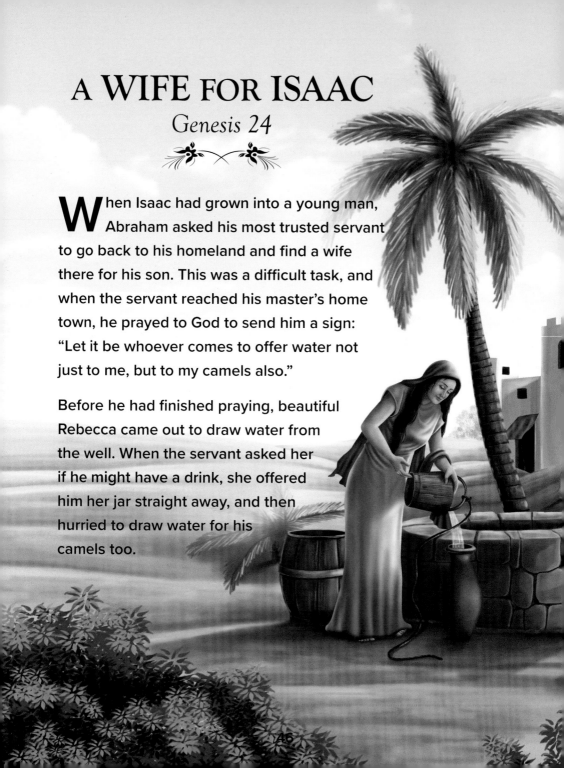

A WIFE FOR ISAAC

Genesis 24

When Isaac had grown into a young man, Abraham asked his most trusted servant to go back to his homeland and find a wife there for his son. This was a difficult task, and when the servant reached his master's home town, he prayed to God to send him a sign: "Let it be whoever comes to offer water not just to me, but to my camels also."

Before he had finished praying, beautiful Rebecca came out to draw water from the well. When the servant asked her if he might have a drink, she offered him her jar straight away, and then hurried to draw water for his camels too.

The servant thanked God for listening to his prayers. He then explained his mission to Rebecca, and when her father was asked, it was agreed that she should become Isaac's wife. When she travelled back to Canaan to meet her new husband, Isaac fell in love with her instantly, and she with him!

JACOB AND ESAU

Genesis 25-27

Rebecca was old before she fell pregnant, and when she did, it was with twins. They seemed to kick and push so much inside her that she was worried, but God told her that the two boys would one day be the fathers of two nations. The first born was a hairy boy, whom they named Esau, and his brother was called Jacob. When they grew up, Esau became a great hunter, while Jacob was quieter and spent more time at home. Isaac loved Esau, but Rebecca was especially fond of Jacob.

One day, Jacob was preparing a stew when his brother came in, ravenous after a long trip. Esau was so hungry that when Jacob told him that he could only have a plate of stew in exchange for his birthright, he agreed!

In later years, Jacob cheated his elder brother out of his father's blessing, too. When Isaac was very old and nearly blind, he wished to give his blessing to his eldest son Esau. Jacob, with the help of his mother, disguised himself as Esau. He wore goatskins around his arms so that he would be hairy like his brother, and when his father touched him, he believed him to be Esau and gave him his blessing to be in charge of the family when he died.

When Esau found out what had happened, he was so angry that he wanted to kill his younger brother, and so Rebecca sent Jacob away from home so that he would be safe.

JACOB'S DREAM

Genesis 28

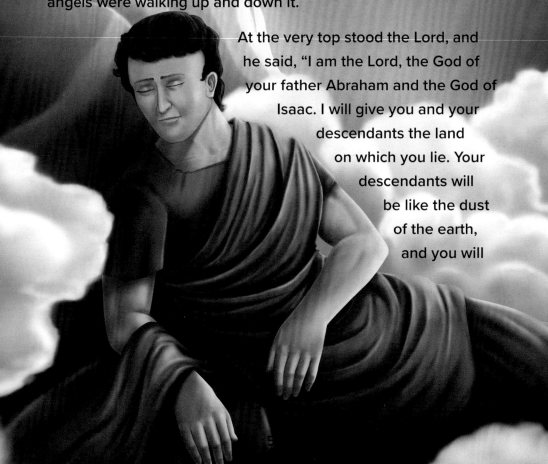

Jacob travelled to the house of his uncle Laban. On the way he stopped for the night. Using a hard stone as a pillow, he lay down to sleep. That night, he had a dream in which he saw a stairway resting on the earth, with its top reaching to heaven, and angels were walking up and down it.

At the very top stood the Lord, and he said, "I am the Lord, the God of your father Abraham and the God of Isaac. I will give you and your descendants the land on which you lie. Your descendants will be like the dust of the earth, and you will spread to the west and the east, to the north and the south. I am with you and will watch over you wherever you go, and I will bring you back to this land. I will not leave you until I have done what I have promised."

TRICKED INTO MARRIAGE

Genesis 29

Jacob worked in the house of his uncle Laban, and he fell in love with Laban's younger daughter, Rachel. His uncle agreed that if he worked for him for seven years, then at the end of that time, he could marry Rachel.

After seven years, the marriage took place, but when Jacob lifted the veil from his wife's face, it was not Rachel standing before him, but her elder sister Leah! He had been tricked!

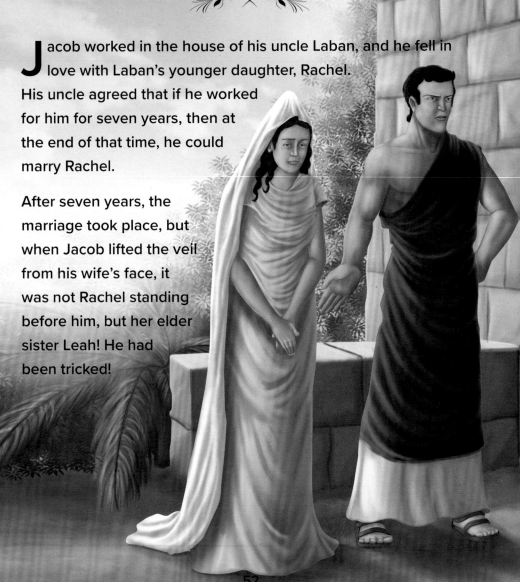

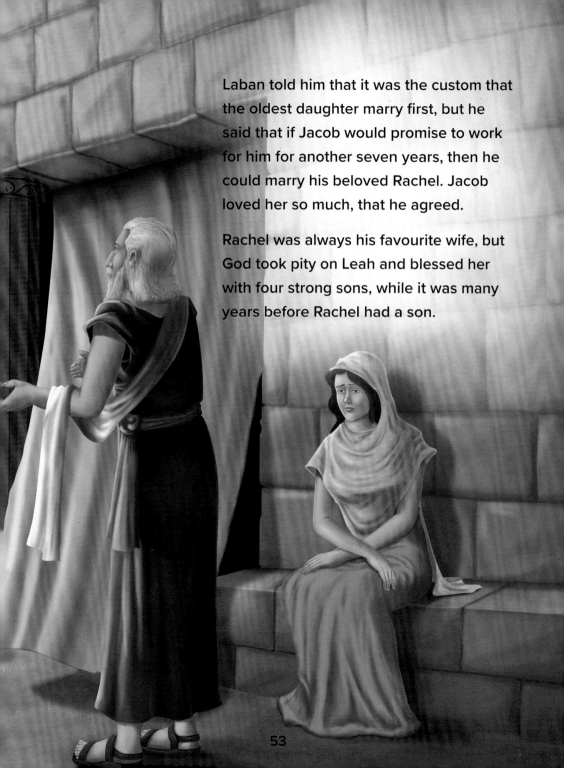

Laban told him that it was the custom that the oldest daughter marry first, but he said that if Jacob would promise to work for him for another seven years, then he could marry his beloved Rachel. Jacob loved her so much, that he agreed.

Rachel was always his favourite wife, but God took pity on Leah and blessed her with four strong sons, while it was many years before Rachel had a son.

PARTING WAYS

Genesis 30-31

Although Jacob felt it was time to return home, his uncle wanted him to stay. He agreed to give him, as his wages, all the marked or speckled animals in the herds, but then tried to cheat Jacob by rounding up any marked animals and sending them away with his sons, so that all the new animals would be born without marks!

But God told Jacob to place some fresh peeled branches in the animals water troughs when the strong, healthy animals came to drink, and all the new animals that were born to them were marked or speckled. In this way all the strong animals went to Jacob and all the weak animals went to Laban.

Jacob knew that his uncle would continue to cheat him, so one day, he set off for home, along with all his family, servants and animals. Laban chased after him, but in the end the two men agreed to let each other be.

WRESTLING WITH GOD

Genesis 32-33

Jacob was worried as he returned home with his family, for he did not know how his brother Esau would greet him. When a messenger said that Esau was coming to meet him with four hundred men, Jacob feared the worst. He sent some of his servants ahead with gifts for his brother to help appease him. Then he sent his family and everything he owned across the river. Jacob himself stayed behind alone to pray.

Suddenly a man appeared and the two of them wrestled together until daybreak. When the man saw that he could not overpower him, he touched Jacob's hip so that it was wrenched. He cried out to Jacob to let him go, but Jacob replied, "Not unless you bless me."

Then the man said, "Your name will no longer be Jacob, but Israel, because you have struggled with God and with men and have overcome."

When Jacob asked his name, he would give no reply, but

blessed Jacob, and Jacob understood that he had wrestled with God himself!

And when Jacob finally came face to face with his brother, he found that Esau had forgiven him and welcomed him with open arms.

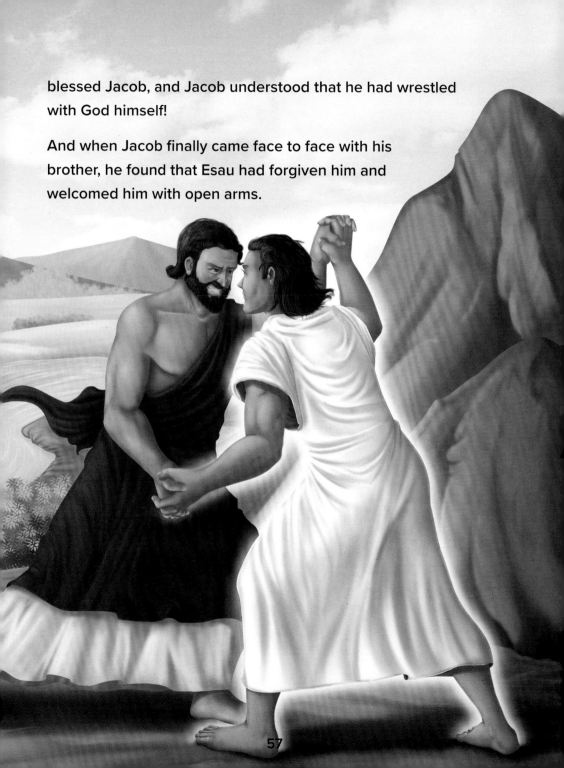

RETURNING TO BETHEL
Genesis 35-36

God spoke to Jacob and told him to go to Bethel. So Jacob travelled with his family and servants to Bethel, where he built an altar to God to thank him for his mercy.

When they left Bethel, Rachel, who was pregnant for the second time, went into labour, but things did not go smoothly. Before she breathed her last breath Rachel saw her lovely baby boy and named him Ben-Oni, although his father called him Benjamin. Jacob was heartbroken and built a pillar over her tomb.

Now Jacob had twelve sons: the sons of Leah, who were Reuben, Simeon, Levi, Judah, Issachar and Zebulun; Joseph and Benjamin who were the sons of

Rachel; Dan and Naphtali who were the sons of Rachel's maidservant; and Gad and Asher who were the sons of Leah's maidservant.

JOSEPH'S DREAMS
Genesis 37

Jacob lived in Canaan. He had twelve sons, but Joseph was his favourite, for he was the first son of Rachel, whom Jacob had loved above all his other wives. To show Joseph just how much he loved him, Jacob had a wonderful coat made for him, a long-sleeved robe covered with colourful embroidery.

His brothers were jealous, but what really angered them was when he began telling them of the dreams he had had: "Last night I dreamt that we were collecting sheaves of grain, when suddenly my sheaf stood up straight and yours all bowed down before it."

"What are you saying?" growled the brothers. "That you're going to rule over us some day? Be off with you!"

Joseph had another dream. "This time the sun and moon and eleven stars were bowing down to me," he told his family. Even Jacob became quite cross when he heard about Joseph's latest dream. "Do you really believe that your mother and I, and all your brothers are going to bow down before you? Don't get too big for your boots!" But Jacob did wonder to himself about what the dream might mean.

BROTHER FOR SALE

Genesis 37

Joseph's brothers had had enough. What with the fabulous coat, and now these dreadful dreams, they felt the time had come to get rid of their annoying brother. One day, when they were out in the fields, the brothers set upon him, tearing off his precious multi-coloured coat and throwing him in a deep pit. Then they sat down nearby to eat, deaf to his cries for help.

Shortly, they saw a caravan of Ishmaelite traders passing by on their camels on their way to Egypt, and quick as a flash they decided to sell Joseph to the traders.

Then they took his beautiful coat, ripped it into pieces and smeared it with the blood of a goat. Afterwards, they trooped home with long faces and showed the coat to their father, saying that Joseph had been killed by a wild animal. Jacob was heartbroken at the death of his beloved son.

POTIPHAR'S WIFE
Genesis 39

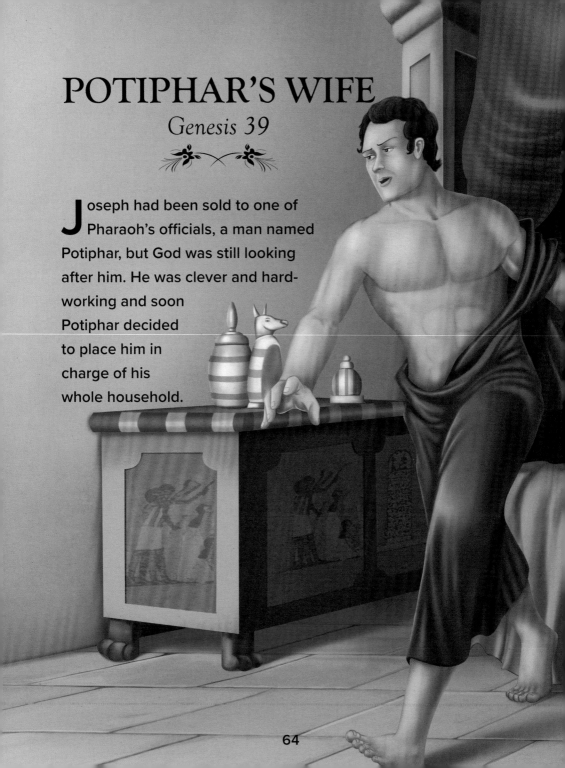

Joseph had been sold to one of Pharaoh's officials, a man named Potiphar, but God was still looking after him. He was clever and hard-working and soon Potiphar decided to place him in charge of his whole household.

But the peaceful times didn't last, for Potiphar's wife took a liking to Joseph, who was a handsome and strong young man. Joseph would have nothing to do with her advances, but one day, when he pulled away from her, in his haste he left his coat behind. When her husband came back, she showed him the coat and told him that Joseph had come to her bedroom to try to take advantage of her, but had run away when she screamed.

Potiphar was furious and threw poor Joseph into jail!

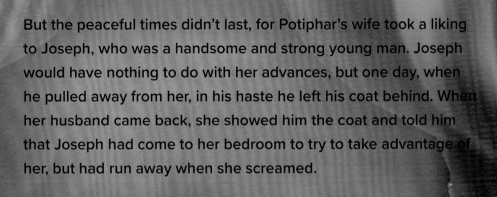

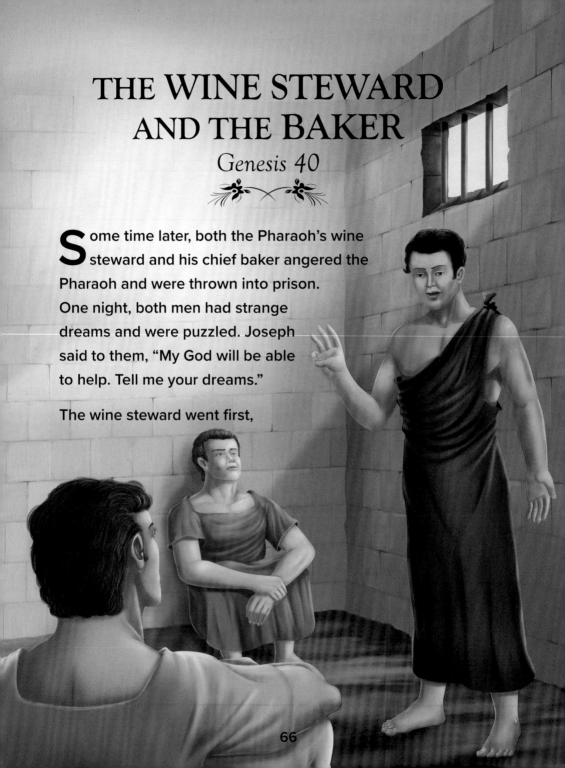

THE WINE STEWARD AND THE BAKER

Genesis 40

Some time later, both the Pharaoh's wine steward and his chief baker angered the Pharaoh and were thrown into prison. One night, both men had strange dreams and were puzzled. Joseph said to them, "My God will be able to help. Tell me your dreams."

The wine steward went first,

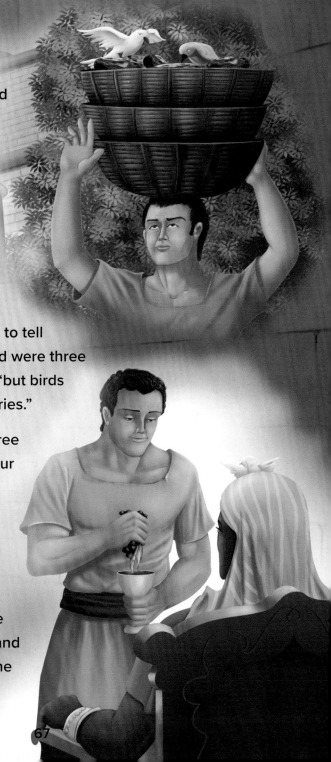

"In my dream I saw a vine, with three branches covered in grapes. I took the grapes and squeezed them into Pharaoh's cup."

Joseph told him that within three days, Pharaoh would pardon him and take him back – and he asked the steward to remember him.

Now the baker was anxious to tell his dream, too. "On my head were three baskets of bread," he said, "but birds were eating Pharaoh's pastries."

Joseph was sad. "Within three days Pharaoh will cut off your head, and the birds will eat your flesh."

Things turned out just as Joseph had foretold, for in three days it was Pharaoh's birthday, and on that day he pardoned the wine bearer and gave him back his job, but he hanged the chief baker.

PHARAOH'S DREAMS
Genesis 41

Joseph asked the wine bearer to remember him when he got out of prison, but two years passed before the Hebrew slave crossed his thoughts, and it happened like this:

One night, Pharaoh had a strange dream. He was standing by the Nile when out of the river came seven cows, healthy and fat, and they grazed among the reeds. After them, seven other

cows, ugly and thin, came up out of the Nile and stood beside them. Then the thin cows ate up the fat cows and yet looked just as thin and sickly as before.

Pharaoh had another dream. Seven healthy heads of grain were growing on a single stalk. Then seven more heads of grain sprouted and these were thin and scorched by the wind. The thin heads of grain swallowed up the seven healthy, full heads.

In the morning, Pharaoh felt worried. He sent for all the magicians and wise men of Egypt, but no one could interpret the dreams.

69

WHAT CAN IT MEAN?

Genesis 41

I t was then that the wine bearer remembered Joseph, and the slave was brought before mighty Pharaoh, who asked him to explain his dream.

"I cannot do it," Joseph replied to Pharaoh, "but God will be able to explain."

Once Pharaoh had told his dream, Joseph replied, "These two dreams are really one and the same. The seven cows and the seven heads of grain are seven years. The land will be blessed with seven years of healthy crops and bountiful harvests, but they will be followed by seven years of dreadful famine. You will need to plan carefully to prepare for what lies ahead."

Pharaoh spoke to his advisors, then turned to Joseph, saying, "It is clear to me that you are the man we need. Since God has made all this known to you, I will put you in charge of my land. You will be second only to me in all of Egypt."

And with that, Pharaoh put his own signet ring on Joseph's finger, a gold chain around his neck and dressed him in fine linen.

A WISE LEADER

Genesis 41

Joseph was thirty years old when he entered the service of Pharaoh, King of Egypt. Riding in a fine chariot, he travelled throughout the land making sure that food was put aside for the times of hardship ahead of them. Just as he had foretold, the country was blessed with seven years of bumper crops, and so much grain was stored in the cities that he gave up counting it.

After seven years, the famine began. When the people of Egypt began to run out of food, Pharaoh told them to go to Joseph.

Now Joseph opened up the storehouses and sold the corn that had been put away so carefully. No one in Egypt went hungry. In fact, there was so much food in Egypt that people from other countries travelled there to buy food, for the famine was severe throughout the world.

THE BROTHERS BUY GRAIN
Genesis 42-43

In Canaan, the famine had hit Joseph's family hard too. Jacob decided to send his sons to buy corn in Egypt. Only Benjamin stayed behind, for Jacob could not bear to lose his youngest son. When they reached Egypt, the brothers bowed down before Joseph. With his golden chain and fine clothes, they did not recognise him, but Joseph could see his dreams becoming reality, as they bowed their heads low and begged to buy food.

Joseph wanted to see if his brothers had changed at all, and so he planned to test their honesty and loyalty. He accused them of being spies, and when they protested their innocence, he agreed to let them go back to Canaan with corn, on condition that they returned with their youngest brother.

Jacob did not want to let Benjamin go, but in the end he had to agree, and so the brothers returned with more money to pay for the grain (for when they had opened the sacks, they had been horrified to find that the money they had taken with them to Egypt the first time to pay for the grain was still in them!)

THE LONG LOST BROTHER

Genesis 44-45

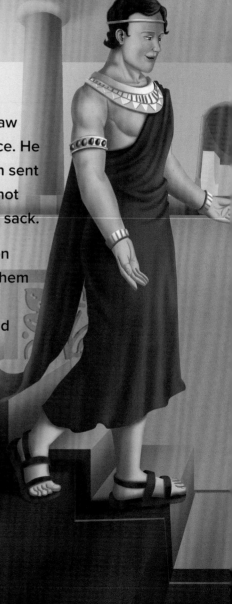

J oseph was so overcome when he saw Benjamin that he had to hide his face. He had his servants feed the brothers, then sent them on their way with more corn, but not before hiding a silver cup in Benjamin's sack.

The brothers were travelling home when guards came upon them and dragged them back to the palace. "Thieves!" shouted Joseph. "I treated you with kindness and you repay me by stealing!"

"There must be some mistake!" cried the brothers, but when the guards checked, there was the silver cup in Benjamin's sack. The brothers fell to their knees. "My Lord!" they cried, "take any one of us, but do not take Benjamin, for his father's heart would break!"

At this, Joseph knew that his brothers' hearts were no longer hard and so he hugged them. Amidst much weeping and amazement, he told them that he was their long lost brother, and that they should not feel too guilty for it had all been part of the Lord's plan. "I was sent to rule in Egypt so that you would not starve in Canaan!" he told them, and then sent for his father.

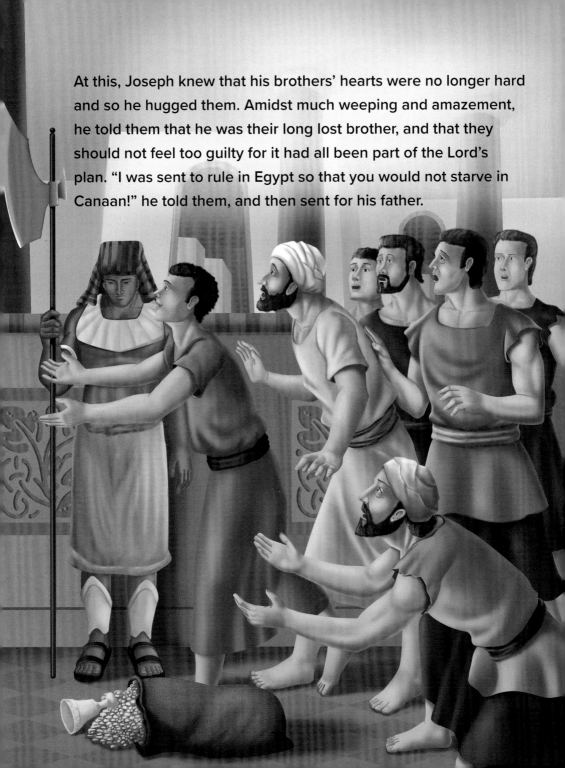

MOVING TO EGYPT

Genesis 46-47

Jacob gathered up all his belongings, his herds, flocks, and his family and travelled to Egypt. God spoke to him, telling him not to be scared of going to Egypt, for he would lead them out of Egypt once again when the time was right. By now, the members of Jacob's family were seventy in all!

Joseph came to meet his father in a great chariot, and led him back to Egypt, where he and his family were well treated and given land near the Canaan border to tend their animals.

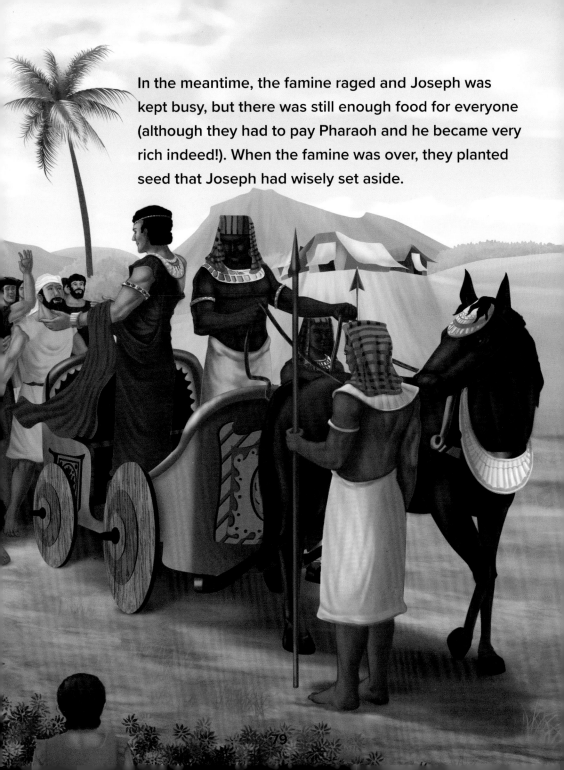

In the meantime, the famine raged and Joseph was kept busy, but there was still enough food for everyone (although they had to pay Pharaoh and he became very rich indeed!). When the famine was over, they planted seed that Joseph had wisely set aside.

THE DEATH OF JACOB

Genesis 48-50

Now Jacob was growing old. Before he died, he called all his sons together to give them each a special blessing, for they were to form the twelve tribes of Israel, and he named Joseph a 'prince among his brothers'.

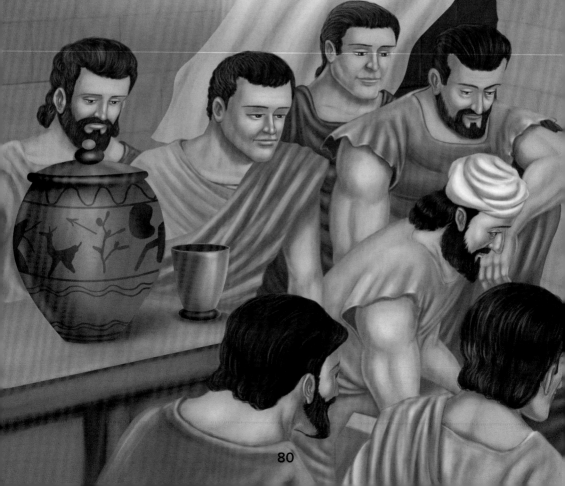

He made Joseph promise to bury him in Canaan, in the spot where
he had buried his wife Leah, and where Isaac and Rebecca were
buried before her, and Abraham and Sarah before them. When
Jacob had breathed his last breath, with Pharaoh's permission,
all Jacob's family, except the children and those who tended the
animals, set off to Canaan, where they buried their father Jacob,
also known as Israel.

SLAVES!

Exodus 1

The years passed, and in time Joseph and his brothers were long dead, but their families continued to grow and by now there were many, many Hebrews in Egypt. The new king believed that there were too many Hebrews in his country, and he feared that they would become too strong, so the Egyptians put guards over the Hebrews and turned them into slaves. They forced them to work the land and build for them.

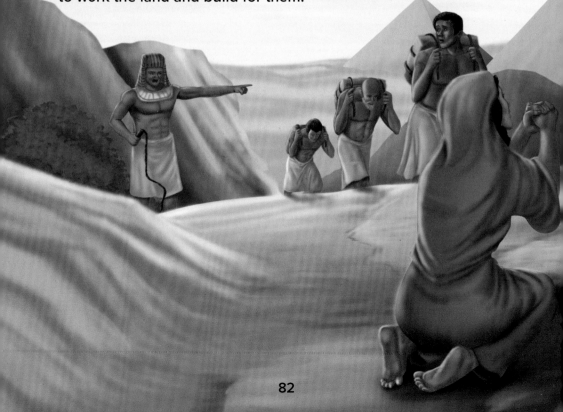

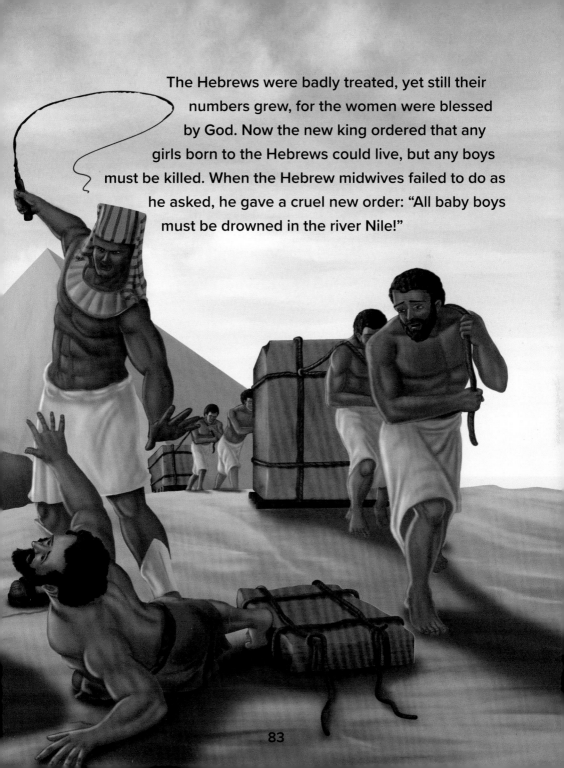

The Hebrews were badly treated, yet still their numbers grew, for the women were blessed by God. Now the new king ordered that any girls born to the Hebrews could live, but any boys must be killed. When the Hebrew midwives failed to do as he asked, he gave a cruel new order: "All baby boys must be drowned in the river Nile!"

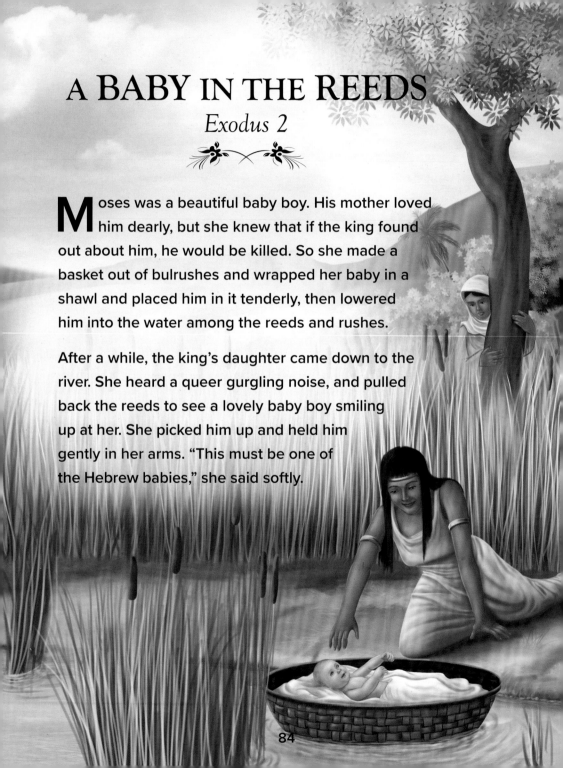

A BABY IN THE REEDS

Exodus 2

Moses was a beautiful baby boy. His mother loved him dearly, but she knew that if the king found out about him, he would be killed. So she made a basket out of bulrushes and wrapped her baby in a shawl and placed him in it tenderly, then lowered him into the water among the reeds and rushes.

After a while, the king's daughter came down to the river. She heard a queer gurgling noise, and pulled back the reeds to see a lovely baby boy smiling up at her. She picked him up and held him gently in her arms. "This must be one of the Hebrew babies," she said softly.

Moses' sister Miriam was secretly watching from nearby. Now she bravely stepped forward and offered to fetch someone to nurse the baby. When the princess nodded, Miriam darted off to find her own mother, and so it was that Miriam's mother looked after her own son, until he was old enough for the princess to take him to the palace.

THE BURNING BUSH

Exodus 3-4

When Moses grew up, he was shocked to see how the Egyptians treated his fellow Hebrews. After killing an Egyptian for beating a Hebrew slave, he had to leave Egypt, and became a shepherd. One day, while Moses was tending his sheep, he noticed that a nearby bush was on fire, yet the leaves of the bush were not burning! As he stepped closer, he heard the voice of God, "Take off your sandals, Moses, for this is holy ground. I am the God of your father, the God of Abraham, of Isaac and of Jacob." Moses hid his face in fear.

The Lord said, "I have come to rescue my people and bring them up out of Egypt into the Promised Land. You must go to Pharaoh and demand that he free them."

Moses was terrified at the thought of speaking to Pharaoh, but God told him that he would be with him, and that he should tell him that it was Yahweh* who sent him. He promised that he would perform many miracles so that in the end Pharaoh would let the Hebrews go.

Moses was scared, but God would not listen to his excuses and sent him back to Egypt, although he did send Moses' brother Aaron to help him.

* The Hebrew word *Yahweh* is a sacred name for God amongst the Jewish people and translates as *'I am who I am.'*

PHARAOH SAYS NO!

Exodus 5-7

When Moses and Aaron came before Pharaoh and said, "The God of Israel asks that you let his people go so that they may hold a festival to him in the desert," Pharaoh could not believe their nerve. "Who is this God of Israel? I don't know him and I will not let the Hebrews go!" He was so angry that he made the slaves work even harder.

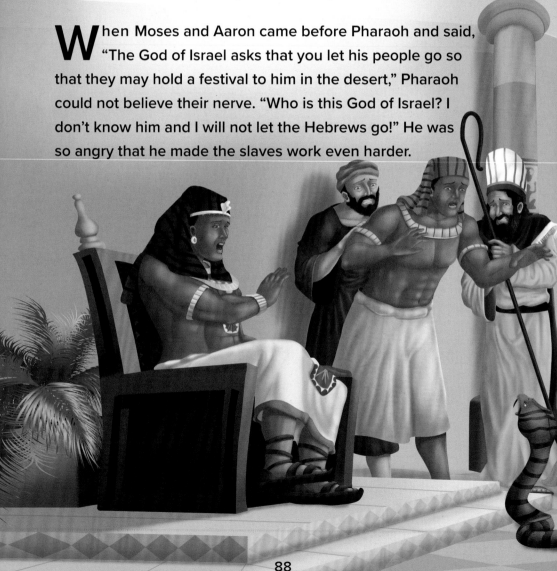

So Moses and Aaron went back to Pharaoh, who demanded some proof of their god. This time Aaron threw down his staff on the ground and it instantly was transformed into a fearsome snake. But the king's magicians huddled together and performed sorcery and when they threw their staffs on the ground, they too turned into snakes, and even though Aaron's snake swallowed them all up, the king's heart was hardened, and he would not let the Hebrews go.

THE PLAGUES
Exodus 7-11

Then the Lord sent a series of plagues upon the Egyptians, each more terrible than the last. First he changed the waters of the Nile into blood, so that all the fish died, and the air stank. He sent a plague of frogs to cover the countryside and fill the houses. Next, the very dust on the ground was turned into gnats, and everything was covered with them, and after them came a swarm of flies, so many that the air was black with them.

He sent a plague among the livestock of the land, but spared those belonging to the Hebrews. Then the Egyptians were afflicted

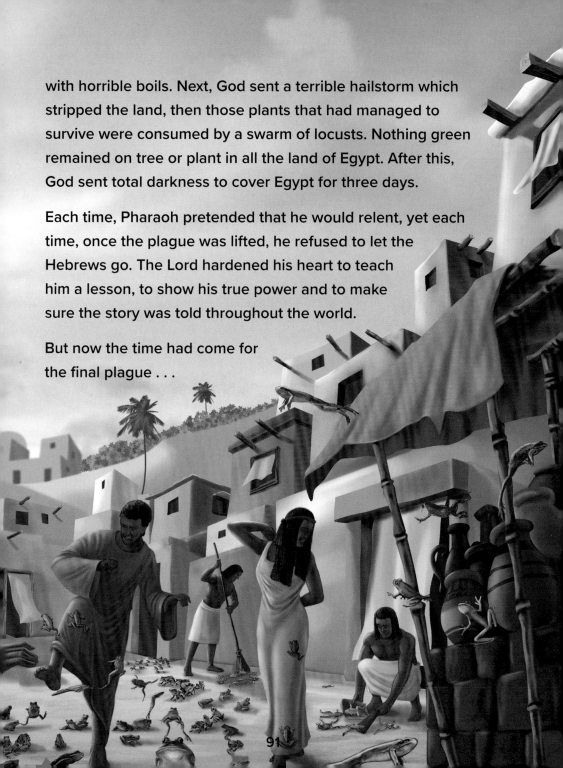

with horrible boils. Next, God sent a terrible hailstorm which stripped the land, then those plants that had managed to survive were consumed by a swarm of locusts. Nothing green remained on tree or plant in all the land of Egypt. After this, God sent total darkness to cover Egypt for three days.

Each time, Pharaoh pretended that he would relent, yet each time, once the plague was lifted, he refused to let the Hebrews go. The Lord hardened his heart to teach him a lesson, to show his true power and to make sure the story was told throughout the world.

But now the time had come for the final plague . . .

THE PASSOVER
Exodus 12

Moses warned Pharaoh that God would pass through the country at midnight and every firstborn son in the land would die, from the son of Pharaoh himself, to the son of the lowliest slave girl, and even the firstborn of the animals as well. But Pharaoh would not listen.

Moses told the Israelites what God wanted them to do to be spared. Each household was to kill a lamb and smear some of the blood on the door frame, and eat the meat in a special way.

That night, God passed throughout Egypt and the next day the land was filled with the sound of mourning, for all the firstborn sons had died, even the son of mighty Pharaoh, but the Hebrews were spared.

Now the Egyptians couldn't get rid of the Hebrews quick enough, and so the Hebrews prepared to leave Egypt.

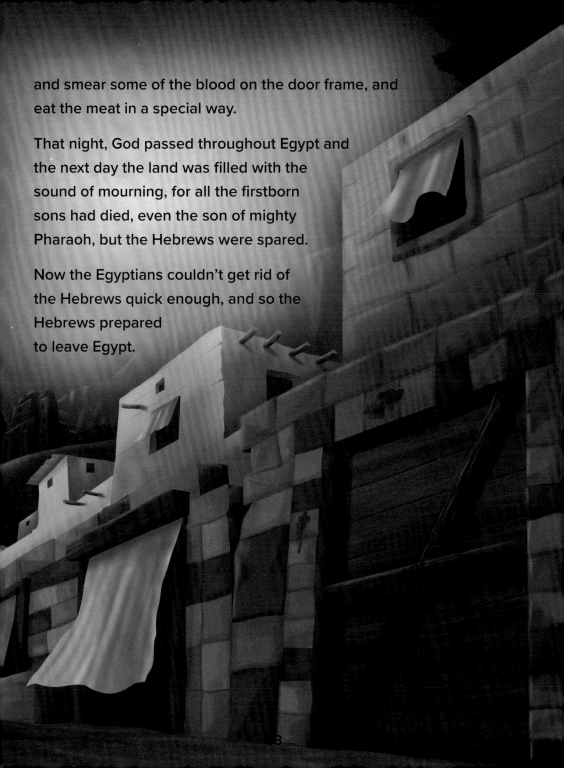

THE EXODUS

Exodus 12-13

The Hebrews travelled southwards across the desert, towards the Red Sea. By day, God sent a great column of cloud to guide them, and by night they followed a pillar of fire. Yet their troubles were far from over, for Pharaoh was regretting his decision to let them go, and had set off with his army to bring them back.

All those flying hooves and grinding wheels set off a huge cloud of dust that the Hebrews could see coming from miles away, and they panicked, for now their way was barred by the waters of the Red Sea. "Why did you bring us all this way, just to have us killed or dragged back into slavery?" cried the terrified Hebrews to Moses. "It would have been better for us to serve the Egyptians than to die in the desert!"

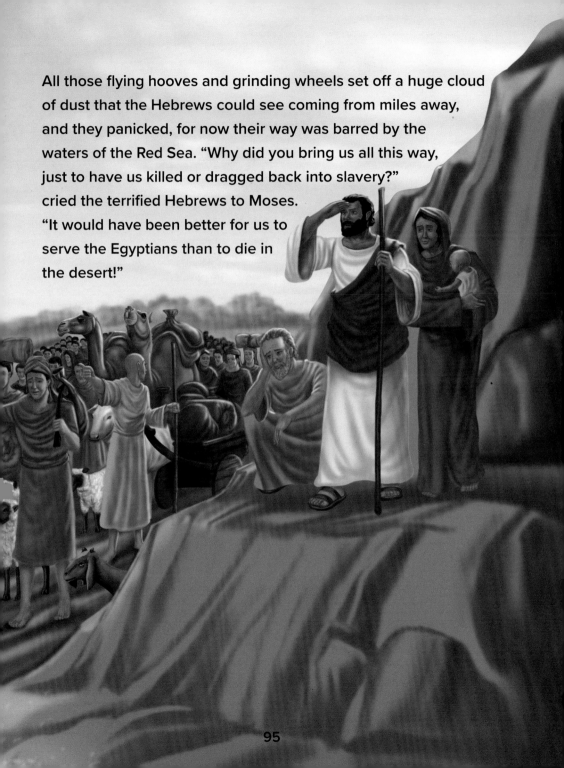

CROSSING THE RED SEA

Exodus 14

The people wrung their hands in fear as the dust thrown up by the Egyptian army grew nearer and nearer, but Moses did not give up his faith in God and stood firm. "God will look after us," he said confidently. "And he will crush our enemy."

Then God told Moses to raise his staff and stretch out his hand over the sea to divide the water so that the Israelites could go through the sea on dry ground. The column of cloud moved between the Hebrews and the Egyptians so that the Egyptians could not see what was happening, and Moses stood before the sea and raised his hand, and all that night, the Lord drove the sea back with a strong east wind and turned it into dry land. The waters were divided, and the Israelites went through the sea on dry ground, with a wall of water on their right and on their left!

97

DROWNED!

Exodus 14-15

The Egyptians were hard on the heels of the Hebrews and, without hesitation, followed them into the sea, along the path that God had made. But God struck them with confusion so that the wheels of the chariots came off and everywhere there was chaos. Then he closed the waters together and the Egyptians were all swept under the water. Of all that mighty army, there were no survivors – not one horse, not one soldier!

And the people of Israel, safe on the other shore of the Red Sea, were filled with gratitude and relief and sang and danced in their joy, and they knew that their God was both mighty and merciful and they praised him greatly.

FOOD AND WATER IN THE DESERT

Exodus 15-17

Moses led his people into the hot, dry desert. For three days they didn't find a drop of water, and when at last they did, it was too bitter to drink. They forgot what God had done for them, and began to complain angrily. God helped Moses to make the water drinkable, but they had to travel onwards and soon they began to complain

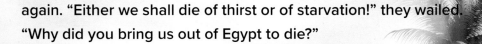

again. "Either we shall die of thirst or of starvation!" they wailed. "Why did you bring us out of Egypt to die?"

Once again God helped his people. In the evenings, quail would come into the camp, and in the mornings, the ground would be covered with white flakes that tasted like wafers made with honey, which they called manna. For all the time that they were in the desert God provided quail and manna for them, and God told Moses to take his staff and strike a rock, and from the rock flowed good, clear, fresh drinking water.

The people of Israel wandered through the desert for many years and the Lord gave them food and water.

THE TEN COMMANDMENTS

Exodus 19-20

Moses led the people to Mount Sinai. There, God spoke to Moses and told him that if the people would honour and obey him, then he would always be with them. The elders agreed to do everything the Lord had told them. Then God told Moses that in three days he would appear to them on Mount Sinai.

On the morning of the third day there was thunder and lightning, with a thick cloud over the mountain, and a loud trumpet blast. The people trembled and waited at the foot of the mountain. Then God called Moses to the top of it and spoke to him, saying: "I am the Lord your God, who brought you out of Egypt.

"You shall have no other gods before me.

"You shall not make any false idols.

"You shall not misuse my name.

"Remember the Sabbath and keep it holy.

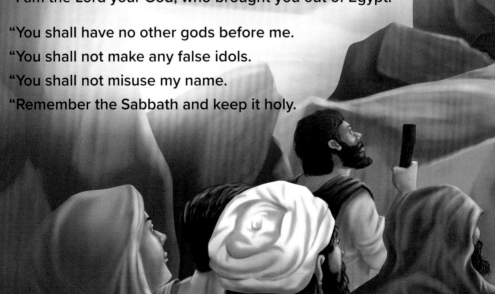

"Honour your father and your mother.

"You shall not murder.

"You shall not commit adultery.

"You shall not steal.

"You shall not tell lies.

"You shall not envy anything that belongs to your neighbour."

Moses told the people what God had commanded and they promised to obey.

A PLACE TO WORSHIP
Exodus 25-27

Moses spent many days on Mount Sinai. God gave him laws for the people to follow so that they should all live in peace and honour God properly – rules concerning food, cleanliness, sacrifices, punishment and many other things. But most important of all were the Ten Commandments written upon two large stone tablets.

God told Moses that the Israelites must build a special place to keep these tablets. They were to be kept inside a wooden chest covered with the purest gold, known as the Ark of the Covenant. This was to be kept inside an inner shrine, inside a large tent known as the Tabernacle. The Tabernacle would travel with the Israelites wherever they went and so they carried the presence of the Lord with them on their travels through the desert.

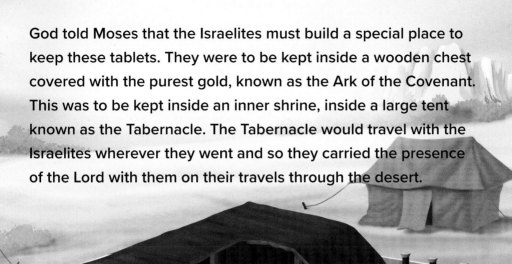

THE GOLDEN CALF

Exodus 32

Moses was gone up the mountain for such a long time that the people began to believe he would never come back down. They asked Aaron to make them gods to lead them, and Aaron told them all to gather their gold jewellery and used it to make a beautiful golden calf, which he placed on an altar. The people gathered round and began to worship it.

God was angry with them and vowed to destroy them, but Moses pleaded with him to forgive them, and God relented.

Then Moses went down from the mountain with the tablets, and when he saw the people singing and dancing around the golden calf, he was so furious that he threw the tablets to the ground, where they shattered. Next, he burned the calf and ground it to powder. God punished those who had sinned with a plague.

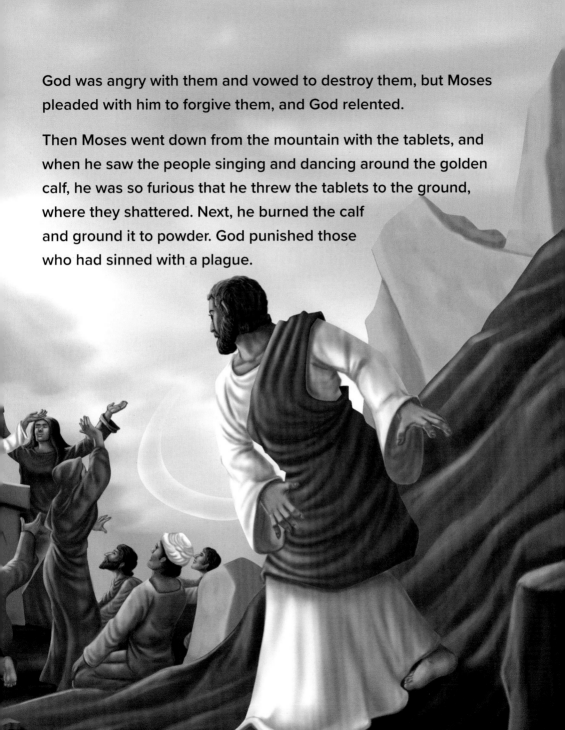

GOD SHOWS HIS GLORY

Exodus 33-34

God told Moses that he and his people must now travel to the land he had promised them, and that he would send an angel to guide them. But Moses begged him to be with them so that the world could see that they were his people, and God promised that he would.

The Ten Commandments were placed on two new stone tablets and when Moses brought them down from Mount Sinai, his face shone so brightly that everyone was scared to come near him, but he called to them and gave them all the commands the Lord had given him.

Now they worked hard on preparing the holy tent and the special place for the tablets. Everyone did what they could and brought anything precious that they owned. When all the work was complete, and everything had been laid out just as God had commanded, then a cloud covered the Tent of Meeting, and the glory of the Lord filled the Tabernacle, and at night it looked like fire.

And in all the travels of the Israelites, whenever the cloud lifted from above the Tabernacle, this was the sign for them to set out.

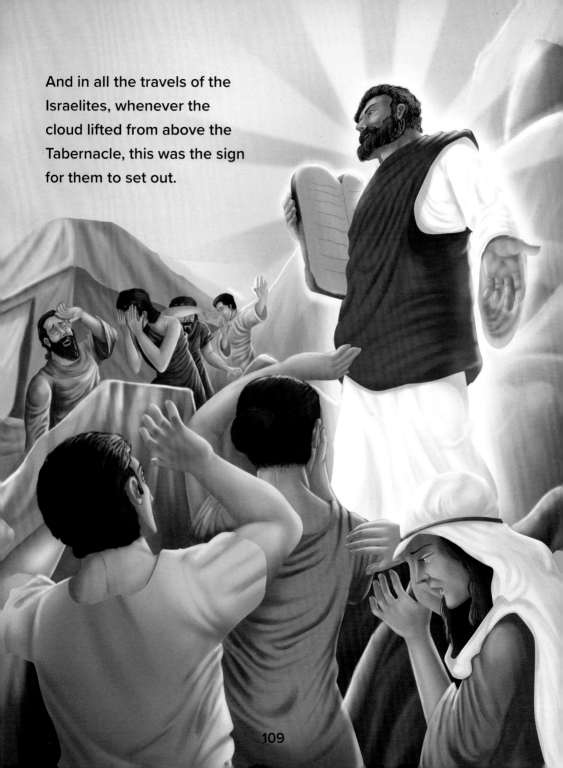

THE DAY OF ATONEMENT

Leviticus 16

Then God gave Moses special instructions for Aaron. Aaron was to make sacrifices to offer atonement for his own sins, and for those of his family and servants. Then he was to take two goats from the people. One was to be sacrificed to God, and the other was to take on all the sins of the Israelites and then to be sent

away into the desert. It was a 'scapegoat' to carry away the sins of all the people.

This ceremony was to take place each year, on the tenth day of the seventh month. It was to be known as the Day of Atonement, and wasn't to be a joyful occasion like many of the other festivals, but was to be serious and sombre, a day of rest to be spent in prayer and thought. It was to be a day to seek forgiveness from God. God commanded the people to fast on the Day of Atonement, which meant that they were not to eat any food or drink any water for one whole day.

"All this you shall do," said God, "because on this day atonement will be made for you. Then, you will be clean from all your sins in my sight."

THE PEOPLE COMPLAIN

Numbers 11-12

O nce again the people began to complain to Moses. They were tired of the hardships and fed up with eating the same food, day after day. "It's not fair!" they moaned. "In Egypt we had cucumbers, melons and onions – we're fed up with manna!"

Moses had had enough of their moaning and grumbling. He went to speak to God. "My Lord," he said, "Why do I have to listen to their wailing all the time? Why is it always me?"

And God took pity on him, and gave some of the Spirit that he had given to Moses, to seventy of the elders. "That way," said God, "they will help you carry the burden of the people."

Now Miriam and Aaron began to complain that Moses wasn't the only important one around. "Hasn't God spoken through us too?" they grumbled. God was angry and told them sternly, "When a prophet of the Lord is among you, I reveal myself to him in visions, and speak to him in dreams. But with Moses I speak face to face. He sees my true form. How can you dare then to speak against my servant Moses?" He was so furious that he punished Miriam with leprosy for seven days.

THE TWELVE SPIES

Numbers 13-14

God told Moses to send some men to explore Canaan, the land he intended for the Israelites, so Moses chose twelve men, one from each of the tribes that came from the sons of Jacob, and he sent them to find out what the land was like. They came back laden with juicy fruit. "The land really does flow with milk and honey, just as God promised!" they enthused. But they also said that there were too many people living there and that the cities were well defended. Only two of them, Caleb and Joshua, were brave enough and trusted God enough to believe they could take the land that God had promised them.

God was angry with the Israelites for not trusting him. He threatened to kill them all, but Moses pleaded on their behalf, and God relented. But he told them that not one of those who had doubted him would ever set foot in the Promised Land, and he struck down those men who had been sent to explore Canaan, and who had doubted him and spread their fear among the people of Israel, and he cursed the rest of the doubting Israelites to wander the desert for another forty years!

REBELLION!

Numbers 16-17

Some of the leaders began to rise up against Moses and Aaron. They gathered with the rest of the elders at the entrance to the Tent of Meeting. Then God told Moses and Aaron to stand aside so he could put an end to them.

But Moses and Aaron begged him not to punish the whole assembly, and so God had the rest of the elders move away from the tents of those who had spoken against Moses and Aaron, and when they had done so, the ground beneath those tents split apart and the earth opened its mouth and swallowed the tents, the rebellious leaders, their families, and all their possessions too!

That night, God told the twelve leaders to each leave a staff in the Tent of Meeting. In the morning, Moses entered to find that Aaron's staff had sprouted leaves, budded and blossomed and even produced almonds! God told Moses, "Put Aaron's staff back in the tent, to be kept as a sign to the rebellious," and that from now on, no one but the members of Aaron's tribe, the Levites, could go near the Tent.

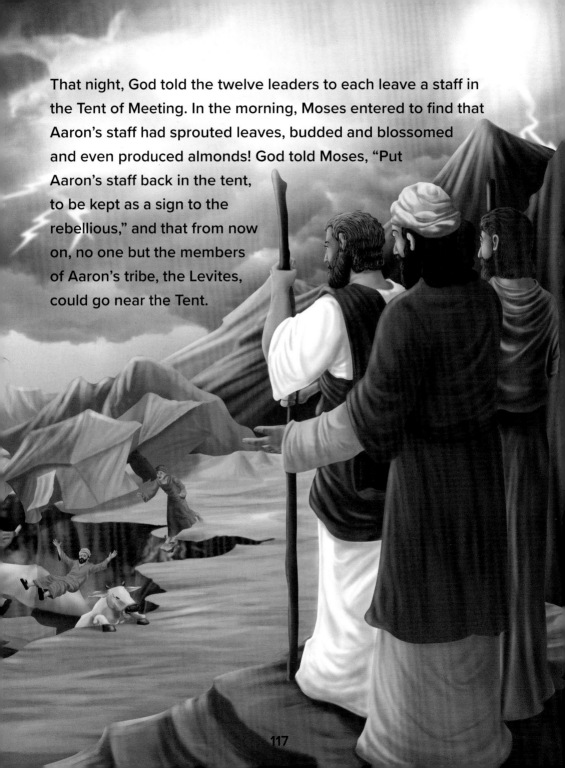

WATER FROM THE ROCK

Numbers 20

Even if the question of leadership was settled, it did not stop the people grumbling, for they were still in the desert and were without water and thirsty. Moses and Aaron asked God to help once more and he told them to take the staff and gather everyone before a large rock. "Speak to that rock before their eyes and it will pour out its water," he commanded them.

Moses and Aaron gathered the people. "Listen, you rebels, must we bring you water out of this rock?" Moses said, then struck the rock twice with his staff. Water gushed out, and everyone was able to drink.

But God was disappointed because Moses hadn't followed his instructions, nor had he given the credit to God, and so he told the brothers that they would never enter the Promised Land.

THE BRONZE SNAKE

Numbers 21

The Israelites had to travel far in the desert. But although God helped them to overcome the people and cities that stood in their way, still the people complained. They spoke against God and against Moses, moaning, "Why have you brought us out of Egypt to die in the desert? There is no bread and hardly any water! And we are sick and tired of this miserable food!"

When God saw their ingratitude, he sent venomous snakes among them and many Israelites died. The people came to Moses and said, "It was wrong of us to speak against God. Please ask him to take the snakes away!" So Moses prayed.

Then God said to him, "Make a snake and put it up on a pole; anyone who is bitten can look at it and live." So Moses made a bronze snake and put it up on a pole. When anyone was bitten by a snake and looked at the bronze snake, he lived.

THE DONKEY AND THE ANGEL

Numbers 22

The Moabites were worried. The Israelites had camped nearby and they feared that if they met them in battle they would be destroyed. Their king, Balak, sent word to a prophet named Balaam to place a curse on the Israelites. Balaam made a living making prophecies and placing curses or blessings for money.

When the messenger came to fetch Balaam, the prophet asked God what he should do, and God said that he must not curse the Israelites, for they were blessed by him, so Balaam told the messengers to go back. Balak sent more messengers and offered more money. Balaam said that he couldn't help, but told them to spend the night and he would speak again to God — even though God had already said 'No!'

That night, God told Balaam he could go, but must say exactly what he was told to say, so the next morning Balaam set off on his donkey. Along the way, the donkey suddenly shied off the road, for an angel stood blocking the way. Balaam could not see it and tried to force the donkey to go on. When it lay down, he began beating it. Then God made the donkey speak. "Why are you beating me?" it asked, and Balaam replied, startled, "Because you are making a fool out of me!"

Then God opened his eyes so that now he, too, could see the angel standing in the road. Balaam fell to his knees in fright. God told him to go the king and to speak only the words that God put in his mouth. In Moab, to the king's horror, Balaam blessed the Israelites instead of cursing them and warned that Israel's enemies would be conquered and that Moab would be crushed!

TIME FOR CHANGE

Numbers 27

God told Moses that it would soon be time for him to leave his people. He said he would let him see the land promised to the Israelites, but would not let him enter it. Moses asked God to choose someone else to lead the people after his death, and the Lord chose Joshua who had already shown his faith in God.

Now, the Reubenites and Gadites had very large herds and flocks. They asked if they could stay on this side of the River Jordan, for

the land was good for grazing. Moses agreed that if all their men helped in the fight to conquer Canaan, then after their victory they could come back and claim this land.

God told the Israelites they must drive out the inhabitants of the land before them, and destroy all their carved images and idols and temples, for God was not giving the Israelites the land because they were good, but because those who lived there were wicked.

CHOOSE LIFE

Deuteronomy 29-30

Moses gathered the people to him, for God wanted them to renew the covenant that he had made with them. Moses reminded them of all that God had done for them and that God would be angry if they ever turned away from him and went off to worship other gods. But if they obeyed God with all their heart and soul, and kept his commandments, then he would look after them wherever they were, and bring them to the land promised to their fathers, and they would be wealthy and successful.

"Today, I set before you a choice between life and death. If you truly love the Lord and obey all his commands, then you and your children will live happily in the Promised Land. But if you do not obey God, if you worship other gods, then you will be destroyed. So choose life, for the Lord is your life, and he will be with you in the land you have been promised!"

HANDING OVER TO JOSHUA

Deuteronomy 31-32

Moses was now very old. He called the people of Israel to him. "God has told me that I may not enter the Promised Land. Joshua will lead you there. You must be brave and strong, for God will not leave you." He said to Joshua in front of all the people, "Be strong and courageous, for you must lead these people into the Promised Land and divide it among them. The Lord himself goes before you and will be with you; he will never leave you nor forsake you, so do not be afraid or discouraged."

God spoke to Moses and Joshua alone outside the Tent of Meeting, and told Moses what to say to the people, for he knew that they would soon turn away from him. Then Moses addressed the people. "You have been stubborn and rebellious with me as your leader. How much worse will you be after I die?" and he

spoke of what had happened and what would happen. "Take my words to heart," he said. "These words are your life – if you obey the words of the law, then God will be with you and your children."

God had some special words for Joshua. "You will lead the people into the land I have promised them. Do not be afraid, Joshua, for I will always be with you."

MOSES SEES
THE PROMISED LAND
Deuteronomy 33-34

I t was time for Moses to leave his people. Before he went, he gathered them to him and said to them, "You are truly blessed! Who is like you, a people saved by the Lord? He is your shield and helper and your glorious sword. Your enemies will cower before you, and you will trample down their high places."

Moses climbed Mount Nebo and the Lord showed him the whole land of Canaan in the distance. Then he died on the mountain and the Lord buried him. He was a hundred and twenty years old when he died, yet his eyes were not weak nor was his strength gone.

The people mourned for thirty days. They knew that there would never be another prophet like him, who had spoken with the Lord face to face.

SPIES IN JERICHO
Joshua 1-4

God had promised the land of Canaan to the Israelites. For many years, they had wandered in the harsh desert, but now it was time to cross the River Jordan into the Promised Land, where food and water were plentiful and the land green and lush.

Joshua sent two spies into the city of Jericho, on the far banks of the river. They spent the night in the home of a woman named Rahab, but the king heard there were spies in his city and sent soldiers to search for them. Kind Rahab hid the men on her roof and when the soldiers came knocking she sent them off on a wild goose chase. Then she gave the spies some rope, so they could lower themselves down, for the house was part of the city wall. "The people of Jericho live in fear of your coming," she told them, "for we have heard how powerful your God is. Please spare me and my family when you attack Jericho!"

The spies told Rahab to tie a piece of red cord to the window and to make sure all her family were inside her house when the Israelites attacked. But they warned her not to speak a word about them, for if she did she would be shown no mercy.

CROSSING THE RIVER
Joshua 3-4

The River Jordan was in flood. The swift-flowing waters were treacherous, and there was no bridge or ford. Yet God had told the people that today they would cross into the Promised Land!

Joshua told everyone to gather their belongings, and then sent the priests ahead, carrying the Ark of the Covenant. As soon as their feet touched the water it stopped flowing and made a huge wall, and a dry path stretched before the priests! They made their way to the middle of the riverbed, and then the people of Israel began to cross safely over. Not a drop of water touched them!

There were so many of them that it took all day to cross, but by nightfall the children of Israel had finally arrived in the land promised to them by God for so many years.

Before the priests finished crossing the river, Joshua had one man from each of the twelve tribes of Israel lift a stone from the middle of the riverbed, where the priests had been standing. As soon as the priests stepped onto the shore, the river came crashing down once more. Then Joshua collected the twelve stones and built them up into a mound as a reminder to the people of how the waters of the river had stopped before the Ark of the Covenant, and how God had brought them safely across it and into the Promised Land.

THE WALLS OF JERICHO

Joshua 6

The Israelites laid siege to Jericho. No one went out and no one came in, and within the walls the people were terrified. Then God told Joshua, "I have delivered Jericho into your hands. March around the city once with all the armed men.

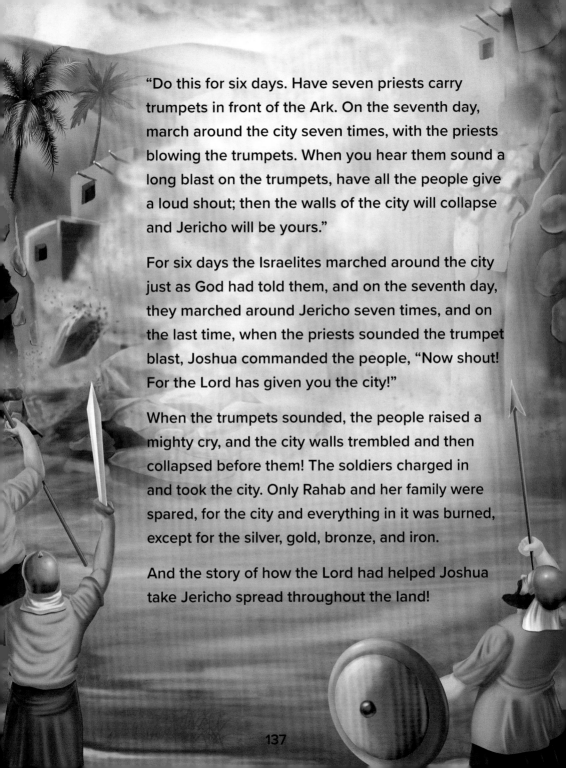

"Do this for six days. Have seven priests carry trumpets in front of the Ark. On the seventh day, march around the city seven times, with the priests blowing the trumpets. When you hear them sound a long blast on the trumpets, have all the people give a loud shout; then the walls of the city will collapse and Jericho will be yours."

For six days the Israelites marched around the city just as God had told them, and on the seventh day, they marched around Jericho seven times, and on the last time, when the priests sounded the trumpet blast, Joshua commanded the people, "Now shout! For the Lord has given you the city!"

When the trumpets sounded, the people raised a mighty cry, and the city walls trembled and then collapsed before them! The soldiers charged in and took the city. Only Rahab and her family were spared, for the city and everything in it was burned, except for the silver, gold, bronze, and iron.

And the story of how the Lord had helped Joshua take Jericho spread throughout the land!

KEEPING A PROMISE

Joshua 9-10

When the people of the nearby town of Gibeon heard how Jericho had fallen, they feared for their own lives. They decided to trick the Israelites into signing a peace treaty with them, by pretending they came from a far off land.

They sent messengers dressed in ragged clothes, with stale bread and leaking waterskins. When Joshua asked who they were, they answered, "We have travelled a long way. This bread was fresh out of our ovens when we started. Now it is stale. And our shoes are almost worn through from walking!"

Joshua drew up a peace treaty with the men of Gibeon and swore an oath to keep it. When the Israelites learned the truth they were furious, but nevertheless, when Gibeon was attacked soon afterwards, the Israelites came to their aid, for Joshua was honourable. God had not been pleased with his rashness in signing the treaty, but he was pleased that he was keeping his word. He helped the Israelites to overcome Gibeon's enemies, and even made the sun and the moon stand still until they had avenged themselves!

The people of Israel had many more battles to win, but, with God's help, the land was finally theirs.

DEBORAH AND BARAK

Judges 4-5

Many years passed. The people turned away from God and fell into wicked ways. God was angry and allowed their enemy, King Jabin, and the commander of his armies, General Sisera, to conquer them. When the people called out once again to God to help them, he spoke to Deborah, a wise woman who he had sent to be a judge over Israel, and told her what to do.

She sent for a soldier named Barak and told him to gather an army of ten thousand men on Mount Tabor, and that she would deliver Sisera and all his soldiers into his hands. Barak agreed to go, but only if Deborah went too! She told him that because he did not trust God, the final victory would be given to a woman.

The Israelites met Sisera and his chariots on the slopes of Mount Tabor, and because the Lord was with them not a single one of the enemy soldiers escaped — all were killed! But Sisera managed to escape and hid in the tent of one of the king's allies, where a woman

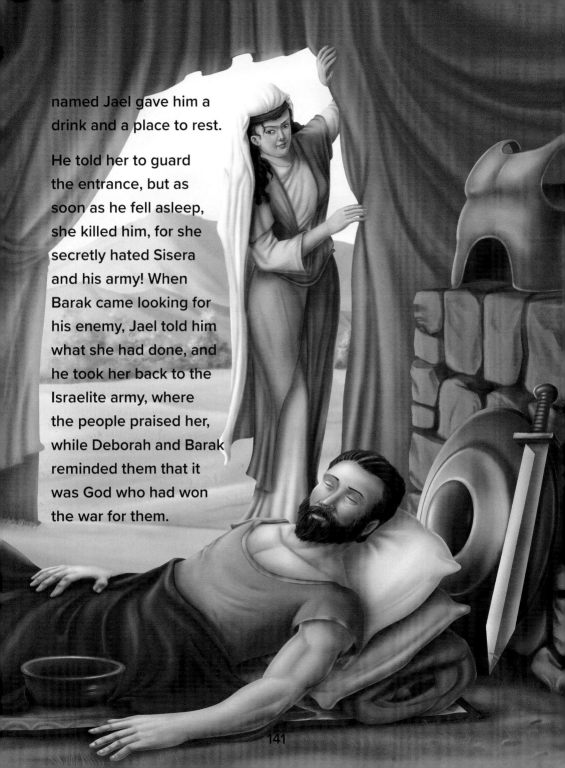

named Jael gave him a drink and a place to rest.

He told her to guard the entrance, but as soon as he fell asleep, she killed him, for she secretly hated Sisera and his army! When Barak came looking for his enemy, Jael told him what she had done, and he took her back to the Israelite army, where the people praised her, while Deborah and Barak reminded them that it was God who had won the war for them.

GOD CALLS GIDEON

Judges 6

❧❧

I n time, the Israelites fell back into their wicked ways, and so, when the terrible Midianites came to take their land, God did not help them. For seven long years the Israelites were forced to hide in the mountains while the Midianites took their crops and

animals. In desperation, the people cried out to God, who sent a messenger to Gideon to tell him that he had been chosen to strike down the Midianites. Gideon was shocked and could hardly believe it. God told him to tear down an altar to Baal in the village and to build a new one to God.

Gideon did the deed with a few servants in the dark of night. When the villagers found out, they wanted to kill him, but his father told them, "If Baal truly is a god, he can defend himself when someone breaks his altar!" and so they left Gideon alone.

Gideon was still not convinced he was the right man for the job. He asked God for a special sign. "I will leave this fleece on the ground. If, in the morning, it is wet, but the ground around it is dry, then I will know that you are going to use me to save Israel."

In the morning the fleece was soaking but the ground was dry. Still Gideon begged for one last sign. "Tomorrow let the fleece be dry, but the ground wet." And so it was – now Gideon was convinced!

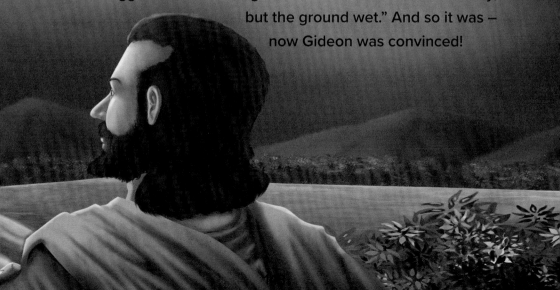

GIDEON AND THE THREE HUNDRED

Judges 7-8

Gideon and the men who had rallied to him looked down on the tents of the Midianites. They stretched as far as the eye could see, covering the ground like a swarm of killer ants! But even so, God said to Gideon, "You have too many men. I do not want the Israelites to think they have won because of their own strength. Tell anyone who is afraid that he can go home."

After Gideon had spoken to his army, only ten thousand remained! But God said, "You still have too many men. Tell them to go and drink from the water, and take with you only those who cup the water in their hands to drink, not those who lap it." When this was done, only three hundred men were left!

That night, Gideon looked down on the sea of tents – how could they ever win? God knew he was anxious and told him to creep down

to the enemy camp where he overheard the soldiers recounting bad dreams about losing! He returned full of confidence and roused his men, giving them all trumpets and empty jars with torches inside.

The men reached the edge of the camp and, following Gideon's signal, they all blew their trumpets and smashed the jars, and shouted out loud. The harsh noise and sudden light startled the Midianites so much that the camp fell into confusion, and the soldiers fled in terror, even turning on one another in their fright!

In this way, Gideon and God defeated the Midianites with just three hundred men!

JEPHTHAH'S PROMISE
Judges 11

Once again, the people of Israel were under attack. This time, their leader was a brave and honourable man named Jephthah. Before he led his people into battle, Jephthah spoke to God. "O God, if you deliver the Ammonites into my hands, I solemnly swear that on my return I shall sacrifice to you the very first thing that comes out of the door of my house to greet me!"

Then Jephthah went out to fight his enemy, and because God was with him, he won.

But on his return home, who should come out to meet him but his lovely daughter, his beloved only child! When he saw her, he tore his clothes and cried out in despair as he told her of his promise to God, to which she replied sadly but gravely, "My father, you have given your word to the Lord, and you must keep your promise. Grant me just one request," she asked. "Give me two months to grieve."

And so for two months Jephthah's daughter went into the hills with her friends and wept for the life she would not have. But at the end of the two months, she returned to her father and he kept his promise to God.

SAMSON THE STRONG
Judges 13

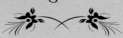

Once again the Israelites returned to their evil ways, and now the Lord delivered them into the hands of the Philistines. For forty years the Israelites had been enslaved by their enemies. One day, God sent a message to a man called Manoah and his wife, who lived in Zorah, "You will have a son who will grow up to deliver you from the Philistines." Now Manoah and his wife had been trying to have a baby for years, without any success, so they were amazed and thrilled at this news. When their son was born, they named him Samson, and they never once cut his hair. It was a sign that he belonged to God in a very special way.

One day, when Samson was older, he was pounced upon by one of the fierce lions that roamed the land of Canaan. Samson was filled with the Spirit of the Lord and he became so strong that he was able to kill the beast with his bare hands!

149

SAMSON AND DELILAH
Judges 16

Samson was a thorn in the side of the Philistines. Although he never led an army, he carried out many attacks against them. But when he fell in love with Delilah, a beautiful Philistine woman, they bribed her to find out the secret of Samson's strength.

Night after night, Delilah would plead with Samson to tell her his secret. In the end, she wore him down, and he said, "If anyone were to cut my hair off, then I would lose all my strength." When Samson awoke, it was to discover that the Philistines had come into his room and cut off his hair. Now he was powerless as they bound and blinded him and threw him into prison!

Over time, Samson's hair grew back. One day, the Philistine rulers were all gathered for a feast in a crowded temple. Samson was brought out to be made fun of. He was chained between the two central pillars of the temple. Then Samson prayed to God with all his heart, "Give me strength just one more time, my Lord, so that I can take revenge upon my enemies!"

Once more Samson was filled with strength. He pushed against the pillars with all his might and they toppled. The temple crashed down, killing everyone inside. Samson killed more of his enemies with this final act than he had killed in all of his life!

FAITHFUL RUTH

Ruth 1-4

Naomi was moving back to Bethlehem. Her husband and sons had died and she wanted to go home, but she begged her beloved daughters-in-law, Orpah and Ruth, to stay behind, for she was penniless and her life would be hard.

Orpah and Ruth loved Naomi dearly, and did not want to stay, but finally Orpah agreed to go home. Loyal Ruth, however, said, "Don't ask me to leave! I will go wherever you go. Your people will be my people and your God will be my God."

So it was that Ruth and Naomi came to Bethlehem. Soon they had no food left, and brave Ruth went out into the fields where workers were harvesting the crops and asked the owner if she could pick up any of the barley that his workers left behind.

This man was Boaz, and he kindly let Ruth work in his fields and told his servants to share their food with her. When Ruth returned with a full basket of food, Naomi knew that the Lord was looking after them, for Boaz was a relation of hers. In time, Ruth married him, and when they had a son, there was no happier woman in the whole of Bethlehem than Naomi!

GOD HEARS HANNAH'S PRAYER

1 Samuel 1-2

Hannah longed to have a child. She could think of nothing else. One day, when she was visiting the temple in Jerusalem, she went to the door of the holy tent and, weeping bitterly, began to pray. "Dear Lord, please give me a child, for I am so unhappy," she begged. "I swear that if you do, I will give him back to you to serve for all his life!" When Eli, the priest, saw Hannah and learnt of her troubles, he sent her on her way gently, saying, "May God answer your prayer."

Hannah left, feeling as if a great weight had left her shoulders. She had spoken to God – now he would decide what was best for her. And how thrilled she was when, some time later, she gave birth to a beautiful baby boy named Samuel!

She did not forget her promise to God, for when the boy was old enough, she took him to the temple, knowing he would be well looked after by the kind priest. Each year she visited him, and God, knowing how difficult it had been for her to give up her son, blessed her with more children to love and cherish at home.

155

A VOICE IN THE NIGHT

1 Samuel 3

Eli grew fond of Samuel, for he was a good boy. One night, Samuel awoke with a start when he heard his name called. He rushed through to Eli's room, but the priest sent him back to bed, saying, "I did not call you, child."

Samuel had barely pulled the covers back over him, when he heard his name called again. As before, he rushed through, but once more Eli sent him away. This happened one more time before Eli realised who was really calling Samuel – God!

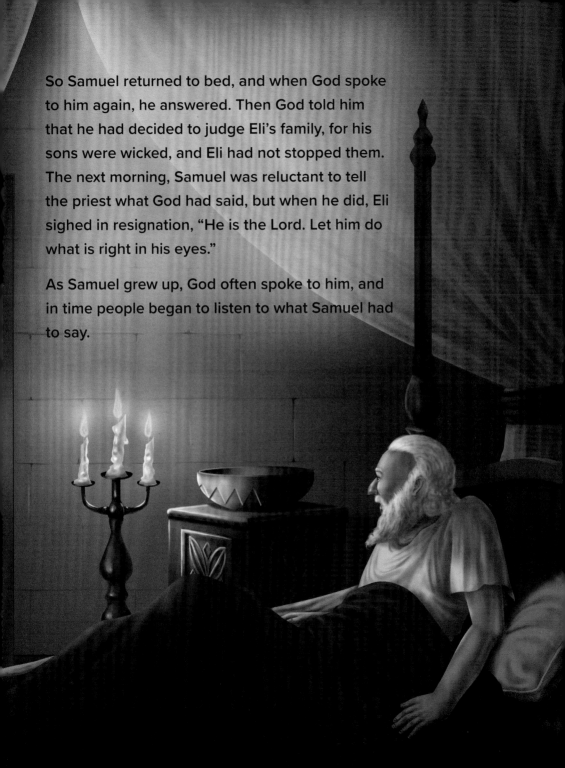

So Samuel returned to bed, and when God spoke to him again, he answered. Then God told him that he had decided to judge Eli's family, for his sons were wicked, and Eli had not stopped them. The next morning, Samuel was reluctant to tell the priest what God had said, but when he did, Eli sighed in resignation, "He is the Lord. Let him do what is right in his eyes."

As Samuel grew up, God often spoke to him, and in time people began to listen to what Samuel had to say.

THE ARK IS CAPTURED!

1 Samuel 4-6

The Israelites were once more at war with the Philistines. Things were not going well, so they decided to take the Ark of the Covenant into battle, for they hoped that it would bring them victory, believing that God would then be with them, but the Philistines fought so fiercely that they slaughtered all the Israelites, and stole the Ark of the Covenant into the bargain!

In triumph, the Philistines placed the Ark inside the temple of their god. In the morning they found the statue had fallen over! They stood it upright once more, but the next morning they found it smashed to pieces! When the people of the city were struck down by a strange illness, they became really scared and moved the Ark to a different city, but everywhere it went, the plague followed it!

The terrified Philistines loaded the Ark and an offering of gold onto a cart pulled by two cows and let them go wherever they would. The cows took the cart straight back to Israel, where the people rejoiced to see the Ark returned safely to them!

ISRAEL DEMANDS A KING

1 Samuel 8-10

Samuel led Israel wisely for many years and brought the people back to God. He was fair and honest and during this time Israel was strong against the Philistines. But when Samuel grew old, the people began to worry about what would happen after he died, and they began to call out for a king.

Samuel knew that they should be happy with God as their King, and he tried to warn them that a king might treat them badly, but the people would not listen – they wanted a king in fine clothes to lead their armies, just like all the other nations around. In the end, Samuel agreed to their demands.

The man God chose was the son of a farmer from the tribe of Benjamin. Saul was a tall, handsome young man. He was shocked when Samuel anointed him, but God sent some special signs, so that he would know that it was the truth.

When Samuel tried to present Saul, the young man was so scared that he hid! When he was found, Samuel announced, "Here is your new king!" and the people cheered and shouted with joy.

SAUL DISOBEYS GOD

1 Samuel 11-15

Saul became a mighty king and had many victories over the Philistines. To begin with, he was good and brave, but over time, Saul became proud and obstinate, and he did not always obey God.

In later years, God called upon Saul to attack the Amalekites, who had once treated the Israelites badly. God told him to destroy Amalek, and everything in it, but Saul spared the best of the animals and brought back the king too.

When Samuel asked why he had disobeyed God, Saul told him that he was going to sacrifice the animals to the Lord. Then Samuel sternly told him that God valued obedience above sacrifice. Saul begged for forgiveness, and when Samuel turned away from him he took hold of his robe and a corner of it tore off in his hands. Samuel told him that in just such a way, the Lord would tear the kingdom away from Saul, for he regretted that he had ever made him king over Israel. Samuel parted from Saul sadly, and never saw him again.

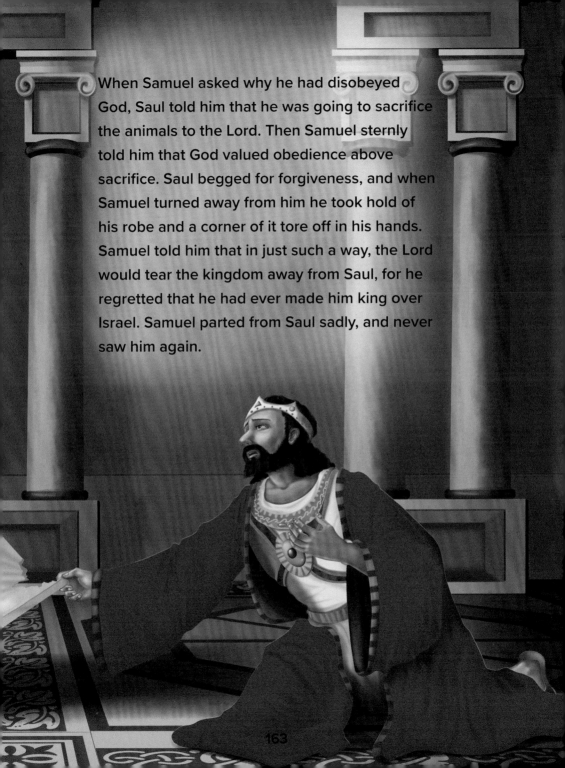

THE SHEPHERD BOY

1 Samuel 16

Samuel went to the house of Jesse in Bethlehem, for God had chosen one of his sons to be king of Israel. When he saw Jesse's eldest son, a fine-looking young man, he thought, "Surely this is God's chosen one," but God told him not to judge by appearances – God looks at the inside of a person, not the outside!

One by one, Jesse brought out his sons, but not one of them was the chosen one. Finally Samuel asked if he had any more sons, and Jesse answered, "There is the youngest, David, but he is tending the sheep in the fields."

When the young shepherd boy was brought before Samuel, the Lord spoke, "This is the one I have chosen!"

Samuel anointed him by sprinkling a few drops of oil on his head, but it was some time yet before David would be king.

For now he stayed at home tending the sheep, passing the hours by playing his harp, and practising with his sling, but from that day onwards, God was always with him.

DAVID AND GOLIATH

1 Samuel 17

Young David stood before Goliath. Mighty Goliath was the fearsome champion of the Philistine army, and he was so big and powerful that he was practically a giant! Goliath had challenged the Israelite soldiers to single combat. Not one of them had dared to fight this terrible warrior, but David did. God had been with him when he had protected his sheep from lions and bears, and David knew that God would be with him now.

The king gave David his own armour and weapons, but they were too big and heavy for the young boy, so David stood before Goliath, with nothing but his staff, a sling, and five smooth stones from a nearby stream.

Goliath laughed when he saw the young shepherd boy, but David fearlessly ran towards him, putting a stone in his sling and flinging it with all his might. It hit Goliath in the middle of his forehead and when he fell to the ground, David raced up and, drawing out Goliath's own sword, cut his head from his body with one strike!

The Philistines were so shocked when they saw their champion killed, that they turned and ran away!

167

SAUL IS JEALOUS

1 Samuel 18-20

David was a hero! He lived in the palace with Saul and his son, Jonathan, who became as fond of him as if he were his own brother. But soon Saul became jealous, for the people seemed to love David more than him. One day, David was playing his harp when evil spirits came upon the king and he threw his spear at David. When it missed, Saul became fearful, for he saw that God had left him and was with David.

Saul tried again and again to have David killed and in the end David had to flee the palace. Jonathan hoped to persuade his father to forgive David, so they agreed on a sign which would show whether it was safe for David to return. "I will go with my servant and fire three arrows," said Jonathan. "Then I will send the boy to fetch them. If I say to him, 'Look, the arrows are on this side of you. Bring them here,' then it is safe to come home. But if I say, 'Look, the arrows are beyond you,' then you must go, for your life is in danger."

Jonathan tried to speak to the king, but Saul became furious and his son realised he would never change his mind. The next day, Jonathan went to the woods where David lay hidden and fired

168

his arrows. As his boy ran to fetch them, he called out, "Isn't the arrow beyond you? Be quick!" and David was filled with sorrow. Jonathan sent the boy back to the palace ahead of him and the two friends hugged one another and said a sad farewell.

DAVID SPARES SAUL
1 Samuel 24, 26

Saul did not forget his hatred of David and searched for him throughout the land. A day came when David held Saul's life in his hands. He and his men were hiding in a cave, when Saul himself came in, needing to go to the toilet! David managed to creep up and cut off a corner of Saul's robe. His soldiers whispered to him that God had delivered his enemy into his hands, but David didn't want to harm Saul. As Saul left the cave, David called after him, and showed him the piece of his robe.

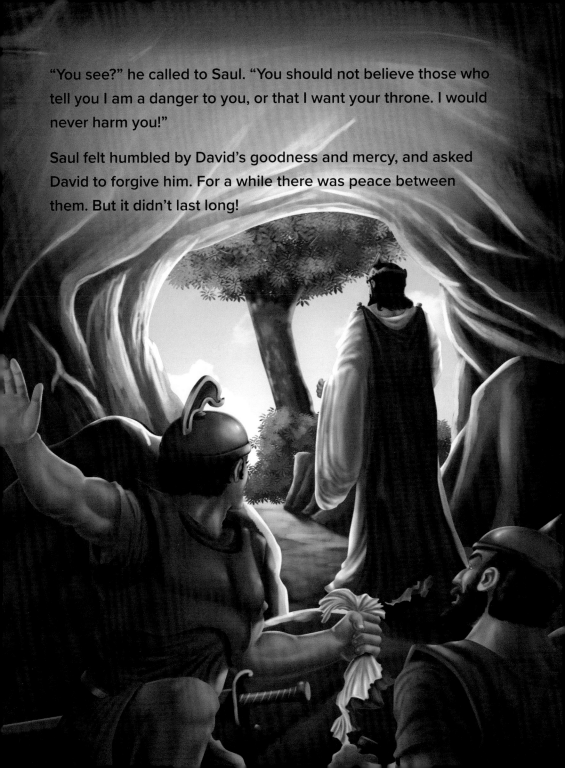

"You see?" he called to Saul. "You should not believe those who tell you I am a danger to you, or that I want your throne. I would never harm you!"

Saul felt humbled by David's goodness and mercy, and asked David to forgive him. For a while there was peace between them. But it didn't last long!

DAVID AND ABIGAIL

1 Samuel 25

One day, David and his men were in the lands of a rich man named Nabal. His wife Abigail was beautiful and wise, but Nabal was evil and selfish. David sent messengers to ask for food and to promise that they meant no harm, but Nabal replied rudely, "Why should I give food to this David?"

David was furious at this, and marched on Nabal's house, but when Abigail learnt of Nabal's rudeness, she gathered together some

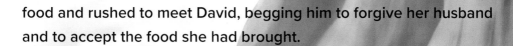

food and rushed to meet David, begging him to forgive her husband and to accept the food she had brought.

David was moved by her plea, and promised there would be no fighting. When Nabal learnt what had happened, he was overcome with shock and died soon afterwards. Then David sent messengers to Abigail, asking her to marry him, which she did with joy.

SAUL AND THE WITCH OF ENDOR

1 Samuel 28

The years passed and Samuel died an old man. When the Philistines once again prepared to attack Israel, Saul felt terrified and helpless. He called out to God to guide him, but he received no answer, for God had turned from him. In desperation, he disguised himself and travelled to see a medium living in Endor who could call up the spirits of the dead.

At first the medium did not want to help, but when Saul swore that she would not be harmed, she agreed. Saul asked her to call up Samuel. Silently the woman began her rites. When she saw the spirit of Samuel, she was frightened, for she guessed now who her visitor was. When Saul realised that the spirit was Samuel, he cried out, "What am I to do? The Philistines are about to attack and God will not tell me what to do!"

"If God will not answer you, then you should not be talking to me," replied Samuel sternly. "You have disobeyed him and you will be punished. Tomorrow, you and your sons will be dead."

The next day, the army of Israel was utterly defeated. One by one, Saul's soldiers were killed or deserted, and by nightfall, Saul and his sons were dead!

DAVID BECOMES KING

2 Samuel 2-5

David was filled with sorrow when he learnt of the deaths of Saul and Jonathan. There was still fighting between Saul's descendants and David, but at long last all the tribes of Israel proclaimed David their king. As one of his first acts, David decided to make the fortress city of Jerusalem his new capital, for he knew that the enemies of Israel were always waiting to pounce.

When David marched his army to Jerusalem, which was still held by a Canaanite tribe, the people there laughed at him, believing that they would be safe behind their high walls. Hills surrounded the city on three sides, and on the fourth it was protected by the huge city gates. "You'll never get inside," they taunted.

But David had God's blessing. He discovered that a water tunnel ran up through the hill to the city. His men climbed up the water shaft, right into the heart of the city, and unlocked the gates from the inside, and so the mighty fortress fell to David and his soldiers!

THE ARK IS BROUGHT TO JERUSALEM

2 Samuel 6; 1 Chronicles 13, 15-16

Once David had conquered the city, he sent for carpenters and stonemasons to enlarge it and to build a grand palace. Jerusalem became known as David's city. But David knew he owed everything to God. He wanted Jerusalem to be known as God's city and so he decided to bring the Ark of the Covenant to Jerusalem.

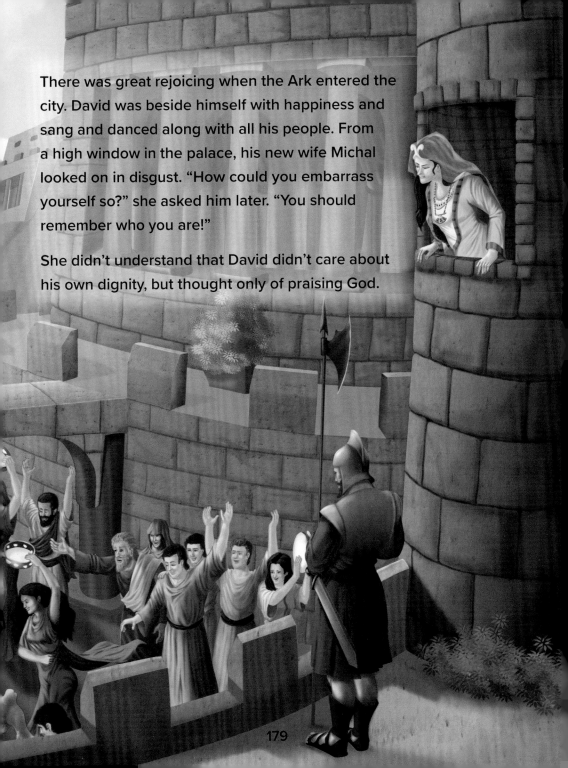

There was great rejoicing when the Ark entered the city. David was beside himself with happiness and sang and danced along with all his people. From a high window in the palace, his new wife Michal looked on in disgust. "How could you embarrass yourself so?" she asked him later. "You should remember who you are!"

She didn't understand that David didn't care about his own dignity, but thought only of praising God.

GOD'S PROMISE TO DAVID

2 Samuel 7; 1 Chronicles 17

One day, David called the prophet Nathan to him. "It does not seem right that I am living in such a splendid palace, while God's covenant chest is in a makeshift tent. I want to build a fine temple for it!"

That night, God spoke to Nathan, and in the morning, the prophet told the king, "God has always travelled with his people in a tent, to be with them wherever they went. He does not want you to build him a temple."

David was bitterly disappointed, but Nathan continued, "God does not want you to build him a house, for it is he who will build a house for you. It is because of him that you left your sheep and fields to become king of all Israel. He promises that he will be with you and help you overcome your enemies. With his guidance you will become the greatest king upon earth, and your sons will be kings of Israel after you for ever more."

David was filled with gratitude. When Nathan had gone, David gave his thanks to God in a heartfelt prayer. He had wanted to do something for God, but God had done something wonderful for him, a simple shepherd boy, instead.

DAVID IS KIND

2 Samuel 9

Even though he was now king, David did not forget his dear friend Jonathan. He asked his advisors to find out if any of Jonathan's family were still living, for he wanted to do something for them if he could. At last they found a servant who told them that a son of Jonathan was still living, but that he was crippled in both feet. His name was Mephibosheth.

David sent for Mephibosheth and when he was brought before the king, he bowed down low before him. "Do not be afraid," said David to Mephibosheth. "I will make sure that all the land that belonged to your grandfather Saul is given back to you, and you will always eat at my table."

Mephibosheth bowed before the king. "Who am I that you should honour me so?"

"You are the son of Jonathan who was my dearest friend," replied David, and so Mephibosheth moved to Jerusalem and was always welcome at David's table.

DAVID AND BATHSHEBA

2 Samuel 11-12

It was early evening in Jerusalem and David was walking on the palace roof when his eyes were drawn to a beautiful woman bathing. His guards told him it was Bathsheba, the wife of one of his soldiers, Uriah, away fighting the Ammonites. David was filled with love for Bathsheba and had her brought to the palace that night. Soon afterwards he learnt that she was expecting his child!

David did not know what to do. Uriah would be furious if he learnt the truth, so David brought him back from the war to be with his wife, hoping he would believe the baby was his own. But when Uriah insisted on sleeping by the palace gates, David sent him back to the front line where the fighting was fiercest, and he was killed. At the end of her mourning period David married Bathsheba and she bore him a son.

God was not pleased. He sent his prophet Nathan to tell David a story about two men, one rich and one poor. One day, the rich man held a feast, and instead of using his own animals, he killed the one lamb that the poor man owned, and gave it to his guests.

"Such a man deserves to die!" exclaimed David in disgust.

But Nathan said sternly, "That man is you. You have everything you could wish for, yet you took that which was not yours!"

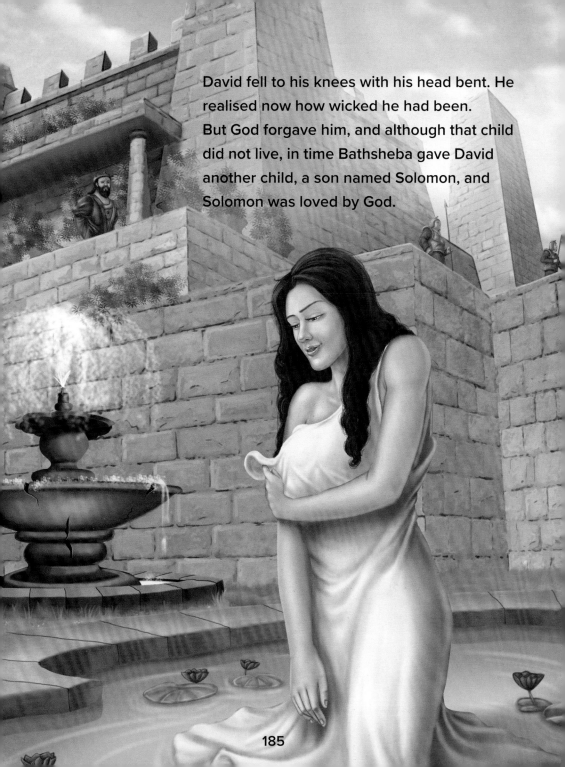

David fell to his knees with his head bent. He realised now how wicked he had been. But God forgave him, and although that child did not live, in time Bathsheba gave David another child, a son named Solomon, and Solomon was loved by God.

ABSALOM REBELS
2 Samuel 15-19

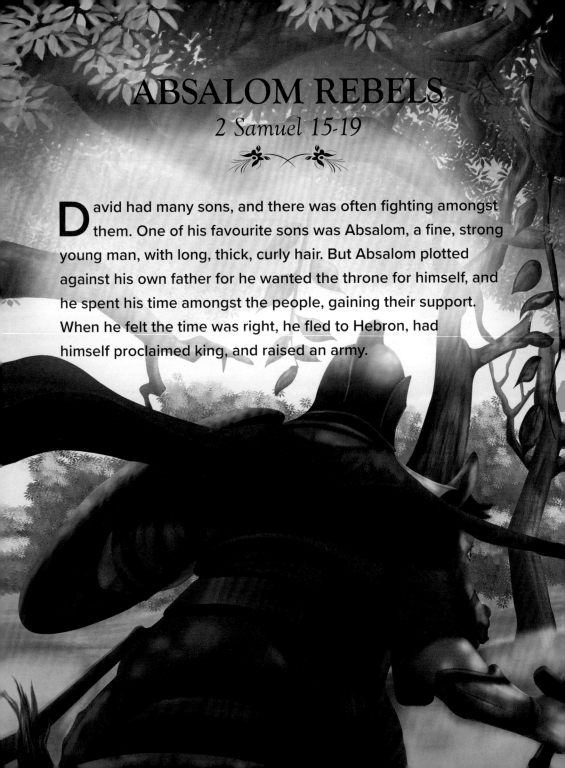

David had many sons, and there was often fighting amongst them. One of his favourite sons was Absalom, a fine, strong young man, with long, thick, curly hair. But Absalom plotted against his own father for he wanted the throne for himself, and he spent his time amongst the people, gaining their support. When he felt the time was right, he fled to Hebron, had himself proclaimed king, and raised an army.

David gathered his soldiers to him and the two armies met in a forest. There was a dreadful battle, but in the end it was clear that David's side would be the victors. Absalom tried to flee, but as his horse passed under a low branch, his long, curly hair caught in the twisted branches and he found himself hanging there, helpless!

David's soldiers found him dangling there and killed him. When David learnt of the death of Absalom, he was filled with anguish and he wished that he himself had died instead of his beloved, treacherous son.

DAVID MAKES WAY FOR SOLOMON

1 Kings 1-2; 1 Chronicles 29

David was old and on his deathbed, and his sons were still fighting over the throne. He had promised it to Solomon, but another of his sons, Adonijah, wanted to be king himself, and tried to claim the throne. The prophet Nathan learnt what was happening, and he and Bathsheba went to tell David the news.

The king told Bathsheba to arrange for Solomon to ride David's own mule to Gihon, where Nathan and Zadok the priest were to anoint him king over Israel. "Blow the trumpet and shout, 'Long live King Solomon!'" commanded David, "for he is to come and sit on my throne and reign in my place."

It happened as King David had ordered, and the people entered the city, cheering and rejoicing. When Adonijah and his fellow conspirators heard the noise and realised that Solomon had been crowned king with David's blessing, they were filled with fear and tried to flee, except for Adonijah who

clung to the altar in the Tabernacle,
terrified his brother would kill him.
But Solomon sent word to him, "As long
as you do no evil, you will live," and
Adonijah returned home in relief.

GOD SPEAKS TO SOLOMON

1 Kings 3; 2 Chronicles 1

Soon after Solomon had been crowned king, God spoke to him in a dream. "What would you like me to give you, Solomon?" he said. "Ask for whatever you want and it shall be yours."

Solomon thought for a moment, then answered humbly, "I am young and have no experience of ruling a nation. I would like to be a great king like my father, but I don't know how. I would ask you to give me wisdom that I might rule over your people wisely and do as you would have me do. Help me to distinguish between what is right and what is wrong."

God was pleased with Solomon's answer. "Most people would have asked for wealth, or long life, or great victories," he said. "You have asked only to be wise. I will give you wisdom. But I will also give you those things you did not ask for. You will be rich and respected, and if you follow in my ways, you will live a long and good life."

When Solomon awoke, he felt comforted and strengthened knowing that God was by his side.

THE WISDOM OF SOLOMON

1 Kings 3

Two women came before Solomon holding a baby between them. "Pardon me, my lord," said one. "This woman and I live in the same house, and we both bore babies within a few days of one another. But her baby died in the night and she took my son from my side and replaced him with her dead son!"

The other woman said, "No! You are lying! The living one is my son; the dead one is yours." And so they argued before the king.

Then the king said, "Bring me a sword." So they brought a sword for the king. He then gave an order: "Cut the child in two and give half to one woman and half to the other."

The woman whose child it really was, cried out in horror, "No! No, my lord! Give her the baby! Don't kill him! I would rather she looked after him than he died!"

But the other said coldly, "No, we should do as the king says. Then neither of us will have him. That will be fair."

Then the king gave his ruling: "Give the baby to the first woman. Do not kill him; she is his true mother."

When all Israel heard the verdict the king had given, they saw how wise and clever God had made him.

193

BUILDING THE TEMPLE
1 Kings 5-8; 2 Chronicles 2-7

Solomon soon began to build the temple that his father David had once dreamed of building. He sent for the finest cedar wood, and the stones were cut at the quarry, so that hammers and chisels would not be heard on the holy site. The temple was wide and long and tall, with many chambers, and the most sacred of all was the Inner Temple. Here, the fine cedar was carved into beautiful shapes and forms, and the doors were exquisitely carved and covered in fine gold.

The temple took thousands of men seven years to build, and when it was finished, King Solomon filled it with fine treasures. But the finest treasure of all was the chest of the Covenant, containing the two stone tablets. It was brought to lie in the Inner Temple, where it rested under the wings of two cherubim made of olive wood and covered in gold, each fifteen feet high, their wings touching in the middle of the room.

The cloud of God's presence filled the temple and the people were full of wonder and thankfulness. Then Solomon thanked God for allowing him to build the temple. "I know that you who created heaven and earth would never live in a building made by man, but I pray that here we can be close to you and hear your word."

And God told Solomon that he had heard his prayer, that his heart and eyes would be in the temple, and that as long as the king walked in God's ways and kept his laws, he would be with him.

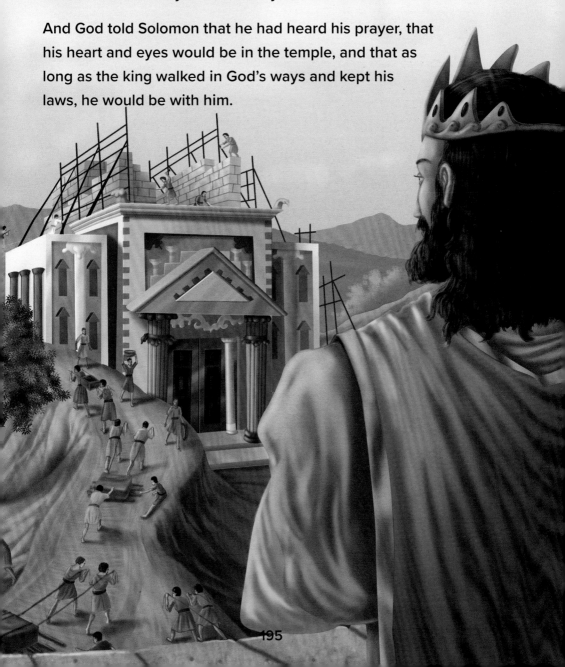

THE QUEEN OF SHEBA
1 Kings 10; 2 Chronicles 9

Solomon grew very rich. After he had built the sacred temple, he built magnificent palaces for himself and one of his wives, the daughter of the Egyptian pharaoh. He ate off gold plates using gold cutlery, and drank from a golden goblet. Even the clothes he wore were threaded with gold.

The stories of his wealth and wisdom travelled far and wide. The Queen of Sheba came to visit him from her kingdom far away. She arrived with a long caravan of camels carrying rare spices, gold, and precious stones to give as gifts.

She asked Solomon many questions, and every question was answered wisely and clearly. "Everything I heard was true!" she told the king. "I thought that people were exaggerating, but now I know they were not. Your people must be proud to have you as their ruler, and it is a sign of your God's love for them that he has made you their king, to rule them with justice and wisdom."

TURNING FROM GOD
1 Kings 11

King Solomon was greater and richer than any other king, and people came from far and wide to hear his wisdom. Yet when he grew old, he turned away from the Lord, for he had married many foreign princesses, and as the years passed, they turned his heart to the strange gods they worshipped. God was angry and sad. For the sake of David, he did not want to take the kingdom in Solomon's own lifetime, but he let his enemies rise up against him.

One day, when Jeroboam, one of the king's officials, was out walking in the country, the prophet Ahijah came to him with a message from God. Ahijah took off the new cloak he was wearing and tore it into twelve pieces. He gave ten to Jeroboam, saying, "These are like the twelve tribes of Israel. I have given you ten pieces, because soon God will take away ten tribes from Solomon, and give them to you. God will punish Solomon and Israel, because they have forsaken him, but he will not take away all the kingdom from David's children; he will give them the tribes of Judah and Benjamin. And if, when you are king, you serve God truly, he will give your kingdom to your sons after you."

When Solomon learnt what Ahijah had said, he was afraid and tried to kill Jeroboam, but Jeroboam escaped to Egypt, where he stayed in safety until Solomon died, and then the kingdom of Israel split in two. In the south, the tribes of Judah and Benjamin stayed loyal to Solomon's son, King Rehoboam, but the ten northern tribes broke away and made Jeroboam their king.

ISRAEL IS DIVIDED
1 Kings 12-14; 2 Chronicles 10-12

In the south, King Rehoboam ruled over Jerusalem and the tribes of Judah and Benjamin. In the north, Jeroboam was king. Israel was divided and the fighting between the tribes was fierce.

Despite Ahijah's message, Jeroboam did not follow God's laws. He had two calves made out of gold for the people to worship, for he was worried that if they travelled to Jerusalem to worship at the holy temple there, they might go back to King Rehoboam.

Things went from bad to worse, and so God sent a holy man to deliver a message. He came to the king at one of the altars and told him God would send a sign: the altar would split open and ashes rain down.

Jeroboam was furious. He stretched out his hand to tell his guards to seize the man, and as he did so his hand shrivelled up and the altar was split apart and its ashes poured out. Yet even after this dire warning, Jeroboam still did not change his ways!

Nor was King Rehoboam in the south much better, for he too had let his people return to the wicked ways of the tribes who had lived in this land before their coming.

ELIJAH AND THE RAVENS
1 Kings 17

Many years passed. Now the rulers of the northern kingdom were wicked Ahab and his cruel wife Jezebel of Sidon. Ahab built a temple for Baal, the god worshipped by Jezebel, and the queen had many prophets killed. But there was one true prophet named Elijah. He warned the king, "For more than two years there will be neither rain nor even dew in this land. You will learn that my God is the one true God," and it happened as he said.

God sent Elijah east of the River Jordan to hide. There, ravens brought him bread and meat, and he drank from the brook. When the brook dried up, God told Elijah to go to Sidon where a widow would help him. When Elijah reached the city gates, he met a woman gathering firewood and asked her for a drink of water. The kind widow went to fetch him a jar of water, even though water was scarce. As she was going, Elijah asked her for some bread.

"I'm afraid I have no bread," she replied, "I have only a handful of flour in a jar and a little olive oil in a jug. I am gathering a few sticks to take home and make one last meal for myself and my son, that we may eat it – and die."

Elijah told her not to worry, but to go home and make a small loaf of bread for him first, and then one for herself and her son, for God had promised that the flour and oil would not run out until the day that rain fell on the land.

The kind widow did as Elijah had asked, and found that when she had made one loaf, she still had enough flour and oil to make another, and so it went on, day after day, and there was always enough food for Elijah, and for the widow and her young son.

THE WIDOW'S SON
1 Kings 17

Elijah and the widow and her son did not go hungry, but one day the boy became ill. Day by day he grew worse, and finally he stopped breathing. Beside herself with sorrow, the widow cried out to Elijah, "Why did you come here? Did you come to punish me and kill my son?"

"Give me your son," Elijah replied calmly, and he took the boy to his room and laid him on the bed. Then he cried out to God, "O Lord, my God, why have you brought tragedy on this widow when she has been so good to me?" Then Elijah stretched himself out on the boy three times and cried, "O Lord, let this boy's life return to him!"

God heard Elijah's cry, and the boy's life returned to him. Elijah carried him down from the room and gave him to his mother and said, "Look, your son is alive!"

The woman fell to her knees in gratitude. "Now I know that you are truly a man of God and that the word you preach is the truth!"

205

THE GREAT CONTEST
1 Kings 18

Three years passed without rain, and King Ahab was desperate. Elijah told him to gather the people of Israel and the prophets of Baal at Mount Carmel. "It is time for you to learn who is the true God of Israel!" he said, and he proposed a test. Both he and the prophets of Baal would prepare a bull for sacrifice. Then each would call upon their god to answer with fire!

First, the many priests of Baal prepared their bull, then called upon their god to send fire. They prayed and prayed, and tore their clothes, but nothing happened. "Perhaps Baal hasn't heard you," mocked Elijah. "Try harder!" But try as they might, there was no answer or sign, and at last they fell to the ground in exhaustion.

Now Elijah went to the broken altar of the Lord, and used twelve stones, one for each of the tribes, to build an altar around which he dug a deep trench. He prepared the bull and laid it on the wood, then got the people to soak the sacrifice and the wood with water until it filled the trench. Then Elijah stepped forward and prayed: "Lord, the God of Abraham, Isaac, and Israel, let it be known today that you are God in Israel and that I have done these things at your command." Then the fire of the Lord fell and burned up the sacrifice, the wood, the stones, the soil, and even the water!

The people fell to their knees. "It's true!" they cried. "The Lord is God!" Elijah made sure that the prophets of Baal were seized and slain, and by evening the rains came and the famine was ended.

NABOTH'S VINEYARD

1 Kings 21

From his elegant palace, King Ahab could see a fine plot of land which his neighbour, Naboth, had made into a vineyard. King Ahab thought that this would make a wonderful vegetable garden for the palace. He offered to buy the land, but Naboth did not want to sell. "This land was given to my ancestors by God. It would not be right to sell it, however much you paid me."

Ahab was used to getting his own way. When his wife Jezebel learnt what was making him cross, she simply decided to get rid of Naboth, and paid a couple of scoundrels to make up false charges against him. Naboth was put on trial, found guilty and stoned to death! And so Ahab got his precious vegetable garden.

But God was not pleased with Ahab and his wife, and sent Elijah to speak to the king. "How could you have had an innocent man killed, just so that you could have something that did not belong to you? God is angry with you and will punish you, and the throne will be taken from you and your family!"

When Elijah had gone, Ahab felt very ashamed. He took off all his fine clothes and ate only plain food. He did everything he could to show that he was sorry. God said to Elijah, "It looks as if Ahab really is sorry for what has happened. Because of this, I will not bring disaster on his family now, but will do it in the time of his sons."

TAKEN TO HEAVEN

2 Kings 2

Elijah and Elisha were walking together by the River Jordan. Elijah was old now, and he knew it was time to hand over his work to Elisha. He took off his cloak and struck the water with it, and a path opened up before him. The two men walked across. Then Elijah turned to his companion, saying, "Soon I shall leave you. Is there anything you would ask of me before I go?"

Elisha thought carefully. "I should like to inherit your spirit, your greatness and power, to help me carry on your work."

Suddenly a chariot of fire drawn by horses of fire appeared before them. As Elisha looked on in amazement, Elijah was taken up to heaven in a whirlwind!

When the sky was empty once again, Elisha noticed that Elijah's cloak had fallen to the ground. He picked it up and walked to the riverbank. He struck the river with the cloak, and the waters parted before him! When the other prophets saw what happened, they bowed to the ground. "The spirit of Elijah has been passed on to Elisha!" they said in wonder.

WASHED CLEAN
2 Kings 5

Naaman, the general of the armies of Syria, was a great soldier, but he was struck with a dreadful skin disease. An Israelite slave girl told him that the wonderful prophet in Samaria might be able to help, so Naaman travelled to Israel.

When Naaman reached Elisha's house, he expected the prophet to come out and perform a spectacular miracle. Instead, Elisha sent his servant to tell the general to bathe in the River Jordan seven times, and he would be cured.

The general was offended. "Why should I wash in that filthy river?" he shouted. "We have plenty of rivers in Syria!" and he would have left in disgust had not his servant calmed him down.

Realising that he was being foolish, Naaman went to the river and bathed in it, and sure enough, when he emerged from the water after the seventh time, his skin was soft and smooth.

He went to thank Elisha. "Yours is the true God. From now on I will worship him too," and he tried to give Elisha a gift. Elisha would take nothing, but his servant went after the general secretly and told him that Elisha had

changed his mind. Naaman gave him
money, and the servant hid it under his bed. But
Elisha knew what had happened and was angry.
"For your greed and lies you will be punished,"
he said sternly. "You will suffer from the
same disease that Naaman had!"

THE BLIND ARMY
2 Kings 6

The king of Aram was at war with Israel, but wherever he planned to set up camp, the Israelites were there before him. His officers told him that the prophet Elisha somehow knew all their secrets and told them to his king.

The king of Aram sent many horses and chariots and soldiers to surround the city where Elisha was staying by night. When Elisha's servant awoke to see a great army surrounding the city, he was dismayed and cried out in fear, but Elisha said calmly, "Don't be afraid. Those who are with us are more than those who are with them." God opened the servant's eyes and he saw that the hills were filled with horses and chariots of fire.

As the enemy began to approach, Elisha prayed to the Lord to strike them with blindness, and all of a sudden the soldiers couldn't see a thing! Elisha went outside and told them that they were going the wrong way. He led them straight to the king of Israel, who asked if he should not kill them. But instead Elisha told him to give them food and water and then send them home. How surprised the terrified soldiers were to be given a feast by their enemies, and after that there were no more raids from Aram!

FAMINE IN SAMARIA

2 Kings 7

The army of Syria was camped outside Samaria. No one could get in or out and there was almost nothing left to eat. The king stormed to Elisha's house. "This is all God's fault!" he complained. "Why doesn't he help us?"

"By tomorrow, there will be food in Samaria!" promised Elisha. The officer with the king was scornful, and told him that was ridiculous, to which Elisha replied calmly, "Ridiculous or not, it will happen, and you will not live to see it!"

Now, outside the city gates were four men who were even worse off than those inside, for they were lepers and were banned from the city. In desperation, they went to the Syrian camp to beg for some food, but when they got there, they were amazed to find it deserted. They went into one of the empty tents and helped themselves to food and drink eagerly.

Then they looked at one another uncomfortably. "This isn't right," said one. "We can't keep this to ourselves." They returned to spread the news. When the king sent out scouts, he found that the Syrians had fled home, for God had made them hear the sound of chariots and horses in the night and they had thought that a great army was about to attack! Their food stores were brought into the city and the people celebrated in delight.

But the officer who had doubted God was knocked down when the people rushed to buy the food, and he was killed instantly!

JEHOSHAPHAT TRUSTS GOD
2 Chronicles 20

King Jehoshaphat had gathered all the people of Judah to Jerusalem. A vast army was on its way to destroy the land. But Jehoshaphat did not despair – he knew who to talk to! He had called his people together to pray to God for help.

As he and the people prayed, the Spirit of the Lord came on one of the priests and he said, "God says: 'Do not be afraid, for this is God's

battle, not yours. Go out to face your enemy tomorrow, and the Lord will be with you.'"

So the next morning, the army of Judah set out for the battlefield, singing God's praises as they went. But as they marched, God made the different groups of the enemy army fight against themselves and by the time the soldiers of Judah came to the place where they had expected to give battle, all they saw before them was a sea of dead bodies! Not one had escaped!

The neighbouring kingdoms were filled with fear at this sign of God's power and for a while, the people of Judah lived in peace.

THE FALL OF JEZEBEL
2 Kings 9-10

Joram, the son of Ahab and Jezebel, now wore the crown, and as he was no better than his parents, God told Elisha that it was time to put a new king on the throne of Israel. Elisha sent one of his followers to the army camp to anoint an officer named Jehu. Immediately Jehu had been anointed, he gathered the soldiers and set off for the city in his chariot. When Joram saw the army approaching, he sent messengers to ask if it came in peace, and when they failed to return, he and his ally, King Ahaziah of Judah, rode to meet the army to ask the same question.

"There can be no peace while you and your mother rule!" shouted Jehu, and he fired an arrow right through Joram's heart, and then he killed King Ahaziah too!

When Jezebel learnt of her son's death, she did her hair carefully and then waited at a palace window. Soon Jehu's chariot drew up before the palace. "You are nothing but a murderer!" she spat.

But Jehu ignored her, shouting up instead, "Who is on my side?" A few faces appeared cautiously in some of the windows. "Throw her down!" ordered Jehu, and they took Jezebel and threw her from the window and she was killed instantly. And now Jehu ordered Ahab's family and all of the priests of Baal killed too!

JOASH, THE BOY KING
2 Kings 11-12; 2 Chronicles 24

When King Ahaziah's mother Athaliah learnt of his death, she tried to gain the throne for herself, and ordered the death of all the royal family. But Ahaziah had left a baby son named Joash, and Joash's aunt took him away and hid him in the temple where he was brought up in secret, until he was seven years old. Then the high priest decided it was time for him to take the throne and put an end to his wicked grandmother's reign.

Before a great crowd, Joash was brought out of hiding and the high priest anointed him and placed the crown on his young head. A great cheer went up, so loud that Athaliah heard and hurried to see what was going on. When she saw the young boy with the crown on his head, she was furious. "Treason!" she cried. But not one soldier came to her aid! Instead, she was taken away and put to death, and the people went to the temple of Baal and smashed the altars and tore down the idols. Joash tried to be a good king and to remember God's laws, and one of the first things he did was to repair the temple of God, for it had been sadly neglected.

GOD CALLS ISAIAH
Isaiah 6

For quite a long time, things were relatively peaceful in Judah and in Israel, but Isaiah knew it wouldn't last. Isaiah was a prophet – one of the greatest that the people of Israel had ever had. He was first called by God in the year that King Uzziah (the grandson of King Joash) died. God sent him an amazing vision.

In his vision, he saw God sitting on a throne. Above him flew winged angels covering their faces and calling to one another, "Holy, holy, holy is the Lord Almighty; the whole earth is full of his glory." The floor shook with the sound of their voices and the temple was filled with smoke.

At first Isaiah was dismayed, for he knew he was a sinner, yet he had looked upon the Lord Almighty. But one of the angels touched his mouth with a live coal taken from the altar, saying, "See, this has touched your lips; your guilt is taken away and your sins are forgiven."

Then he heard the voice of the Lord saying, "Whom can I send? Who will be my messenger?"

Isaiah called out, "Here am I, Lord. Send me!"

Then God gave Isaiah a message for his people. He warned Isaiah that people wouldn't want to listen, that they would close their ears — and their hearts too — but Isaiah was still willing to be God's prophet.

CAPTURED BY ASSYRIA
2 Kings 17

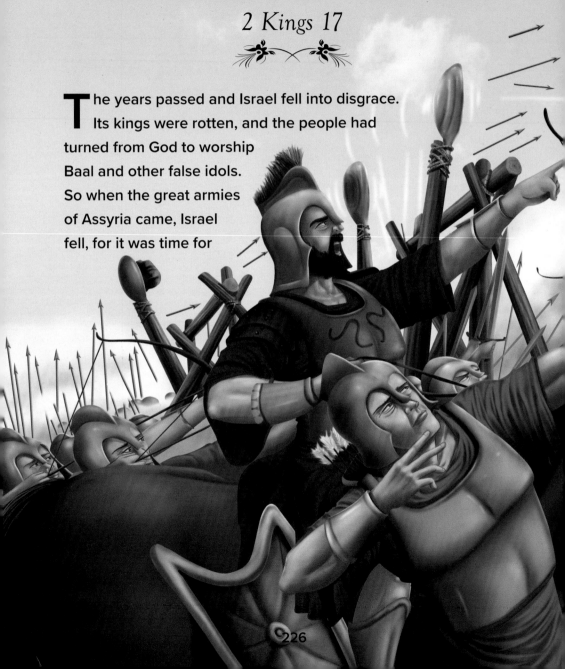

The years passed and Israel fell into disgrace. Its kings were rotten, and the people had turned from God to worship Baal and other false idols. So when the great armies of Assyria came, Israel fell, for it was time for

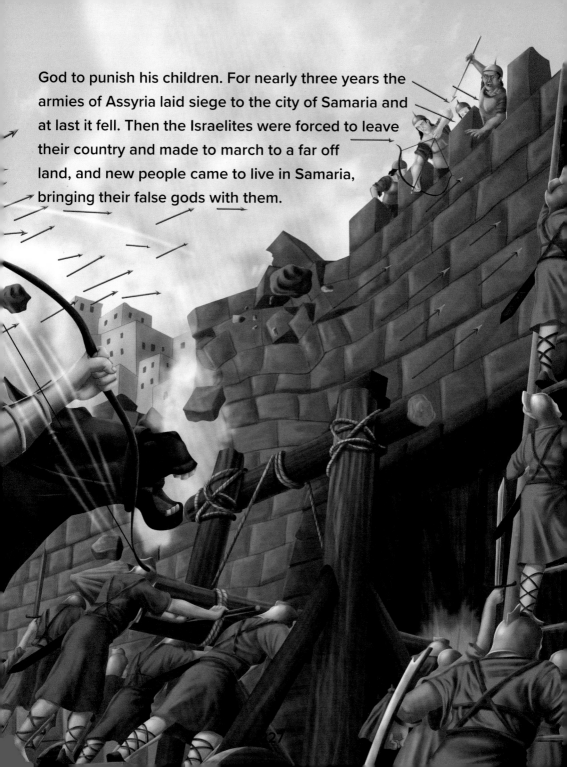

God to punish his children. For nearly three years the armies of Assyria laid siege to the city of Samaria and at last it fell. Then the Israelites were forced to leave their country and made to march to a far off land, and new people came to live in Samaria, bringing their false gods with them.

HEZEKIAH'S PRAYER

2 Kings 18-19; 2 Chronicles 32

Further south, Hezekiah was king of Judah. He was a good man and refused to make an alliance with Assyria, choosing to depend upon God alone for protection. Before long, the mighty army of Assyria came before the walls of Jerusalem and demanded that the city surrender. The people cowered in fear, but Isaiah said, "Do not be afraid. Do not make the same mistake as Israel. Trust in God, for he will save us."

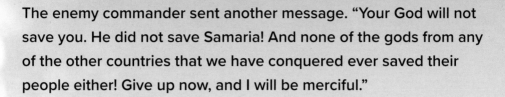

The enemy commander sent another message. "Your God will not save you. He did not save Samaria! And none of the gods from any of the other countries that we have conquered ever saved their people either! Give up now, and I will be merciful."

Hezekiah went to the temple and prayed to God. "You are the only true God," he said. "I place all my trust in you. Deliver us from these Assyrians who insult you, so that all the kingdoms may know that you alone, Lord, are God."

That night, the angel of the Lord passed through the Assyrian camp, and when the sun came up the next morning, it rose on the dead bodies of thousands and thousands of Assyrian soldiers. After that, those Assyrians still alive packed up their things and marched home as quickly as they could!

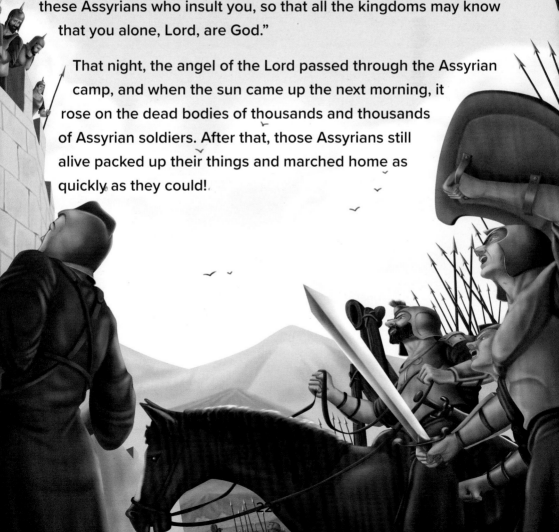

CRYING OUT FOR HEALING
Isaiah 38; 2 Kings 20

Hezekiah needed to be strong to rule Judah, but instead he became ill. A boil on his skin spread infection through his body like poison, until he was close to death. Isaiah told him that God had said he must try to put his affairs in order.

Hezekiah was dismayed. He turned to the wall, weeping, and said a heartfelt prayer to God, "Remember, Lord, how I have always loved you and tried to serve you faithfully."

Then Isaiah told the king, "The Lord has heard your prayer. He will let you live for another fifteen years, and he will save you from your enemy, Assyria. And this is the Lord's sign to you: he will make the shadow cast by the sun go back the ten steps it has gone down on the stairway of Ahaz." And so the sunlight went back the ten steps it had gone down!

Isaiah told the servants to prepare a paste from figs and place it on the boil, and by morning, Hezekiah was cured! Filled with gratitude, he promised to spend the rest of his life praising God.

JOSIAH AND THE BOOK OF LAW
2 Kings 22-23; 2 Chronicles 34-35

Josiah was only eight years old when he first sat on the throne of Judah. The land had once again fallen into evil ways, but Josiah was a good king who tried to bring his people back to God's way. He sent men to repair the Lord's temple, for it had, once again, been neglected. One of the workmen came across the Book of Law and a priest took it to the king.

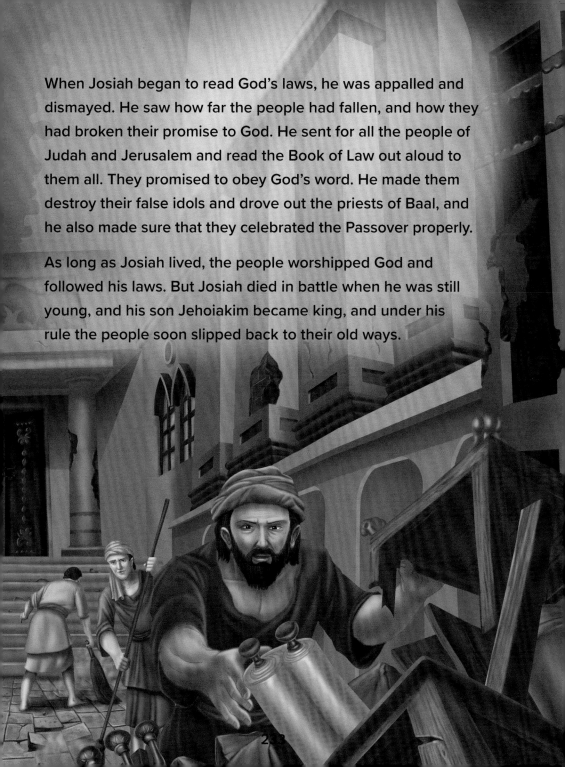

When Josiah began to read God's laws, he was appalled and dismayed. He saw how far the people had fallen, and how they had broken their promise to God. He sent for all the people of Judah and Jerusalem and read the Book of Law out aloud to them all. They promised to obey God's word. He made them destroy their false idols and drove out the priests of Baal, and he also made sure that they celebrated the Passover properly.

As long as Josiah lived, the people worshipped God and followed his laws. But Josiah died in battle when he was still young, and his son Jehoiakim became king, and under his rule the people soon slipped back to their old ways.

JEREMIAH IS CALLED

Jeremiah 1

One of the greatest prophets of the Lord was Jeremiah. He was chosen by God to pass on his message to the kings and people of Judah in a very difficult time. When Jeremiah first heard God speak to him, he thought he was far too young and inexperienced to be a prophet. But God said, "Do not worry. I will be with you, and I will put the words into your mouth."

God wanted to warn his people that a great enemy would come upon them. He showed Jeremiah a large cooking pot over a blazing fire. As Jeremiah watched, the liquid in the pot began to boil, spilling over in a huge rush of steaming liquid.

"In just such a way will an enemy from the north spill over into the lands of Judah and Jerusalem, and destroy all that lies in its path," warned God. "You must warn the people so that they turn from their wicked ways, back to my laws, for only then will they be saved."

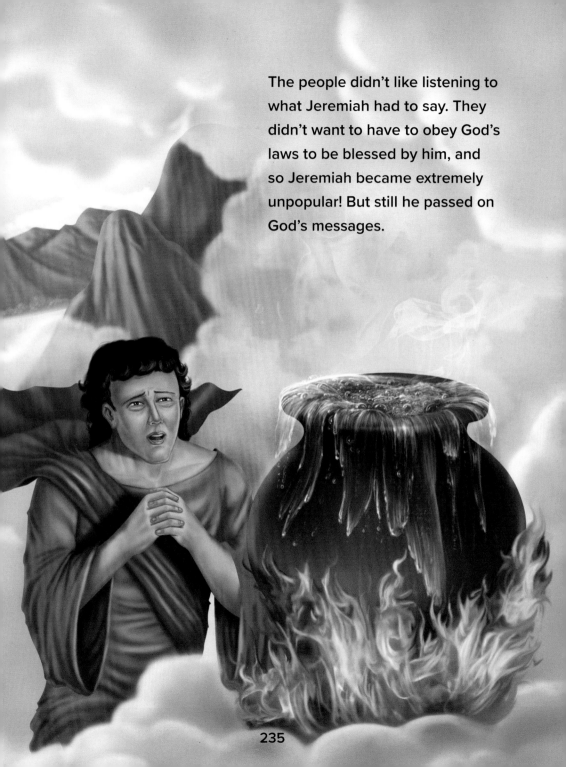

The people didn't like listening to what Jeremiah had to say. They didn't want to have to obey God's laws to be blessed by him, and so Jeremiah became extremely unpopular! But still he passed on God's messages.

THE POTTER'S CLAY

Jeremiah 18-20

Jeremiah watched a potter mould pieces of rough clay into beautiful vases and useful jugs. Sometimes the clay did not do what the potter wanted it to, so he would start again and make it into something different. "Israel is like the clay," God said. "If Israel does evil, I will change whatever good thing I had planned for it, but if Israel repents, then I will relent."

God told Jeremiah to warn the people that disaster was coming, and that only by being truly sorry could they stop it. But he knew they would not listen. Jeremiah took some priests and elders to the Valley of Ben Hinnom. He warned them that God was going to punish his people for their wrongdoing. Judah and Jerusalem would fall to their enemies' swords and their bodies would carpet the ground. The place would become known as the Valley of Slaughter. Then Jeremiah broke a clay jar into many pieces and said, "God will smash this nation and this city just like this jar."

The priests were so cross that they put Jeremiah in stocks!

237

THE SCROLL
Jeremiah 36

For more than twenty years, Jeremiah continued faithfully to warn the people of Judah to turn back to God. God told Jeremiah to write down everything he had said on a scroll. When everything had been written down, Jeremiah asked his friend if he would read from the scroll at the temple, for Jeremiah was not allowed to enter it any more.

When King Jehoiakim's officials found out, they knew the king would be furious. They brought the scroll to him, and as they read to him from the scroll his face grew redder and redder with anger. Each time the official read part of the scroll, the hard-hearted king took his knife and cut off the section and threw it into the fire. When the entire scroll was burnt, he sent his guards to arrest Jeremiah and his friend, but they were safely hidden.

The king thought that he had got rid of God's words, but God simply told Jeremiah to write them out again and he told Jeremiah to tell the king that he and his children and all Judah would be punished.

CONQUERED!

Jeremiah 29

For too long the people of Judah had ignored God's warnings. It was time for them to be punished. There came a new enemy from the north, more terrifying than before – Babylon! Just as Jeremiah had warned, Jerusalem fell to mighty Nebuchadnezzar and his army, and all the strong, skilled people were sent away to Babylon, while Nebuchadnezzar chose his own puppet king to put on the throne, and stripped the temple of its treasures.

God knew that the Israelites exiled in Babylon would be in the depths of despair, so Jeremiah, who had stayed behind, wrote a letter to comfort them and give them hope:

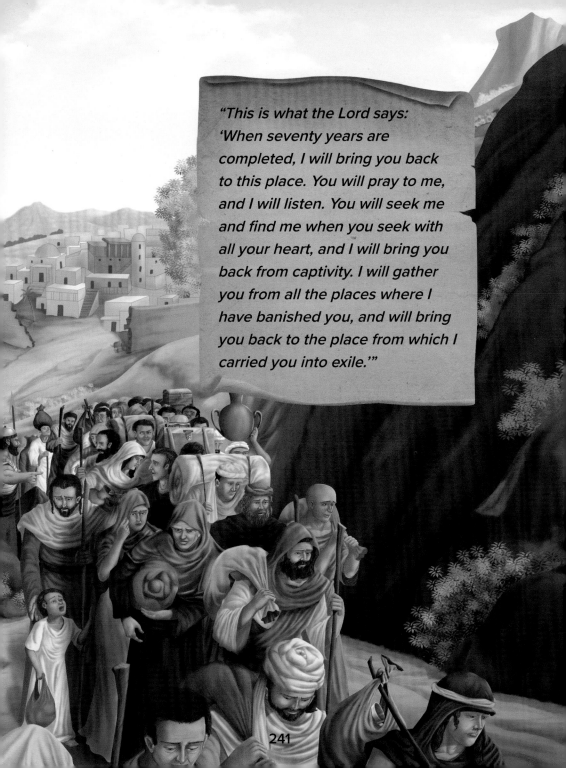

"This is what the Lord says: 'When seventy years are completed, I will bring you back to this place. You will pray to me, and I will listen. You will seek me and find me when you seek with all your heart, and I will bring you back from captivity. I will gather you from all the places where I have banished you, and will bring you back to the place from which I carried you into exile.'"

GOOD AND BAD FIGS

Jeremiah 24

The people left in the city were feeling rather pleased with themselves. They had been beaten by a foreign ruler, but at least they hadn't been captured and taken away. Jeremiah asked God why he did not punish them, for they were proud and had not changed their wicked ways.

God showed Jeremiah two baskets of figs, and asked him what he saw. Jeremiah replied rather puzzled, "I see one basket full of ripe, tasty-looking figs, and another full of figs so rotten that nobody would ever want to eat them."

"The people of Jerusalem are like those good figs," God told him. "Those already taken from Jerusalem to Babylon have begun to repent and are learning to come back to me. I will look after them, and one day I will bring them back to their own land.

"But the people left in Jerusalem are like the figs in the second basket. They are rotten, and will never change their ways. Whether by sword or famine or plague, they shall all be wiped from this land, every last one of them!"

DOWN A WELL

Jeremiah 37-38

Time after time Jeremiah tried to warn the new king that Judah was not strong enough to rebel against the might of Babylon. For now, they would have to do as Nebuchadnezzar ordered. But King Zedekiah and his officials were angry when Jeremiah tried to tell them things like that.

One day, when he was leaving the city, the guards arrested him and he was accused of trying to run off to the enemy. They put him in chains and locked him up in prison. Some people still came to listen to the prophet! In frustration, the officials threw him into the bottom of an unused cistern, where water was sometimes stored. It was deep and dark and muddy.

But one of the king's officials had a conscience. He went to ask the king if he could let Jeremiah out, for otherwise he would surely starve, and the king agreed. Taking some men with him, the good official went to the cistern and carefully pulled poor Jeremiah back out into the fresh air.

THE FALL OF JERUSALEM
2 Kings 25; 2 Chronicles 36

Zedekiah refused to listen to Jeremiah, and tried to rebel against Nebuchadnezzar. Then, once again, the mighty forces of Babylon came against Judah, and camped outside Jerusalem. Zedekiah was terrified. This time he begged Jeremiah for his advice, and Jeremiah told him, "God says: 'If you surrender, your life will be spared and the city will not be burned down. But if you will not surrender, the city will be given to the Babylonians and they will burn it down and you will not escape.'"

Even now, Zedekiah would not listen to Jeremiah. Instead, he tried to flee the city with his army in the middle of the night. But the Babylonians cut them down, then destroyed the city utterly. They set fire to the temple, the palace and all the houses, and the rest of the people were taken away as slaves. They had refused to listen to God and now they were being punished.

COMFORT IN DESPAIR
Isaiah 40

Jerusalem was destroyed. God had punished his disobedient children. But he had not stopped loving them. Years before, Isaiah had known this would happen, and he had a message of hope for the exiles from God:

"'Comfort my people,' says your God. 'Speak tenderly to Jerusalem, and tell her she has paid for her sins.'

"A voice calls out, 'Prepare a way in the wilderness for the Lord. His glory will be revealed, and all will see it together. The people are like grass, their faithfulness like flowers. Grass withers and flowers fall, but the word of our God lasts forever."

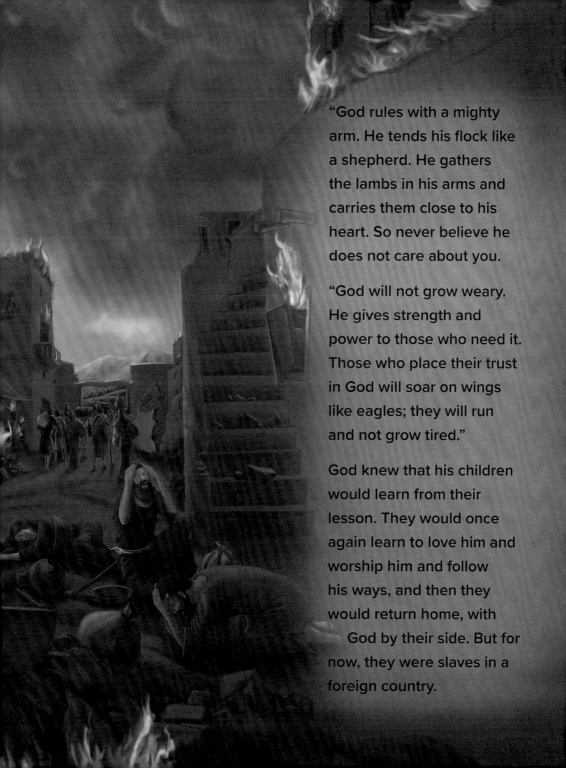

"God rules with a mighty arm. He tends his flock like a shepherd. He gathers the lambs in his arms and carries them close to his heart. So never believe he does not care about you.

"God will not grow weary. He gives strength and power to those who need it. Those who place their trust in God will soar on wings like eagles; they will run and not grow tired."

God knew that his children would learn from their lesson. They would once again learn to love him and worship him and follow his ways, and then they would return home, with God by their side. But for now, they were slaves in a foreign country.

EZEKIEL'S AMAZING VISION
Ezekiel 1

I t was five years since Ezekiel had seen his beloved homeland. Now he lived in Babylon, among the other captives. At this time, the final fall of Jerusalem and its temple had not yet happened, but most of the skilled people had been forced to leave the city.

Ezekiel was a good man, who loved God. One day, he was by the river, when an enormous cloud appeared in the sky encircled by brilliant light, and within it Ezekiel saw the most amazing vision.

Within the cloud there appeared four creatures surrounded by fire. Lightning flashed all around. Each had four faces — human, lion, ox and eagle — and four wings. The sound of the wings was like rushing water. Beside each creature was a wheel and within that there was another wheel, and the wheels sparkled like topaz and moved with the creatures, which stood under a sparkling vault. Above this was

a throne of startling blue lapis lazuli upon which sat a figure like a man, but glowing as if of fire, surrounded by light. Then God spoke to Ezekiel and told him he had been chosen to pass God's message on to his people, however obstinate and rebellious they might be.

EZEKIEL'S WARNING

Ezekiel 4-5

God told Ezekiel to take a clay brick and draw a picture of Jerusalem on it. Next, he was to lay siege to the city by setting up enemy camps and battering rams around it, and then he was to take an iron pan and place it between himself and the brick like a wall. Finally, he was to lie on his side for many, many days to bear the sins of the people of Israel and Judah, and was to eat only a small loaf of bread, which he was to make each day, and to drink only a little water. God was showing the people that Jerusalem would be under siege once again, and that the people would have little to eat or drink.

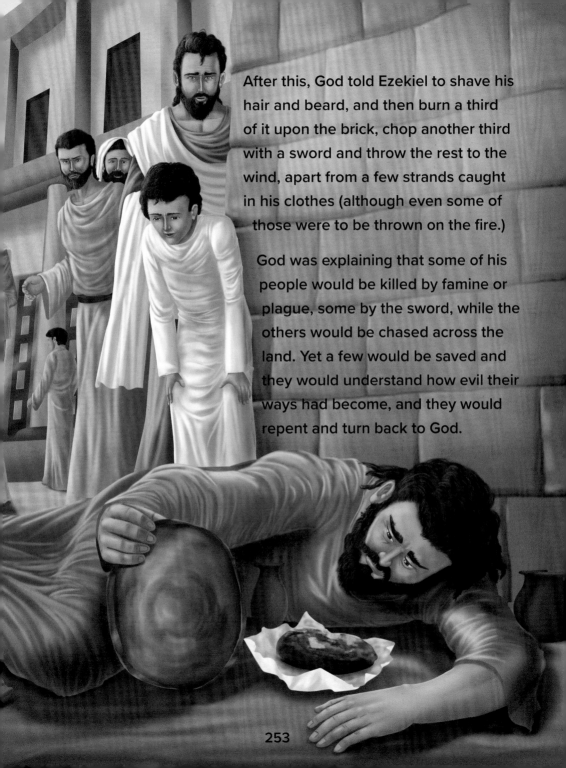

After this, God told Ezekiel to shave his hair and beard, and then burn a third of it upon the brick, chop another third with a sword and throw the rest to the wind, apart from a few strands caught in his clothes (although even some of those were to be thrown on the fire.)

God was explaining that some of his people would be killed by famine or plague, some by the sword, while the others would be chased across the land. Yet a few would be saved and they would understand how evil their ways had become, and they would repent and turn back to God.

THE LOST SHEEP

Ezekiel 34

A s Ezekiel had warned, Nebuchadnezzar's armies once again attacked Jerusalem, and this time they destroyed everything. The walls were razed to the ground, the holy temple was ransacked and burned, and everyone left was killed or taken captive.

Ezekiel told the leaders of those in exile that they had failed their people. They should have been looking after them like shepherds with their sheep, caring for the weak and healing the sick, looking for those who were lost or who had strayed.

Instead, they had been harsh and cruel, and the sheep had strayed and become prey for the wild animals that roamed the land.

Now God himself would gather his stray sheep, rescuing them from the dark places whence they had scattered, and bringing them back to Israel, where he would look after them.

THE VALLEY OF BONES

Ezekiel 37

When the exiles learnt of the fall of Jerusalem they felt certain that God had abandoned them. God wanted them to know that once they had learnt their lesson, he would cleanse them of their sins, and they could start afresh. He took Ezekiel to a valley covered in bones and asked him if they could live.

"You alone know, my Lord," Ezekiel replied, upon which God told him to prophesy to the bones, saying God would bring them to life.

When Ezekiel finished speaking, he heard a scraping sound, then a rattling, and before his eyes the bones came together to make whole skeletons. Then he saw that muscles and ligaments were joining the bones and the skeletons became covered in skin.

God said, "Tell the winds to blow breath into these bodies," and Ezekiel did so. There came a whistling sound as the winds breathed life into the still bodies. First their chests began to move, then their legs and arms, and soon before him stood a vast army of men. Then God told Ezekiel, "My people are like these bones. They have lost all hope and are as if lifeless. But you must tell them that I will breathe new life into my people."

VEGETABLES AND WATER
Daniel 1

Daniel was another exile living in Babylon, but because he came from a good family, and was clever and strong, he had been chosen to live in the royal palace, where he and his three friends were well-treated and taught the language, science and philosophy of Babylon.

Daniel was unhappy about eating the king's fancy food and wine, for God had forbidden

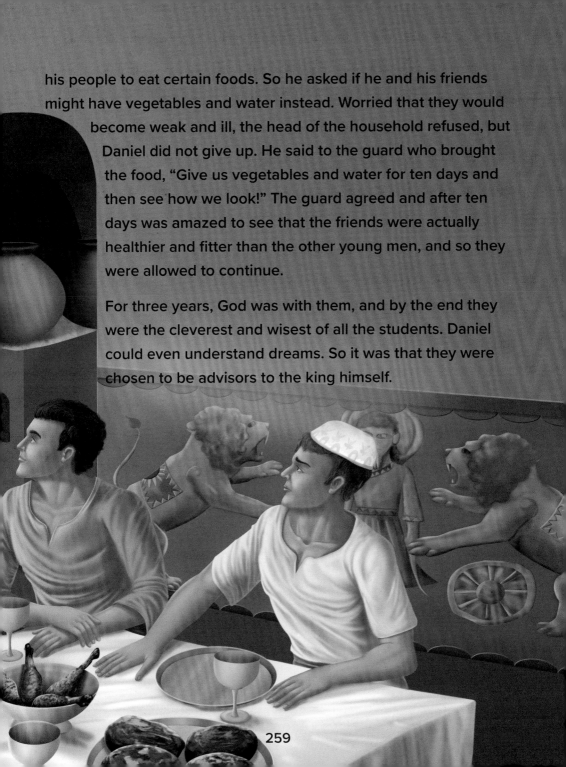

his people to eat certain foods. So he asked if he and his friends might have vegetables and water instead. Worried that they would become weak and ill, the head of the household refused, but Daniel did not give up. He said to the guard who brought the food, "Give us vegetables and water for ten days and then see how we look!" The guard agreed and after ten days was amazed to see that the friends were actually healthier and fitter than the other young men, and so they were allowed to continue.

For three years, God was with them, and by the end they were the cleverest and wisest of all the students. Daniel could even understand dreams. So it was that they were chosen to be advisors to the king himself.

THE MYSTERIOUS DREAM
Daniel 2

Not long after this, the king began having bad dreams — in fact, he had the same horrible dream over and over again. He was so worried and upset about it that he called all his fortune-tellers and wizards to him, saying, "My dream is worrying me. Tell me what it means."

His advisors looked puzzled. They asked him to describe the dream, but the king wanted them to work it out themselves, and then tell him the meaning. "No king has ever asked such a thing!" exclaimed the bemused wizards. "What you ask is impossible! Only the gods could do this!"

The king was so furious that he ordered them all executed – and all his advisors, including Daniel and his friends!

THE DREAM EXPLAINED

Daniel 2

Daniel begged for time to interpret the dream, then he and his friends prayed to God. That night, the mystery was revealed to him. The next day, he explained it foretold the future:

"You saw a terrible and massive statue standing before you. Its head was made of shining gold; its chest and arms of silver; its waist and hips of bronze, its legs of iron, and its feet partly of iron and partly of clay. While you watched, a great stone fell, smashing into its feet and shattering them. Then the whole statue crumbled, disappearing into dust born away by the wind. But the stone grew into a mountain that covered the whole earth.

"This is what it means. The mighty kingdom of Babylon is the gold head, and the other parts of the statue are empires yet to come. There will be another empire, then another, which will rule the whole earth. Then yet another empire will emerge, as strong as iron, crushing all the earlier ones. Yet it will be divided, for the feet were made of iron and of clay. But God will establish another kingdom which will never be conquered and which will destroy all those before it. God's kingdom will never end. That is the stone that will become a mountain."

The impressed king declared that Daniel's God truly was the wisest and greatest, and he made Daniel his chief advisor.

THE GOLD STATUE

Daniel 3

King Nebuchadnezzar's humility did not last long. Some time later he decided to have a great statue built out of gold, ninety feet high and nine feet wide. When it was completed, a special ceremony was held. A herald announced in a loud voice:

"People of the Empire! Shortly you will hear trumpets and other instruments. You must bow down and worship the statue. If you do not, you will be thrown into a blazing furnace!"

As soon as the fanfare sounded, everyone bowed down and worshipped the
gold statue. But among the crowd were
Daniel's three friends, Shadrach,
Meshach, and Abednego, who
refused to bow down before the
statue, for to do so would be
to disobey God's
commandment
to worship him
alone.

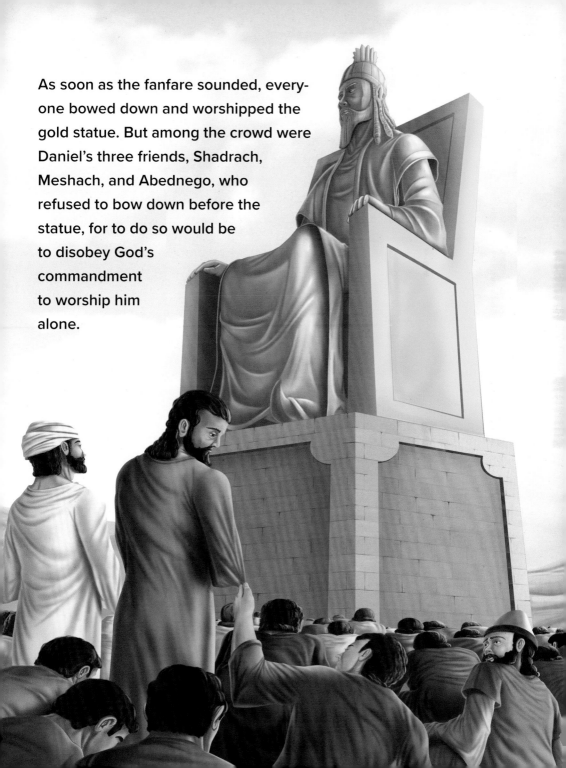

THE FIERY FURNACE

Daniel 3

When the king learnt of the three men's defiance, he was furious. He offered them one more chance to obey, but the young men still refused, saying, "Your Majesty, we will not bow down to anyone but our God. He can save us from the furnace, but even if he doesn't, we will never worship your statue."

The angry king told his guards to tie them up tightly with ropes, and to stoke up the furnace until it was seven times hotter than usual. Then they were thrown into the flames. The furnace was so hot that the guards themselves were scorched to death!

Nebuchadnezzar looked on. Suddenly he leapt up in disbelief, for within the furnace he could see four men: Shadrach, Meshach, and Abednego were no longer bound, but walked around freely, and with them was a fourth man who looked like the Son of God!

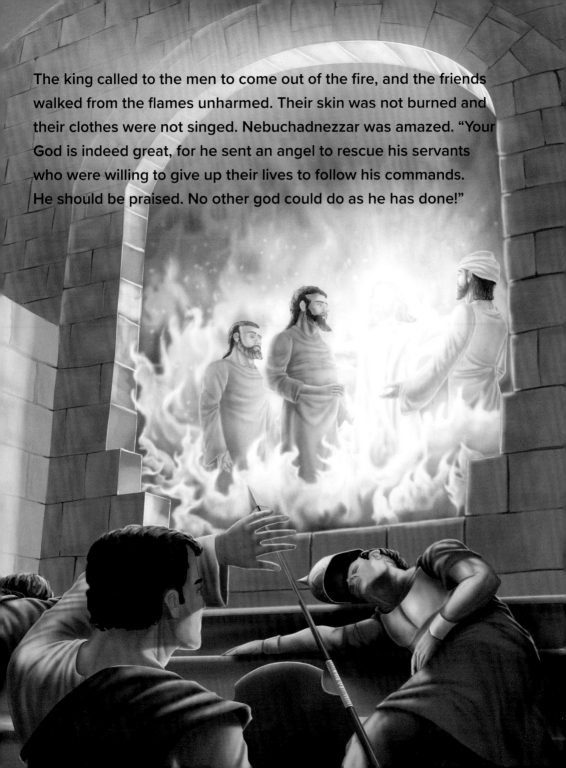

The king called to the men to come out of the fire, and the friends walked from the flames unharmed. Their skin was not burned and their clothes were not singed. Nebuchadnezzar was amazed. "Your God is indeed great, for he sent an angel to rescue his servants who were willing to give up their lives to follow his commands. He should be praised. No other god could do as he has done!"

THE GREAT TREE
Daniel 4

King Nebuchadnezzar had had yet another terrifying dream. None of his advisors could help, so he sent for Daniel, saying, "I know that your God can solve all mysteries. Last night I had a dreadful dream. There stood before me an enormous tree, towering above the land, strong and tall, with its topmost branches touching the sky. It could be seen to the very ends of the earth. The leaves were green and the branches were laden with fruit for every living creature. Animals sheltered beneath its boughs and birds lived happily in the branches.

"Then came a messenger from heaven who cried out that it must be cut down and the fruit scattered. The birds and the animals were to flee, but the stump and its roots were to remain. And the messenger said, 'Let him live outside among the animals for seven long years, with the mind of a wild animal, so all will know that God alone controls all kingdoms and chooses their rulers.'"

Daniel hardly knew what to say! "Your Majesty," he replied, clearly upset, "How I wish that this dream was not meant for you! You see, you are that tree. Your empire is strong and great and covers the earth. Yet unless you learn to honour God, you will be cut down and become mad and will be forced to

live like a wild animal for seven years! But the stump of the tree will
remain, and if you lose your pride and worship God, then he will
give you back your greatness again, so please, Your Majesty," he
begged, "take heed now and follow God's will and then maybe this
will never come to pass!"

THE WILD MAN

Daniel 4

Nebuchadnezzar was shaken at first, but little by little he fell back into his old habits. One day, about a year later, Nebuchadnezzar was walking on the roof of the royal palace, looking down upon Babylon. He was filled with pride, "All this is my doing!" he said arrogantly. "How powerful and great I am!"

No sooner had he said this than his ears were filled with a great booming sound. "King Nebuchadnezzar, this kingdom is no longer yours. You will be forced to leave the places of men and go and live with the wild animals, until you learn that God is in control of all earthly kingdoms and that he chooses their rulers."

Then the king was taken by a terrible madness and he was forced to flee the city and live in the fields, eating grass like a wild animal. His hair grew long and his fingernails looked like the claws of a bird and he did not remember that he had once been a mighty king living in a fine palace.

After seven long years, his mind cleared and he understood at last that he had nothing to be proud about — everything on earth was given by the goodness of God. God alone was mighty and powerful. Then Nebuchadnezzar humbly returned to his palace and once again became the ruler of the kingdom.

THE WRITING ON THE WALL
Daniel 5

After Nebuchadnezzar, Belshazzar was king. One evening he held a grand banquet with exotic food and fine wine and he sent for the gold and silver goblets taken from the holy temple in Jerusalem, so that he and his guests could drink wine out of them, as they praised the false idols they had created.

Suddenly the fingers of a human hand appeared and began to write on the plaster of the wall. The king turned white with terror and began to shake. He asked his advisors what the strange writing meant, and promised to reward them richly if they could explain it, but not one of them had a clue.

At the queen's suggestion he sent for Daniel, who told him that he did not want any reward but would tell him what the writing meant because of what God showed him.

"King Nebuchadnezzar was mighty and proud, but he learnt that God alone rules over this world and chooses who shall be king. You have not learnt this lesson. Your heart is hard and you are full of pride. You do not honour God who has given you all you have, but use goblets taken from God's holy temple, and bow down before false idols.

"This hand was sent by God. He has written, 'Mene, Mene, Tekel, Parsin,' and this is what it means: Mene – the days of your kingdom have been numbered; Tekel – you have been weighed on the scales and found wanting; Parsin – your kingdom will be divided."

That very night, Belshazzar was killed and Darius the Mede took over the kingdom.

THE SNEAKY TRAP
Daniel 6

Darius was impressed with Daniel, for he was wise and honest, and soon Darius put him in charge of his whole kingdom. The other officials were jealous. They knew Daniel prayed to his God every day at his window, and they came up with a plan.

"Your Majesty," said one of them. "We have written a new law. It states that for the next thirty days whoever asks anything of any god or any man, except of you, our King, shall be thrown into a den of lions. Please sign your name to the decree, so that it is official and cannot be changed." So the king signed his name, for he did not realise that they were setting a trap for Daniel!

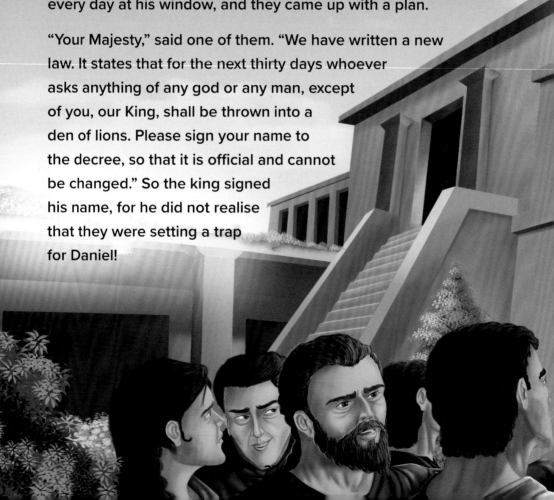

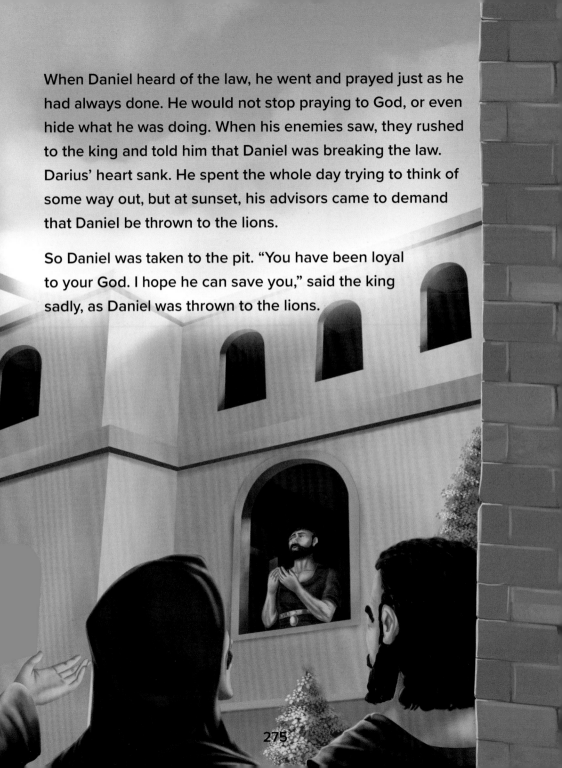

When Daniel heard of the law, he went and prayed just as he had always done. He would not stop praying to God, or even hide what he was doing. When his enemies saw, they rushed to the king and told him that Daniel was breaking the law. Darius' heart sank. He spent the whole day trying to think of some way out, but at sunset, his advisors came to demand that Daniel be thrown to the lions.

So Daniel was taken to the pit. "You have been loyal to your God. I hope he can save you," said the king sadly, as Daniel was thrown to the lions.

DANIEL IN THE LIONS' DEN
Daniel 6

That evening the king did not sleep a wink. At first light, he rushed down to the pit. "Daniel!" he cried out, more in desperation than hope. "Has your God been able to save you?"

He could not believe his ears when Daniel answered, "My God sent an angel and shut the mouths of the lions. They have not hurt me, for I was found innocent. Nor have I ever wronged you." The king was overjoyed and had Daniel brought out immediately. Then he ordered the men who had tricked him to be thrown into the pit themselves – and this time the lions were ruthless!

After this, Darius ordered his people to respect and honour Daniel's God, "For he can do wonderful things in heaven and on earth, and he rescued Daniel from the power of the lions!"

DANIEL'S VISIONS

Daniel 7-12

Daniel had many visions. They told of the future of the land. In one, he saw the winds of heaven churning up the sea, and four great beasts coming forth. He described them: "The first was like a lion with the wings of an eagle; the second was like a bear with three ribs in its mouth; the third was like a leopard with four heads and four wings; while the final beast, with iron teeth and ten horns, was more terrifying than all the others. It crushed and devoured its victims and trampled underfoot whatever was left.

"As I looked, the Ancient of Days was seated in a flaming throne, and a river of fire flowed before him. The first three beasts were stripped of their authority yet allowed to live a while longer, but the fourth was slain and thrown into the fire.

"As I watched there appeared one like the Son of Man. He was given glory and power and all people and nations worshipped him. His kingdom is everlasting and cannot be destroyed.

"I was told that the four beasts are four kingdoms that will rise up, each conquering the one before, and the fourth will crush the whole earth. Yet in the end, it will be judged and all the kingdoms under heaven will be handed over to the holy people of the Most High. His kingdom will be everlasting, and all rulers will worship and obey him, and his people will possess his kingdom for ever."

RETURN TO JERUSALEM
Ezra 1

When Daniel was an old man, King Cyrus took the throne. His Persian empire stretched far and wide, but God touched his heart and the mighty king issued a decree that the exiles from Judah could at last return home. He also sent for the precious treasures taken from God's temple so many years ago, and gave them to the exiles to take back.

Great was the excitement and the rejoicing among the people. They couldn't believe that they were finally going to return home! But not everybody was able to return to Jerusalem. The journey would be long and hard, and it would take time to rebuild the temple and city. Only the strongest and fittest were able to go.

Daniel was one of those who stayed behind. But his heart was filled with joy as he saw his people set out on their way, singing praises to God and laughing and smiling, and he gave thanks to God for allowing his people to return home and start again.

THE TASK AHEAD

Ezra 3

When the exiles returned to Jerusalem, they were shocked and saddened. The walls and buildings were ruined and the holy temple was no more than a pile of rubble. Still, everyone pulled together to help, and gave whatever they could spare.

It took time to get everyone settled, but they put up an altar where the temple had once stood, so they could worship God properly. When the foundations for God's temple were finally laid, people cheered and celebrated, but many also wept, for the eldest among them had seen the wonderful temple that had once stood there so proudly, and they knew it could never be equalled.

NASTY NEIGHBOURS

Ezra 4

When the Israelites had been exiled, new people had come to live on the rich, fertile land. They were known as Samaritans and were not thrilled to see the return of the Jews. However, they offered to help build the temple. "Let us help," they said. "We worship God too!" But Prince Zerubbabel refused, for they also worshipped false idols. God would not want him to accept their help.

This angered them and now they were determined to make trouble for their new neighbours. They tried to frighten them into stopping work, they bribed officials to work against them, and in the end they sent a letter to the new king of Persia:

"Your Majesty, we thought you should know that the Jews have settled in Jerusalem and are rebuilding that evil city. Jerusalem has always been a rebellious city, and if they manage to rebuild it, then they will surely give you trouble, and will stop paying your taxes. As your loyal subjects, we felt obliged to warn you about the situation."

The king of Persia commanded that all work on rebuilding the city was to cease, and for sixteen years, work on the temple stopped altogether.

REBUILDING THE TEMPLE
Ezra 5; Haggai 2; Zechariah 8

God did not want his people to give up so easily, so he sent two prophets to speak to them: Zechariah reminded the people that God was with them, and would protect them against their enemies; while Haggai told them it was wrong to be making their own homes comfortable when God's temple was not finished. Haggai also said that God had promised that the new temple would be so full of his presence that it would be even more glorious than King Solomon's temple!

The Jews began work once more. When the Samaritans questioned them, they replied that they were doing as King Cyrus had commanded. The Samaritans sent yet another letter to Persia telling the king what the Jews had said. But a new king was on the throne, and he checked through the royal records and found the original order. Then he told the Samaritans to stop interfering and to give the Jews whatever they asked for!

Now the Jews were able to work properly on the temple, and when at last it was finished, everyone gave thanks to God.

THE SAME MISTAKES
Ezra 7-10

Many years later, when yet another mighty king sat on the throne of Persia, there was a man named Ezra. He was worried that the people in Judah were not obeying God's law as they should, and he asked the king if he might go back to Jerusalem to guide them. Ezra had God's blessing, and the king respected him greatly. He sent him back to Jerusalem and gave him silver and gold for the temple to take with him.

When he got to Jerusalem, Ezra realised that he had been right to worry. The men had married foreign wives who had gods of their own. This was what had got his people into trouble before! Ezra felt so ashamed that they had made such a stupid mistake when they had been given such a wonderful second chance.

He spoke to the leaders. They agreed that they must put things right, and the foreign wives were sent away. The people promised God that they would try to honour his commandments.

NEHEMIAH WEEPS
Nehemiah 1-2

Nehemiah was Emperor Araxerxes' wine steward. He was a Jew in Babylonia, but was well-respected. He learnt that although the temple had been rebuilt in Jerusalem, the walls were still ruined, the city was without gates, and people were still struggling. Nehemiah was sad. He sat down and wept. He wanted to be with his people and to help them. He prayed to God to soften the emperor's heart, so that he would help.

One day, some time later, when he was serving the emperor his wine, Araxerxes looked closely at him. "You look dreadful," he said. "Is something making you unhappy?"

Servants were not supposed to show any expression, but the emperor looked concerned, and so Nehemiah decided to speak. "Your Majesty," he replied humbly, "how can I not be sad when I learn that my city is still in ruins?" and then he begged for permission to return to his homeland to help rebuild the city.

The emperor looked at him for a moment and then smiled. "Tell me what you need," he said, and Nehemiah thanked God for answering his prayers.

291

NEHEMIAH IN JERUSALEM
Nehemiah 2

When Nehemiah arrived in Jerusalem, he didn't tell anyone that he was there. He wanted to see what was happening for himself. One night, he took a trip around the walls to see what state they were in. In some places there was so much rubble on the ground that his donkey couldn't pass.

The next morning he went to the leaders of the people and said to them, "This is a disgrace! We need to rebuild the walls and make new gates. God answered my prayers when I wanted to come back here, and he will help us now!" and so work began on the city walls.

REBUILDING THE WALLS
Nehemiah 3-4

E veryone who could helped out on the walls. But even now the Samaritans tried to discourage them. "You'll never be able to rebuild those walls!" they taunted. "You think you can pray to your God and it will all be done overnight! And what sort of a pathetic wall will you be able to build anyway?" But the men of Judah turned their backs and carried on. It was hard work, but they refused to give in.

The Samaritans were worried. They didn't want Jerusalem to be strong and safe, so they plotted an attack. But Nehemiah divided his men into two – half worked, and half stood guard, and

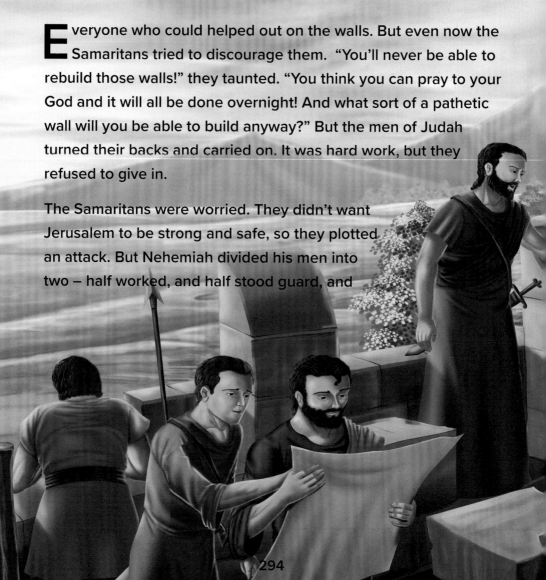

those who worked carried weapons – and he told them not to worry, for God was with them.

They worked from first light until the stars came out, always watching for the enemy, and in fifty-two days the walls were finished and the city was protected!

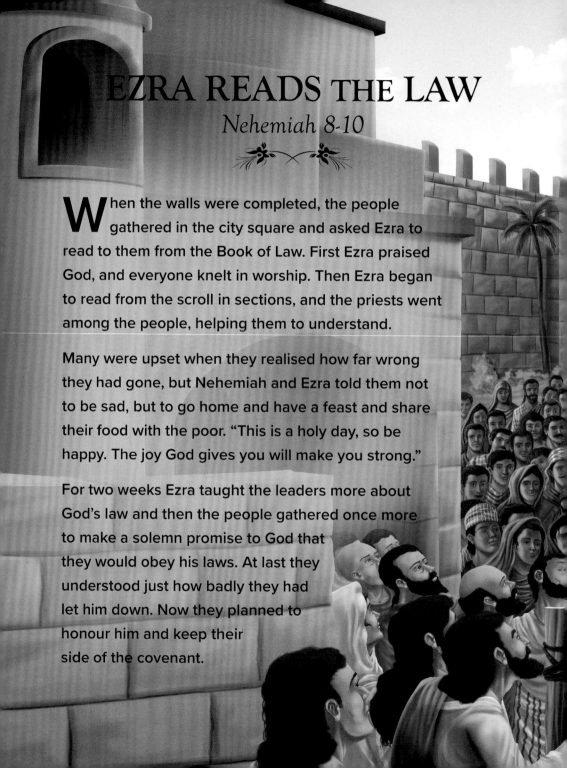

EZRA READS THE LAW
Nehemiah 8-10

When the walls were completed, the people gathered in the city square and asked Ezra to read to them from the Book of Law. First Ezra praised God, and everyone knelt in worship. Then Ezra began to read from the scroll in sections, and the priests went among the people, helping them to understand.

Many were upset when they realised how far wrong they had gone, but Nehemiah and Ezra told them not to be sad, but to go home and have a feast and share their food with the poor. "This is a holy day, so be happy. The joy God gives you will make you strong."

For two weeks Ezra taught the leaders more about God's law and then the people gathered once more to make a solemn promise to God that they would obey his laws. At last they understood just how badly they had let him down. Now they planned to honour him and keep their side of the covenant.

THE ANGRY KING

Esther 1

There was a new king in Persia. Foolish King Xerxes wanted to impress all the princes and nobles of his mighty empire so he invited them to a fabulous feast – it lasted six months! The guests were served the finest food, on gold plates, and they drank the finest wine. He drank rather too much himself, and decided to send for his beautiful wife, Queen Vashti, to show her off!

Queen Vashti didn't want to be paraded and refused to come down. The king was furious and his advisors suggested he should make an example of her. "You should stop her from being queen," they told him. "Otherwise all the women will think it's fine to disobey their husbands!" The king agreed and had a proclamation sent out that every husband should be the master of his home!

BEAUTIFUL ESTHER

Esther 2

King Xerxes needed a new queen, and so servants were sent out to find all the beautiful young maidens of the land and bring them to the palace.

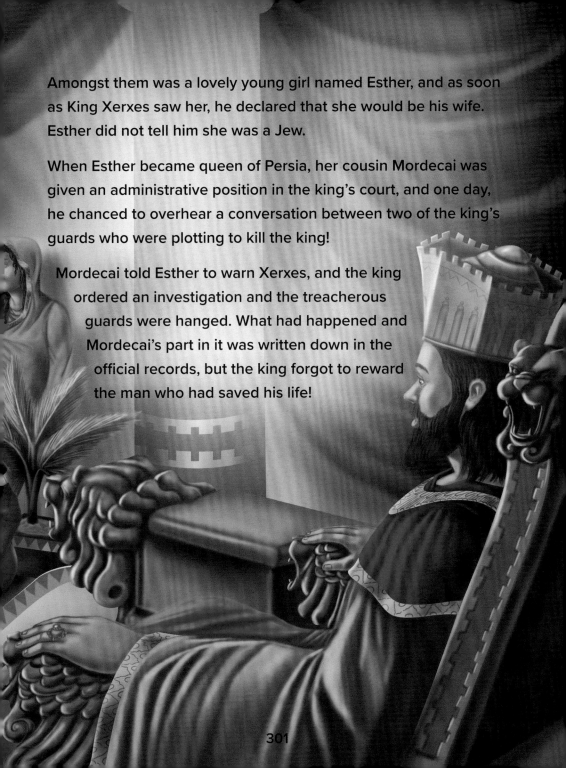

Amongst them was a lovely young girl named Esther, and as soon as King Xerxes saw her, he declared that she would be his wife. Esther did not tell him she was a Jew.

When Esther became queen of Persia, her cousin Mordecai was given an administrative position in the king's court, and one day, he chanced to overhear a conversation between two of the king's guards who were plotting to kill the king!

Mordecai told Esther to warn Xerxes, and the king ordered an investigation and the treacherous guards were hanged. What had happened and Mordecai's part in it was written down in the official records, but the king forgot to reward the man who had saved his life!

HAMAN BEARS A GRUDGE

Esther 3

The king's prime minister, Haman, thought very well of himself. He loved to ride through the streets and see the people bow before him. It made him feel powerful. And it truly annoyed him that Mordecai would never bow before him. When Haman found out that Mordecai was a Jew, he decided to punish not only him, but all the other Jews as well.

Haman was cunning. "Your Majesty," he said to the king. "There is a race of people in your empire that does not obey your laws. I would advise you to issue a decree that they be put to death."

The king agreed, and so Haman sent out a decree, stamped with the royal ring, stating that on the thirteenth day of the twelfth month of that year, all Jews – young and old, women and children – were to be killed throughout the empire!

THE BRAVE QUEEN
Esther 4-5

Never before had the Jewish people faced such annihilation! When Mordecai learnt of the decree, he tore his clothes and put on sackcloth and ashes. He sent a message to his cousin, begging that Esther plead their case before the king.

Esther was terrified. To go before the king without a summons was punishable by death! Only if the king held out his sceptre would the person be spared. But Mordecai sent another message, saying, "You must help the Jews or God will be angry. Maybe he made you queen precisely so that you can save his people."

Esther was scared, but made up her mind to go to the king. When he saw her, he smiled and held out his golden sceptre,

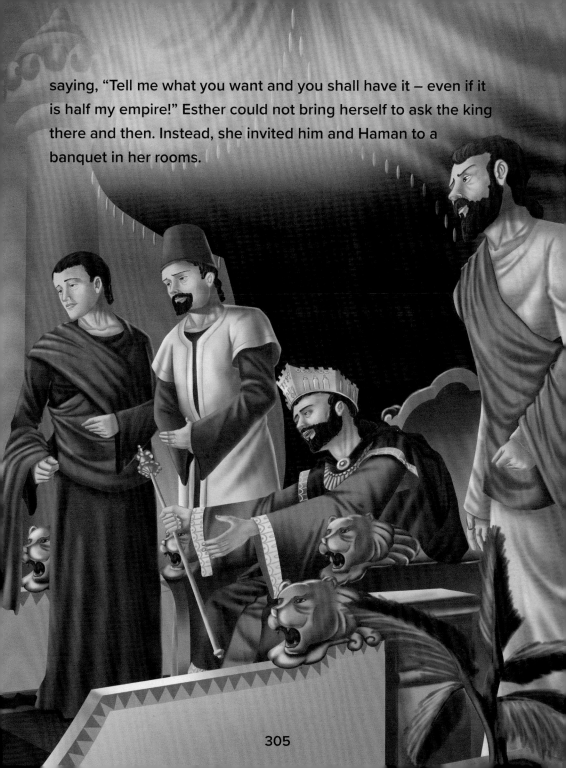

saying, "Tell me what you want and you shall have it — even if it is half my empire!" Esther could not bring herself to ask the king there and then. Instead, she invited him and Haman to a banquet in her rooms.

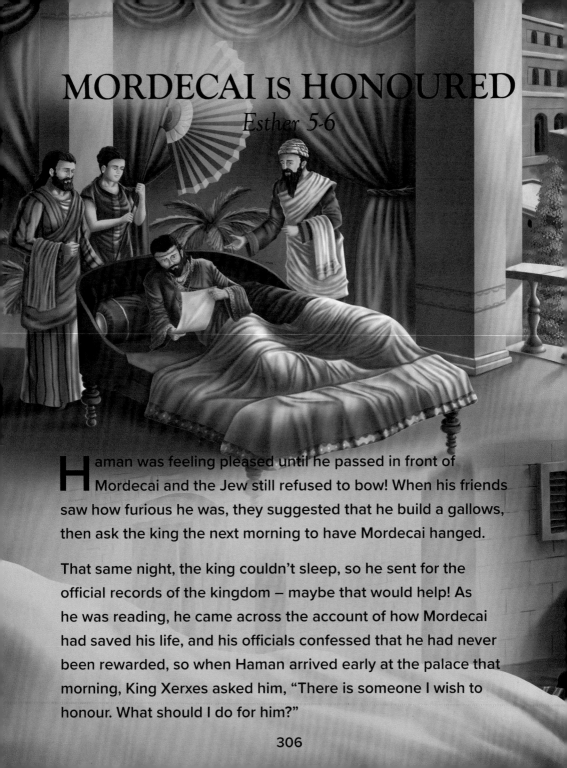

MORDECAI IS HONOURED
Esther 5-6

Haman was feeling pleased until he passed in front of Mordecai and the Jew still refused to bow! When his friends saw how furious he was, they suggested that he build a gallows, then ask the king the next morning to have Mordecai hanged.

That same night, the king couldn't sleep, so he sent for the official records of the kingdom — maybe that would help! As he was reading, he came across the account of how Mordecai had saved his life, and his officials confessed that he had never been rewarded, so when Haman arrived early at the palace that morning, King Xerxes asked him, "There is someone I wish to honour. What should I do for him?"

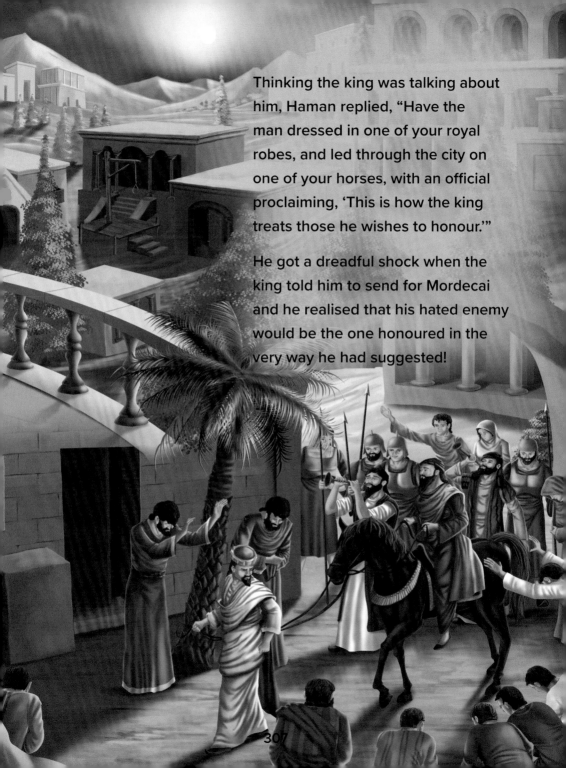

Thinking the king was talking about him, Haman replied, "Have the man dressed in one of your royal robes, and led through the city on one of your horses, with an official proclaiming, 'This is how the king treats those he wishes to honour.'"

He got a dreadful shock when the king told him to send for Mordecai and he realised that his hated enemy would be the one honoured in the very way he had suggested!

307

HAMAN IS PUNISHED
Esther 7

H aman was still seething when he arrived for the queen's
banquet. But things were only going to get worse! During the
banquet, the king again asked Esther what it was that she wanted.
This time the queen was brave enough to ask, "Your Majesty, if I
have found favour in your sight, I beg you to save my life and that
of my people, for we have been sold for slaughter!"

"Who has dared to do such a thing?" roared the king, and Esther
pointed to Haman. The king was so furious that he left the room

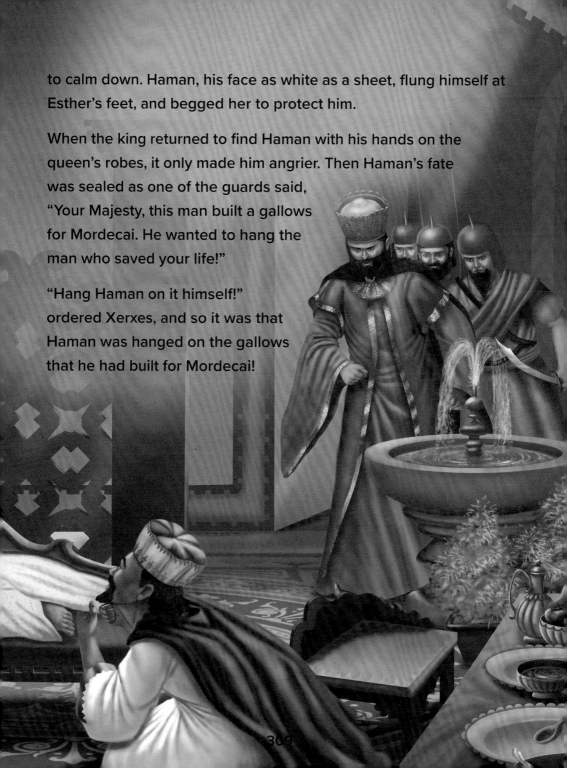

to calm down. Haman, his face as white as a sheet, flung himself at Esther's feet, and begged her to protect him.

When the king returned to find Haman with his hands on the queen's robes, it only made him angrier. Then Haman's fate was sealed as one of the guards said, "Your Majesty, this man built a gallows for Mordecai. He wanted to hang the man who saved your life!"

"Hang Haman on it himself!" ordered Xerxes, and so it was that Haman was hanged on the gallows that he had built for Mordecai!

ARM YOURSELVES!

Esther 8-9

Haman was dead, but the danger was not over. A decree stamped with the royal seal could not be changed. The Jews were still sentenced to death. Once again, brave Esther begged the king for help.

The king thought carefully, and then got Mordecai to send out another proclamation across the empire. This time it stated that all Jews might arm themselves, and if they were attacked, they might fight back and destroy the attackers and take all their possessions.

So it was that when the followers of Haman tried to massacre the Jewish people, the Jews fought back and destroyed them. Haman's ten sons were hanged and throughout the land, in every province, the enemies of the Jews were destroyed. The Jewish people were saved! And ever since, the Jews have celebrated the holy festival of Purim each year, in gratitude for God's deliverance of them through Esther and Mordecai.

JONAH DISOBEYS GOD

Jonah 1

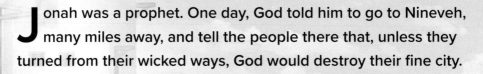

Jonah was a prophet. One day, God told him to go to Nineveh, many miles away, and tell the people there that, unless they turned from their wicked ways, God would destroy their fine city.

Now, the people of Nineveh were enemies of the Jews, and Jonah did not want to go and warn them, just so that God could spare them. He thought they deserved to be punished! So, instead of doing as God had told him, Jonah boarded a ship heading in the opposite direction to Nineveh! He was trying to run away from God, but of course, God is everywhere!

THE DREADFUL STORM
Jonah 1-2

A dreadful storm sprang up from nowhere. The winds howled and the waves towered above the ship. The terrified sailors threw their cargo over the side to lighten the ship, and they prayed to their gods. The captain found Jonah asleep in his cabin. He woke him roughly, saying, "How can you sleep when we are in such danger? Pray to your god to save us!"

The sailors drew straws to see which of them had angered the gods. When Jonah picked the short straw, they asked him what he had done, and Jonah told them that he was running away from his God, and that he was being punished. As he spoke, he realised how foolish and wicked he had been. He told them that they must cast him over the side, for God was only angry with him.

The sea became rougher and rougher and, in the end, the sailors lowered Jonah over the side with heavy hearts. Instantly, the sea became calm! The sailors were filled with awe, and began to pray to God with all their hearts, to thank him for sparing them and to promise to worship only him from that day forward.

THE BIG FISH

Jonah 2

But what about Jonah? The prophet sank swiftly to the bottom of the sea, certain he was going to die. But before he could take his last breath, God sent an enormous fish. The fish opened its mouth and swallowed Jonah whole, and there inside the fish Jonah could breath once again and was safe.

For three days and nights Jonah sat inside the belly of the fish. He had plenty of time to think about his mistakes and to feel very sorry for having disobeyed God. He prayed to God, thanking him for delivering him from the sea and letting him know how remorseful he felt.

After three days, God commanded the fish to spit Jonah up, unharmed, onto dry land. And when God once again asked him to take his message to Nineveh, Jonah was ready to do his will.

GOD'S MERCY

Jonah 3-4

When the people of Nineveh heard Jonah's message they were appalled and frightened. The king issued a royal proclamation that everyone should fast and wear sackcloth, and the people prayed to God and vowed to give up their evil ways. When God saw how sorry they were, he was filled with compassion and forgave them. The city was spared! But this made Jonah angry, for he felt that the people of Nineveh did not deserve to be saved and he went to sulk in the desert!

The desert was hot and God made a large, leafy plant grow up to protect Jonah from the fierce sun. But the next day God told a worm to nibble at the plant, and soon it withered and died. Jonah was cross, but God asked him what right he had to be angry.

"Every right!" replied Jonah indignantly. "I might as well die now that that plant has gone!"

Then God answered, "Jonah, you are unhappy about losing that plant, even though you did not plant it yourself, or tend it, and even though it was here one day, and gone the next!

"Nineveh has more than a hundred and twenty thousand people living there – men, women and children that I have made and cared about over the years. Do I not have the right to be concerned and to take pity on them?"

A GOOD MAN
Job 1

Job lived in the days of Abraham. He was wealthy, but was not boastful or selfish. He worshipped God and obeyed all his laws, and God was pleased with him. One day, Satan said, "It's easy for Job to be good when things are going so well. I bet if life got hard, he would change his tune!" And God agreed that Satan could test Job's faith.

One day, shortly after this, when Job's children were all feasting at his eldest son's house, a messenger came running up in a dreadful state to tell Job that all his cattle had been stolen. He had hardly finished speaking when another servant came to tell him that a ball of fire had fallen from the sky and burnt all the sheep. But the worst was yet to come, for now another servant came to tell Job that all his children had been killed when a mighty wind from the desert had struck his son's house, and it had collapsed, killing all inside.

Job tore his hair and clothes and sank to the ground in sorrow, but he said, "Everything I have was given to me by God. What he has given, he can take away. I still praise his name."

Job had passed the first test.

THE SECOND TEST
Job 2-31

Satan went back to God. "That's all very well," he said, "but it would be a different story if Job himself had to suffer." God agreed that he could test him again, and the very next day Job woke up covered in boils from head to toe. They stung and itched so much that all he could do was sit in a corner with a broken piece of pottery and use it to scrape his skin.

When his wife asked why he wasn't cursing God, Job replied, "If we take all the good things God sends, then we should take the bad things, too."

Job's friends came to see him. "You must have done something very wrong for God to be punishing you like this!" they said. "Tell him you are sorry and ask for forgiveness!"

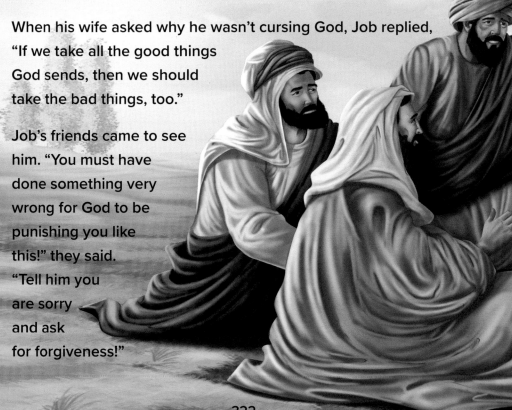

They were trying to help, but they only made it worse. Job knew he hadn't done anything wrong, but their words troubled him, and at last he broke out in frustration, "Curse the day that I was born! It would have been better to have died, then I wouldn't have to suffer like this! Oh, God, what have I done to make you so angry with me? How can you do this to me?"

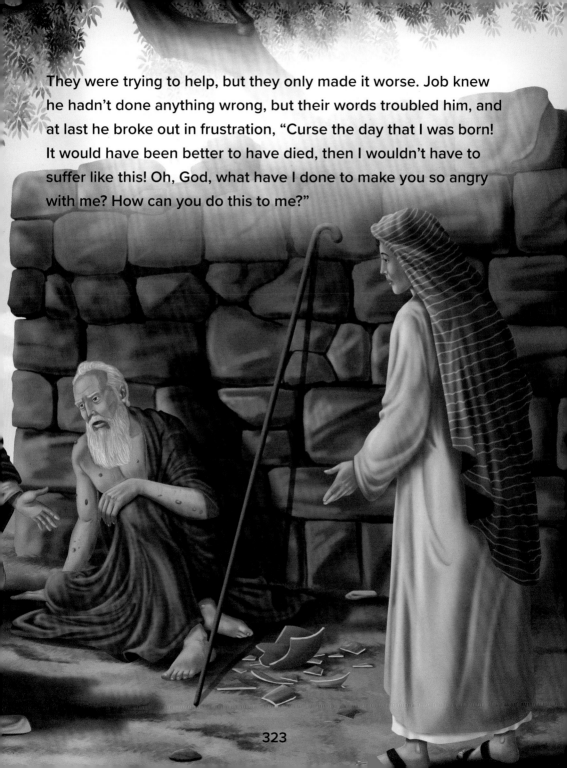

GOD TALKS TO JOB

Job 32-42

Another of Job's friends said, "I kept quiet up till now, because I am younger and I thought you would all be wiser than me. But wisdom clearly comes from God — not from old age! Job, you have no right to criticise God. Think of how great and powerful he is. You cannot begin to understand his ways. God is always just and merciful. Think of all the wonderful things he has done!"

Just then, a dreadful storm began to rage. Lightning filled the sky and thunder filled their ears. Then out of the storm came the voice of God, "Job, who are you to question Me? Were you there when I made the world? Can you command the day to dawn or the rain to fall on the land? How can you dare to question My wisdom?"

Then Job was ashamed. "Oh Lord," he said. "I am foolish and ignorant. Please forgive me!"

God was pleased with Job. He healed him and blessed the last part of his life even more than the first. Job had many more children, and lived happily for many more years.

A MESSENGER IS COMING
Malachi 1-4

Years had passed since the Jews had returned to Jerusalem. To start with, they had been full of good intentions, but things had begun to slip. They didn't realise how much they had to be thankful for. Instead, they wanted things to be easier, and felt that God had forgotten them. God sent Malachi to speak to them:

"You complain that God isn't blessing you. Yet you have stopped loving him with all your heart. Love and honour him and then you will receive his full blessing.

"One day, he will send a messenger to prepare the way for him. He will be like a scouring soap, a blazing fire that burns away everything impure, leaving behind only those who will worship God properly. For one day, God's judgement will come upon those who do wrong. But those of you who obey him will feel his power shine on you like the warm rays of the sun! Just remember to obey his laws!

"God has also promised that before the Day of the Lord, Elijah will return to earth to bring fathers and children together in order that people might follow in God's ways."

Now the people of Israel knew that one day, a mighty messenger would come to prepare the way for the Lord!

A TREE BY A STREAM
Psalm 1

*The Psalms are a wonderful collection of prayers, songs and poetry.
Many were written by King David. They are full of different emotions, such as
despair, sorrow, joy and love, and they praise God for his mercy and blessings.*

How happy and blessed is the person who doesn't
hang around with wicked people,
or do what they do,
or listen to what they say,
But who instead loves God's law
and thinks about his words every day and every night.

That person is like a tree planted by a stream of water,
which bears its fruit in the right season
and whose leaves do not wither.
That person will succeed in everything he does.

But not the wicked people!
They are like straw that the wind blows away.
The wicked people will be judged by God,
and will not be allowed to stand with God's own people.
God watches over those who try to be good and obey his laws,
but wicked people are heading towards destruction!

YOUR NAME IS WONDERFUL!

Psalm 8

Oh Lord, how wonderful is your name!

Your glory shines down from heaven,
it is seen everywhere on earth.
The praise of young children
silences your enemies and makes you strong.
When I think about how you made the heavens,
how you placed the moon and stars in the sky,
I wonder how you can care about human beings –
we are so small!

Yet you have made us only a little lower than the angels,
you have made us rulers over everything you created:
the birds and the beasts, the fish in the sea.
We rule over all of them.

Oh Lord, how wonderful is your name!

GOD IS MY FORTRESS
Psalm 18 and 91

How I love you, Lord!
You are my fortress and my rescuer,
with you I can always be safe,
you are like a shield to me.
The danger of death was all around me,
I was overwhelmed.
When I cried out to you, you heard me
And you reached down from the heavens
and pulled me out of deep waters.
Oh Lord, with your help I can do anything.
You make me strong and keep me safe,
you hold me up,
so that I can stand strong and secure.

Lord, I will sing your praises across the land,
I will praise your name wherever I go!

*King David sang Psalm 18 when God saved him
from his enemies.*

If you make the Lord your fortress,
no harm will come upon you,
no disaster will befall you.
For the Lord says,
I will save those who love me.
When they call to me,
I will answer them;
when they are in trouble,
I will be with them.

Psalm 91

DO NOT BE FAR FROM ME
Psalm 22

This is another of King David's psalms, which many Christians read or sing on Good Friday, because they believe that it is not only about the suffering of King David, but that it is also about the suffering of Jesus.

My God, why have you forsaken me?
I cry out every day, but you do not answer,
every night, but I find no rest.
Yet you saved our ancestors.
When they cried out to you they were saved.
They trusted you and you did not let them down.
But I am nothing but a worm,
Everyone mocks me, saying,
"If he trusts in the Lord, then let the Lord save him!"
Yet it was you that brought me into this world.

Do not be far from me,
for I am surrounded by trouble
and there is no one to help me.
My enemies encircle me like wild beasts,
waiting to pounce, ready to destroy me.
Like a pack of dogs they close in on me;
tearing at my hands and feet.

So do not stay away, my Lord, come quickly to help me.
Rescue me from these wild beasts!
I will tell everyone what you have done; I will praise your name.
For you do not neglect the poor or ignore their suffering;
but answer when they call for help.

Everyone will bow down before you,
and future generations will be told,
that the Lord saved his people.

THE LORD IS MY SHEPHERD

Psalm 23

The Lord is my shepherd,
he will make sure I have everything I need.
He lets me rest in green meadows,
he leads me beside quiet streams to drink,
he refreshes my soul.
He shows me the right way to go,
so that I can bring honour to his name.
Even though I walk through the darkest of valleys,
I will fear nothing, for you are with me;
your rod and your shepherd's crook make me feel safe.
You prepare a feast for me in front of my enemies.
You anoint my head with oil;
I feel so honoured that I am overwhelmed.
Surely your goodness and love will be with me
every day of my life,
and I will live in the house of the Lord forever.

YOUR DAY WILL COME
Psalm 37

Don't waste time worrying about people who do bad things,
for they won't last long.
Trust in God and do good,
love him and you will have everything you need.
Follow his ways and your reward will shine like the brightest sun.
Be calm and patient and your day will come.

God looks after those who love him.
Even though they may stumble, he keeps them from falling,
He holds them up with his hand.
God never lets them down.

God will always make sure those who love him have enough.
Bad people hold on tight to what they have and it is taken away.
But good people want to share the things they have,
and they will be blessed.
One day, those who do bad things will be punished.
Then God's followers will inherit the land.

God will always take care of his people
He will look after them when times are bad,
He will rescue them from wicked people
because they turn to him for help.

WATER IN THE DESERT
Psalm 63

You, God, are my God,
I seek you with all my heart;
I need you just like a dry, parched desert needs water.
I have seen how wonderful and glorious you are.
Your love is better than life itself, and I will praise you.
I will praise you as long as I live, and I will pray to you.

King David wrote this psalm when he was in the Desert of Judah.

Your love will satisfy me like the richest food.
When I lie in my bed I will remember you,
and I will think of you all night long.
You have always been there to help me,
your wings protect me,
and when I cling to you, your hand keeps me safe.

A LAMP FOR MY FEET
Psalm 119

How blessed are they who are good;
who follow the ways of the Lord
and seek him with all their heart.

But how can young people keep their lives pure?
By obeying your commands.
I seek you with all my heart
and love your laws.
Please give me understanding
and keep me strong
that I may follow your laws.
Your words taste sweet in my mouth,
they are a lamp for my feet,
a light on the path on which I travel.
You are my refuge and my shield,
I put all my hope and trust in you.
Steady me with your hand,
and help me to honour you.
I am like a sheep that was lost:
please come and look for me,
for I remember all your commands.

HE WILL NEVER SLEEP

Psalm 121

I lift up my eyes to the mountains –
where will my help come from?
My help comes from the Lord,
the Maker of heaven and earth.
He will not let me stumble or fall,
He will never sleep while he is watching over me.
The protector of all Israel never sleeps.

The Lord watches over you,
He is right beside you, shading you;
the sun will not harm you by day,
nor the moon by night.
The Lord will keep you from all harm,
He will watch over you your whole life long;
He will watch over you in your daily life
now and always.

BY THE RIVERS OF BABYLON

Psalm 137

By the rivers of Babylon we sat and wept
when we remembered Zion.
There on the willow trees
we hung our harps,
for our captors wanted us to entertain them,
our tormentors ordered us to sing songs of joy!
They said, "Sing us one of the songs of Zion!"
How can we sing the songs of the Lord
in a foreign land?
If I forget you, Jerusalem,
may my right hand forget its cleverness,
and let my tongue stick to the roof of my mouth,
if I do not remember you —
if I do not think about Jerusalem
above everything else.

*This psalm expresses the yearning and sorrow
of the Jewish people in exile.*

347

PRAISE HIM WITH MUSIC
Psalm 150

Praise the Lord.
Praise God in his Temple,
praise him in his mighty heavens.
Praise him for his acts of power;
praise him for his surpassing greatness.
Praise him with trumpets,
praise him with harps and lyres,
praise him with drums and dancing,
praise him with stringed instruments and flutes,
praise him with the clash of cymbals.
Let everything that breathes praise the Lord!

WISE SAYINGS
from the Book of Proverbs

The Bible is a wonderful place to look for words of wisdom. The Book of Proverbs is filled with wise sayings, many composed by King Solomon, while others were passed down through the ages, or written by other wise men.

God

Trust in God with all your heart: never rely on what
you think you know.

We may make our plans, but God has the last word.

God sees everything that we do, whether good or bad:
He can see what is inside our hearts.

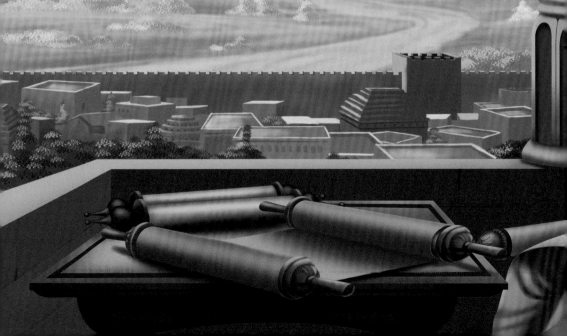

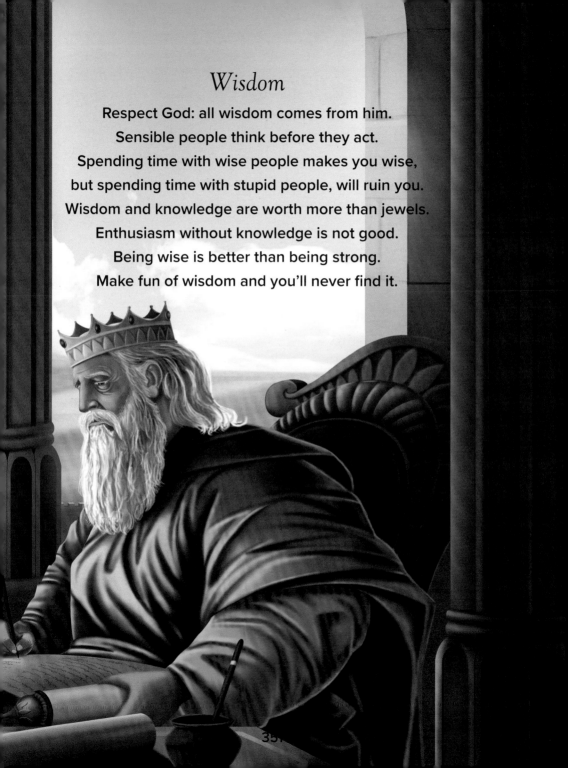

Wisdom

Respect God: all wisdom comes from him.

Sensible people think before they act.

Spending time with wise people makes you wise,

but spending time with stupid people, will ruin you.

Wisdom and knowledge are worth more than jewels.

Enthusiasm without knowledge is not good.

Being wise is better than being strong.

Make fun of wisdom and you'll never find it.

Wealth and Money

The easier you get money, the sooner you will lose it.

Better to eat a dry crust of bread with peace of mind
than a banquet in a house full of trouble.

If you have to choose between reputation and wealth,
choose reputation.

Rich and poor were all created by God.

Some people spend their money freely and still grow richer:
others are cautious, yet grow poorer.

Don't spend all your time trying to get rich: money can disappear
overnight, as if it had grown wings and flown away.

It's far better to be wise and sensible than to be rich.

Borrow money and you become the lender's slave.

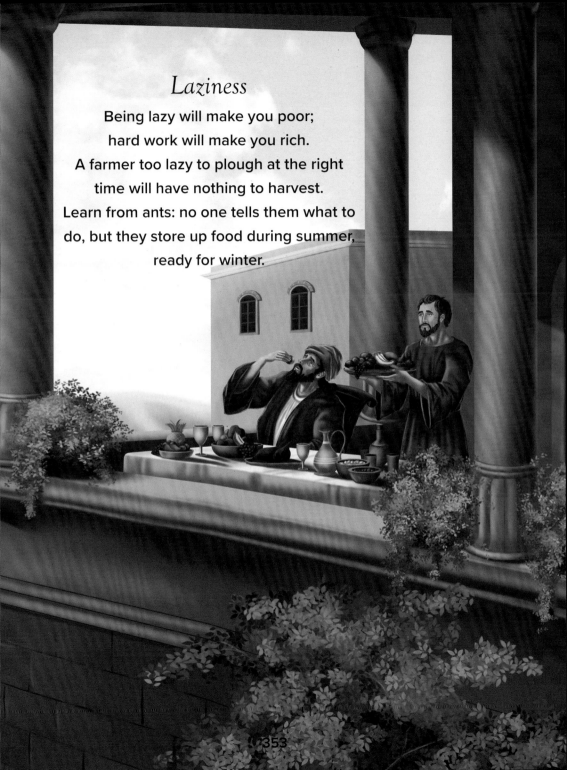

Laziness

Being lazy will make you poor;
hard work will make you rich.
A farmer too lazy to plough at the right
time will have nothing to harvest.
Learn from ants: no one tells them what to
do, but they store up food during summer,
ready for winter.

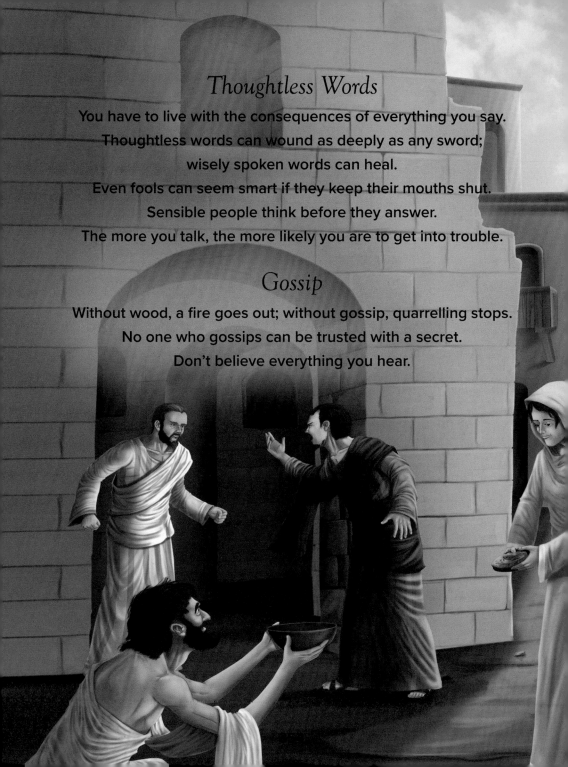

Thoughtless Words

You have to live with the consequences of everything you say.
Thoughtless words can wound as deeply as any sword;
wisely spoken words can heal.
Even fools can seem smart if they keep their mouths shut.
Sensible people think before they answer.
The more you talk, the more likely you are to get into trouble.

Gossip

Without wood, a fire goes out; without gossip, quarrelling stops.
No one who gossips can be trusted with a secret.
Don't believe everything you hear.

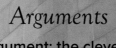

Arguments

Any fool can start an argument: the clever thing is to avoid them.

If you're wronged, don't try to get even: trust God to make it right.

The start of an argument is like the first break in a dam; stop it before it goes any further.

Getting involved in an argument that is none of your business is like grabbing a fierce dog by the ears.

Curses cannot hurt you unless you deserve them.

It is better to win control over yourself than over whole cities.

If you want people to like you, be forgiving.

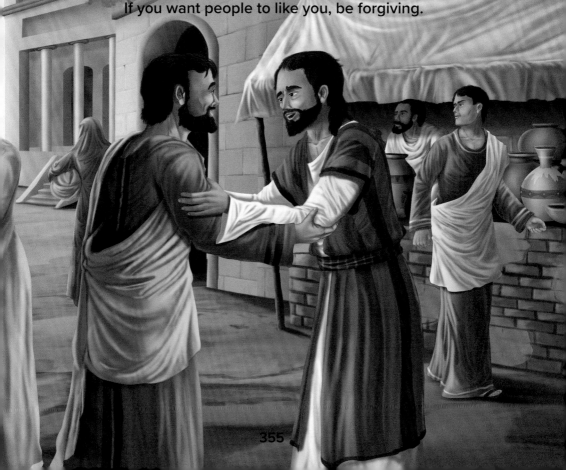

Family

Respect your parents and show them your appreciation:
make them proud of you and you'll make them happy.
When parents correct their children, it shows
that they love them.
Sensible children listen when their parents correct them:
stubborn children will ignore them.
A helpful wife is her husband's greatest treasure.
Better to live on the roof than share a house
with a nagging wife.

Correction and Advice

Listen when God corrects you: He corrects
those he loves.
Sensible people accept good advice and want to be told
when they're wrong: it is stupid to hate being corrected.
An intelligent person learns more from one rebuke than a
fool learns from being beaten a hundred times.
Bad advice is a deadly trap, but good advice is a shield.

Jealousy

Anger is cruel and destructive, but jealousy is far worse.
Peace of mind makes the body healthy;
jealousy is like a cancer.

357

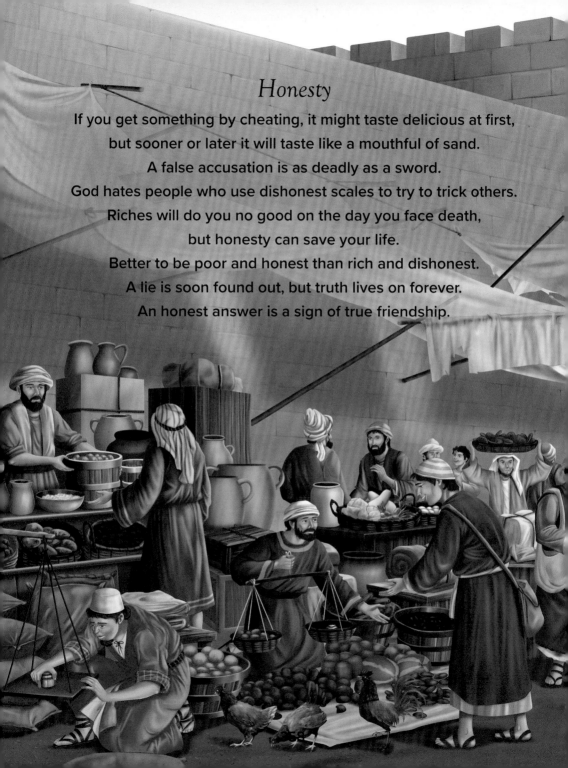

Honesty

If you get something by cheating, it might taste delicious at first,
but sooner or later it will taste like a mouthful of sand.
A false accusation is as deadly as a sword.
God hates people who use dishonest scales to try to trick others.
Riches will do you no good on the day you face death,
but honesty can save your life.
Better to be poor and honest than rich and dishonest.
A lie is soon found out, but truth lives on forever.
An honest answer is a sign of true friendship.

Praise and Flattery

Insincere talk that hides what you are really
thinking is like a fine glaze on a cheap clay pot.
Let other people praise you: never do it yourself!
Too much honey is bad for you, and so is
trying to win too much praise.

Love

A simple meal with people you love is better than
a feast where there is hatred.
Love is always ready to overlook the wrongs
that people do.

Compassion

When you give to the poor, it is like lending
to God, and God will pay you back.
If you don't listen to the cry of the poor,
your own cry for help will not be heard.
Whenever you possibly can, do good to those
who need it, even if they are your enemies.
You do yourself a favour when you are kind:
if you are cruel, you hurt yourself.
Don't be glad when your enemies are in
difficulties: God will know you are gloating, and
won't like it; and maybe he won't punish them.

Friends

Friends mean well, even when they hurt you;
but when an enemy puts his arm around your
shoulder – watch out!
Some friends are more loyal than brothers.
Don't mix with people who'll pass on bad habits.

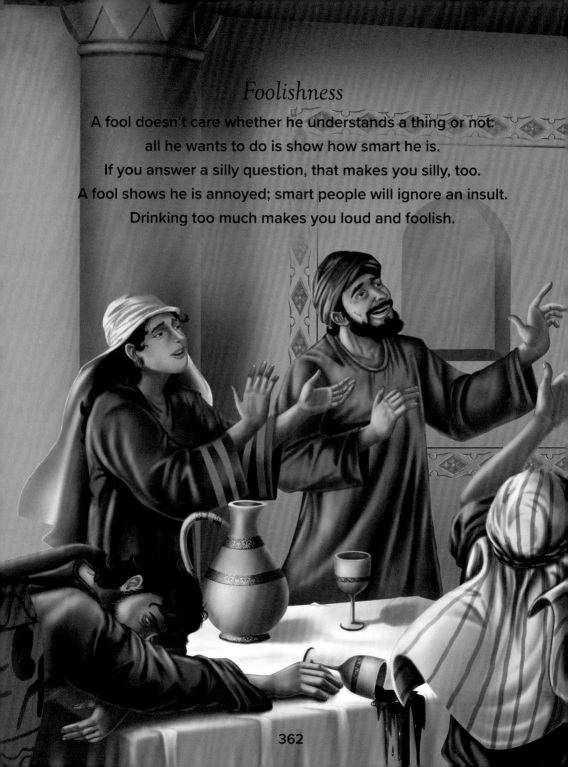

Foolishness

A fool doesn't care whether he understands a thing or not:
all he wants to do is show how smart he is.
If you answer a silly question, that makes you silly, too.
A fool shows he is annoyed; smart people will ignore an insult.
Drinking too much makes you loud and foolish.

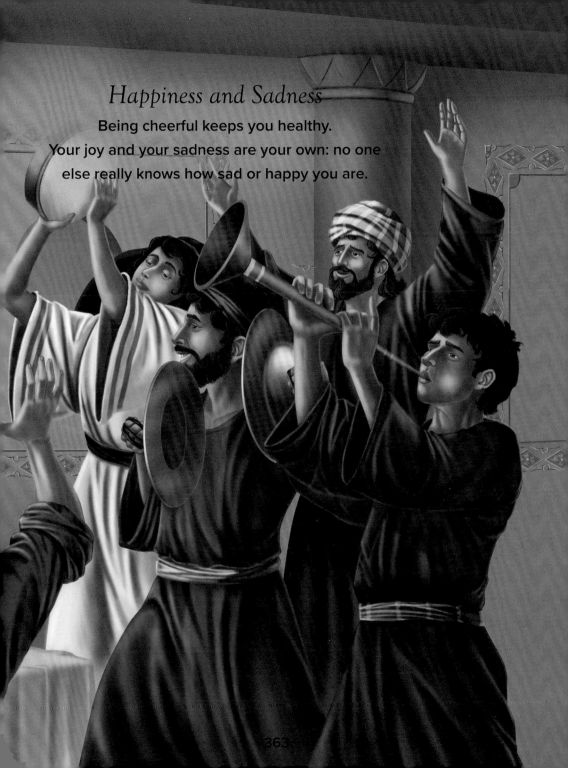

Happiness and Sadness

Being cheerful keeps you healthy.
Your joy and your sadness are your own: no one
else really knows how sad or happy you are.

More Wise Sayings

The road good people travel is like the sunrise, getting brighter
and brighter, but the road of the wicked is dark as night.
Sometimes only a painful experience makes us change our ways.
Pride leads to destruction, and arrogance to downfall.
Depending on an unreliable person in a crisis is like trying to chew
with a loose tooth or walk with a crippled foot.
If someone powerful invites you to eat, don't take too much
of what he offers you – he might be trying to trick you.
The poor have a hard life, but happiness lies
in being content.

A TIME FOR EVERYTHING

Ecclesiastes 3

The writer of the Book of Ecclesiastes believed that everything that happens does so at the time God chooses, that we should spend our lives doing the best we can and trying to be happy, and that we should enjoy the things that we work to get, because life is God's gift to us. This is what he wrote:

There is a time and a season for everything:
A time to be born, and a time to die;
A time to plant, and a time to uproot;
A time to kill, and a time to heal;
A time to break down, and a time to build up;
A time to weep, and a time to laugh;
A time to mourn, and a time to dance;

A time to scatter stones, and a time to gather stones together;
A time to embrace, and a time to refrain from embracing;
A time to seek, and a time to lose;
A time to keep, and a time to throw away;
A time to rend, and a time to sew;
A time to keep silence, and a time to speak;
A time to love, and a time to hate;
A time for war, and a time for peace.

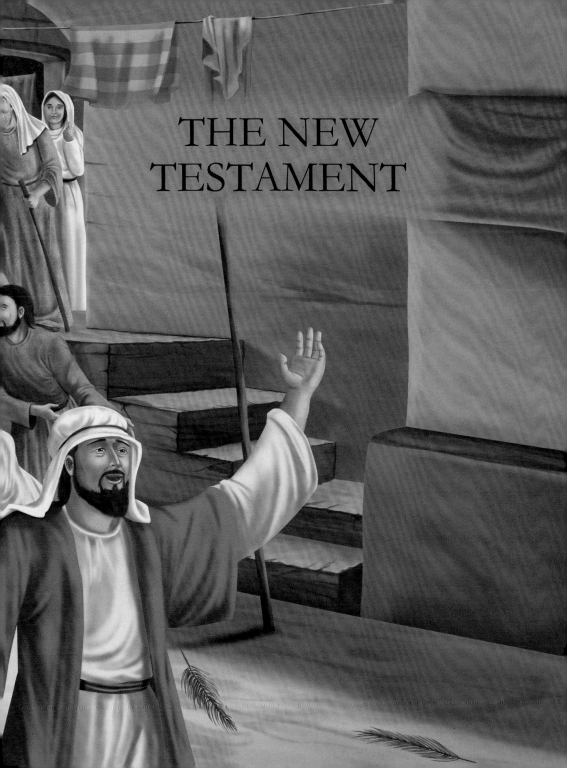

THE NEW TESTAMENT

THE HOLY LAND
IN THE TIME OF JESUS

Sidon •

Tyre • PHOENICIA

GALILE

Capernau
Bethsaida
Mt Carmel ▲ Cana •

Nazareth •
Nain • Mt
Tabo ▲

The Great Sea
(Mediterranean)

Caesarea •

SAMARIA

Samaria •

Shechem •
(Sychar)

EPHRAIM

Jericho •
Emmaus •
Jerusalem • ▲ Mt of Oli
Bethlehem • • Bethany

JUDAH

Dea
Sea

IDUMAEA

370

ABILENE

● *Damascus*

SYRIA

● *Caesarea Philippi*

TETRARCHY OF
PHILIP

● *Bethsaida Julias*

Sea of
Galilee

DECAPOLIS

PERAEA

thabara

NABATAEA

371

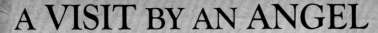

A VISIT BY AN ANGEL
Luke 1

Four hundred years had passed since Malachi had warned the people of Israel. Now evil King Herod sat on the throne of Judah, but even he answered to Augustus Caesar, the emperor of the mighty Roman empire.

Zechariah was burning incense inside the holy temple in Jerusalem, when an angel appeared before him! Zechariah was terrified, but the angel said gently, "Do not be afraid. God has heard your prayers. Your wife Elizabeth will bear you a son, and you are to call him John. He will be a great man, and will prepare the way for the one who comes after him."

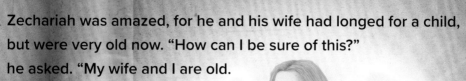

Zechariah was amazed, for he and his wife had longed for a child, but were very old now. "How can I be sure of this?" he asked. "My wife and I are old. How can this be?"

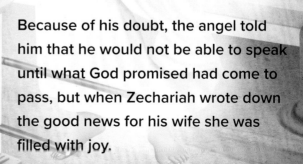

Because of his doubt, the angel told him that he would not be able to speak until what God promised had come to pass, but when Zechariah wrote down the good news for his wife she was filled with joy.

MARY IS CHOSEN BY GOD
Luke 1

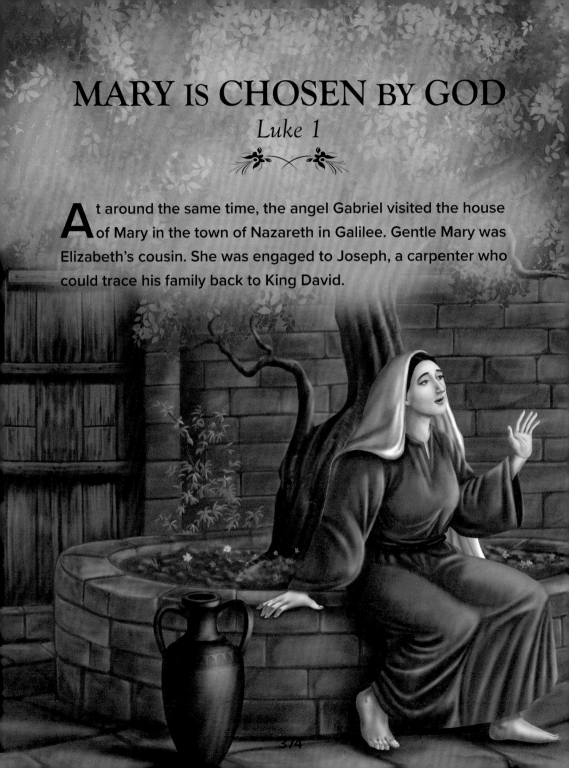

A t around the same time, the angel Gabriel visited the house of Mary in the town of Nazareth in Galilee. Gentle Mary was Elizabeth's cousin. She was engaged to Joseph, a carpenter who could trace his family back to King David.

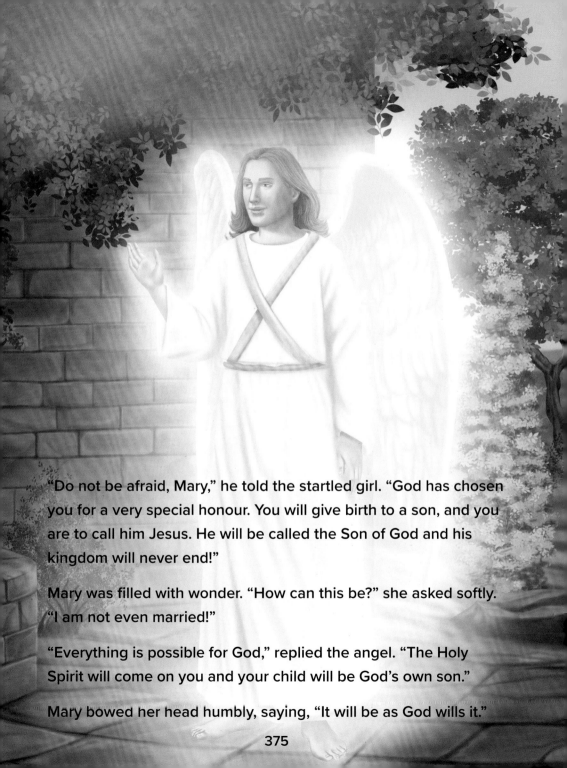

"Do not be afraid, Mary," he told the startled girl. "God has chosen you for a very special honour. You will give birth to a son, and you are to call him Jesus. He will be called the Son of God and his kingdom will never end!"

Mary was filled with wonder. "How can this be?" she asked softly. "I am not even married!"

"Everything is possible for God," replied the angel. "The Holy Spirit will come on you and your child will be God's own son."

Mary bowed her head humbly, saying, "It will be as God wills it."

MARY VISITS ELIZABETH
Luke 1

Mary couldn't wait to tell her cousin the good news, and travelled to see her. No sooner had she said 'Hello', than Elizabeth exclaimed: "Oh Mary, you are truly blessed among women, and so is the child you will bear! How honoured I feel, when the mother of my Lord visits me! When you greeted me, the baby in my womb leaped for joy. We are so lucky, cousin!"

Mary was so full of thanks and joy that she broke out into a song of praise, thanking God with all her heart. The two women had so much to share that Mary stayed with Elizabeth for several months before returning home.

377

JOSEPH LISTENS TO GOD
Matthew 1

Not surprisingly, when Joseph found out that Mary was pregnant, he thought she had been unfaithful to him and was bitterly disappointed. He decided to break off the marriage, but before he could do anything, God spoke to him in a dream: "Mary has not been unfaithful. The baby she is carrying was conceived from the Holy Spirit. She will give birth to a son, and you will call him Jesus, for he will save his people from their sins."

When Joseph awoke, he felt much happier. Mary had been true to him, and now he would do all he could to keep her and the child safe, and so he married her without delay.

HIS NAME IS JOHN

Luke 1

Soon Elizabeth gave birth to a boy. Her friends and relatives were thrilled, and asked what she was going to call him. When she told them he would be named John, they were rather taken aback, for they had expected the child would be named after his father – no one else in the family was called John!

They asked Zechariah, and were amazed when he took a tablet and wrote on it in clear, bold letters, "His name is John." At that moment, Zechariah's tongue was freed — and the very first words that he spoke were all in praise of the Lord: "Let us praise the Lord, the God of Israel! He has sent his people a mighty Saviour, from the house of his servant David, who will go before the Lord to prepare the way for him, to let his people know that they will be saved, for their sins will be forgiven."

The people looked at one another in wonder. It was clear that this child would grow up to be very special indeed.

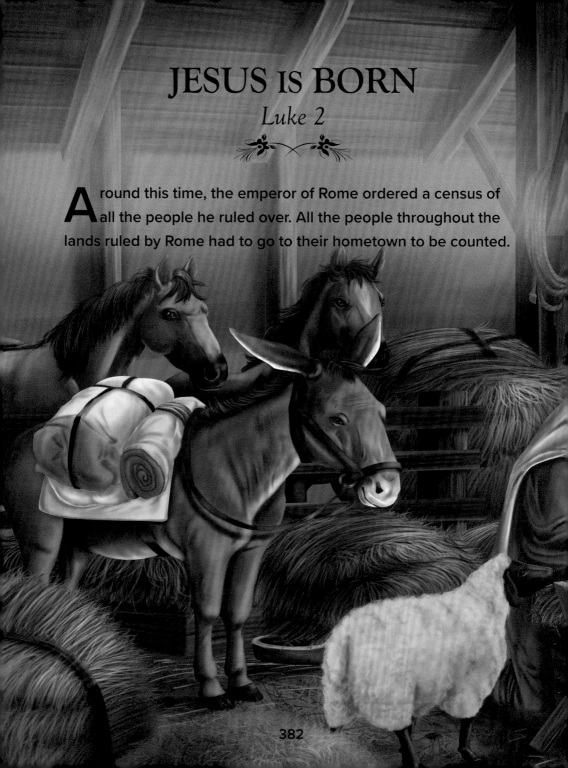

JESUS IS BORN
Luke 2

Around this time, the emperor of Rome ordered a census of all the people he ruled over. All the people throughout the lands ruled by Rome had to go to their hometown to be counted.

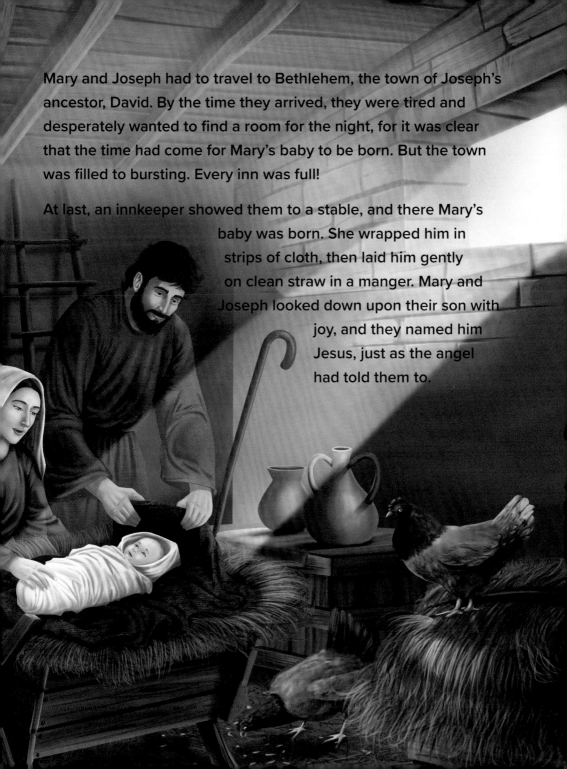

Mary and Joseph had to travel to Bethlehem, the town of Joseph's ancestor, David. By the time they arrived, they were tired and desperately wanted to find a room for the night, for it was clear that the time had come for Mary's baby to be born. But the town was filled to bursting. Every inn was full!

At last, an innkeeper showed them to a stable, and there Mary's baby was born. She wrapped him in strips of cloth, then laid him gently on clean straw in a manger. Mary and Joseph looked down upon their son with joy, and they named him Jesus, just as the angel had told them to.

THE SHEPHERDS' STORY

Luke 2

That same night, an angel appeared to some shepherds in the hills above Bethlehem. As they fell to the ground in fear, the angel said, "Do not be afraid. I bring you good news. Today, in the town of David, a Saviour has been born to you; he is the Messiah, the Lord. Go and see for yourselves. You will find him wrapped in cloths and lying in a manger." Then the sky was filled with angels praising God!

When the angels had left, the shepherds
hurried to Bethlehem where they found
the baby lying in the manger just as they
had been told. And when
they had seen him, and knelt
before him, they rushed off to tell
everyone about this special baby
and the wonderful news!

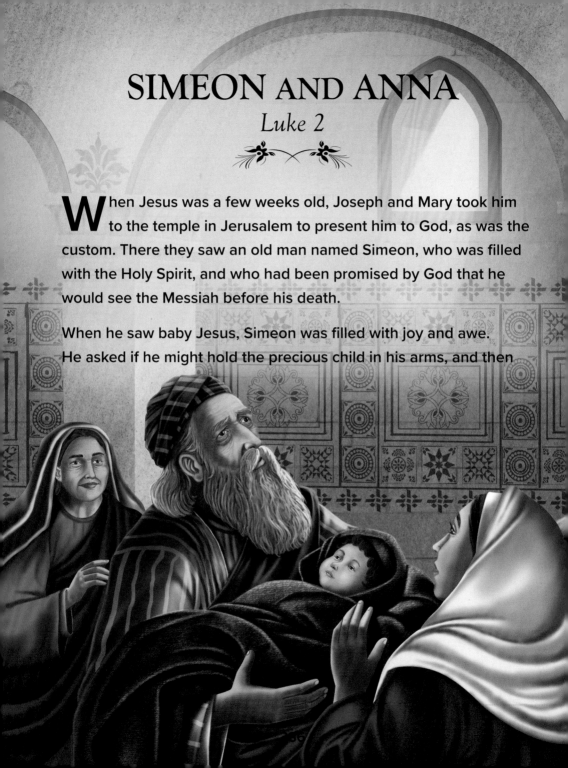

SIMEON AND ANNA

Luke 2

When Jesus was a few weeks old, Joseph and Mary took him to the temple in Jerusalem to present him to God, as was the custom. There they saw an old man named Simeon, who was filled with the Holy Spirit, and who had been promised by God that he would see the Messiah before his death.

When he saw baby Jesus, Simeon was filled with joy and awe. He asked if he might hold the precious child in his arms, and then he cried out in gratitude, "Lord, you have kept your promise, and you may let your servant go in peace. With my own eyes I have seen the child who will bring salvation to your people!" Then he turned to Mary, "Your child has been chosen by God to bring about both the destruction and salvation of many people in Israel!"

While they stood there, another stranger came up. Anna was an old widow, who spent her life worshipping in the temple. She too recognised how special Jesus was and gave thanks to God. Jesus meant so much to so many people!

THE BRIGHT STAR
Matthew 2

In a distant land, three wise men had been studying the stars. When a really bright star was discovered shining in the skies, they followed it all the way to Judah, for they believed it was a sign that a great king had been born.

They went first to the court of King Herod, and asked if he could show them the way to the baby who would be the king of the Jews. Worried Herod called for his advisors, and they told him that a prophet had foretold that the new king would be born in the city of King David, in Bethlehem.

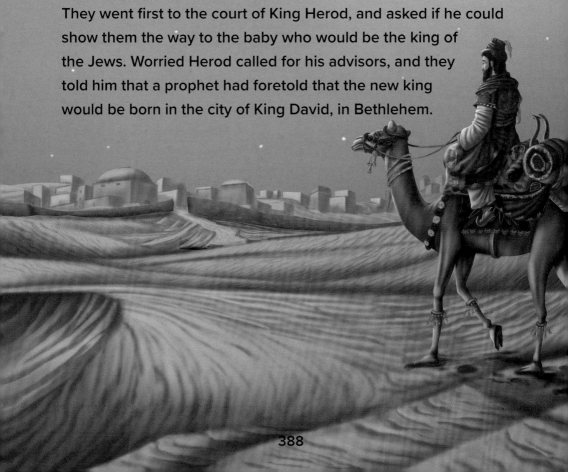

Then the cunning king directed the wise men to Bethlehem, saying, "Once you have found him, come back and tell me where he is, so that I can visit him too."

The wise men followed the star to Bethlehem, where they found baby Jesus in a humble house. They knelt before him, and presented him with fine gifts of gold, frankincense and myrrh before returning home. But they did not stop off at Herod's palace, for God had warned them in a dream not to go there.

ESCAPE TO EGYPT
Matthew 2

Herod was furious when he realised the wise men weren't coming back. He was determined to put an end to this threat to his power, and gave an order that all boys under the age of two be killed.

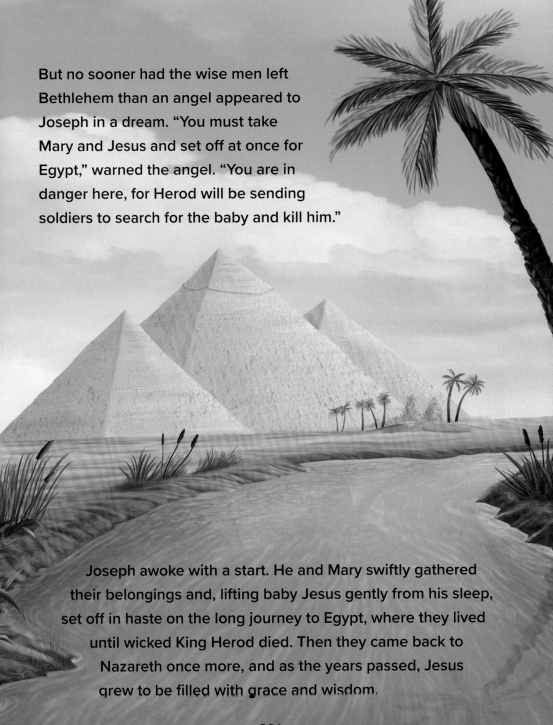

But no sooner had the wise men left Bethlehem than an angel appeared to Joseph in a dream. "You must take Mary and Jesus and set off at once for Egypt," warned the angel. "You are in danger here, for Herod will be sending soldiers to search for the baby and kill him."

Joseph awoke with a start. He and Mary swiftly gathered their belongings and, lifting baby Jesus gently from his sleep, set off in haste on the long journey to Egypt, where they lived until wicked King Herod died. Then they came back to Nazareth once more, and as the years passed, Jesus grew to be filled with grace and wisdom.

"MY FATHER'S HOUSE"

Luke 2

When Jesus was about twelve years old, his mother and father took him to Jerusalem to celebrate Passover – the festival which reminded the Jews of how God had rescued them from slavery in Egypt so many years before. For one whole week the city was filled to bursting.

At the end of this time, Mary and Joseph set off home with a host of other people, but on the way they realised Jesus was missing. Frantic with worry, they rushed back to the crowded city to search for him. At last, on the third day of searching, they found him in the temple courts, talking with the teachers of the law, who were amazed by how much he knew.

"Jesus!" cried his parents. "We've been so worried about you!"

"But why were you looking for me?" answered the young boy. "Surely you knew that I would be in my Father's house?" For while Jesus loved Mary and Joseph dearly, he understood that God was his Father in a very special way.

393

A VOICE IN THE WILDERNESS
Matthew 3; Mark 1; Luke 3

Jesus' cousin, John, was living in the desert when God called him. He wore clothes made of camels' hair and lived on locusts and wild honey. God wanted John to prepare the people for the coming of his Son, so John travelled throughout the land preaching to people.

"Be sorry for your sins and God will forgive you," he would say. He told those who came to hear him that it wasn't enough to say that they were descended from Abraham to be saved. They needed to truly repent, and to change their ways.

People came from all around to listen. Many were truly sorry, and John baptised them in the River Jordan, as a sign that their sins had been washed away and that they could start afresh.

Some wondered if John himself could be the promised King, but he said, "I baptise you with water, but the one who comes after me will baptise you with the Holy Spirit and with fire! I'm not even worthy to tie up his sandals!"

JESUS IS BAPTISED
Matthew 3; Mark 1; Luke 3

A t that time, Jesus came from Nazareth to the River Jordan where John was preaching. John knew at once that this was the promised King, the 'Lamb of God.' So when Jesus asked him to baptise him, John was shocked.

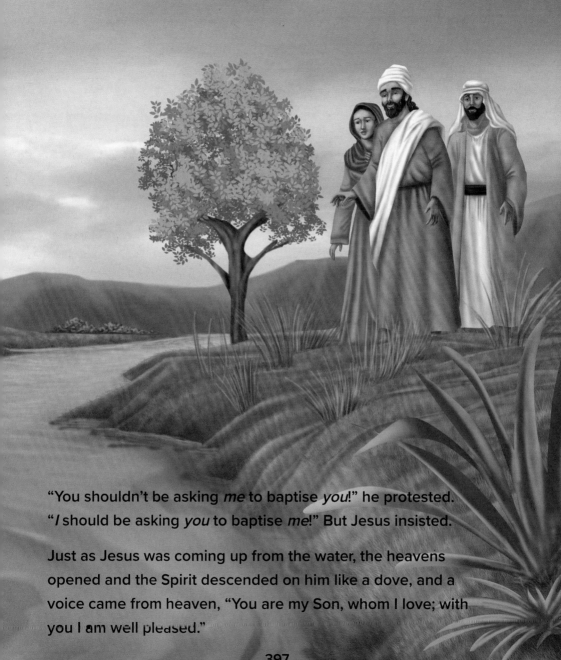

"You shouldn't be asking *me* to baptise *you*!" he protested. "*I* should be asking *you* to baptise *me*!" But Jesus insisted.

Just as Jesus was coming up from the water, the heavens opened and the Spirit descended on him like a dove, and a voice came from heaven, "You are my Son, whom I love; with you I am well pleased."

TESTED IN THE DESERT
Matthew 4; Mark 1; Luke 4

Jesus spent forty days and nights in the dry, hot desert as a test. He ate nothing and was desperately hungry. The devil came to him and said, "If you are the Son of God, surely you can do anything. Why don't you tell these stones to become bread?"

Jesus answered calmly, "It is written: 'Man shall not live on bread alone, but on every word that comes from the mouth of God.'" Jesus knew that food wasn't the most important thing in life.

The devil took Jesus to the top of a temple and told him to throw himself off, for surely angels would rescue him. But Jesus said, "It is also written: 'Do not put the Lord your God to the test.'"

From a high mountain the devil offered him all the kingdoms of the world, if Jesus would simply bow down and worship him, but Jesus replied, "Away from me, Satan! For it is written: 'Worship the Lord your God, and serve him alone.'"

When the devil realised that he could not tempt Jesus, he gave up and left him, and God sent his angels to Jesus to help him to recover.

FISHING FOR MEN
Matthew 4; Mark 1; Luke 5

Now Jesus returned to Galilee and began to preach. Word soon spread, and people travelled to hear him. One day, on the shore of Lake Galilee, the crowd was so large that Jesus asked a fisherman if he would take him out in his boat a little way, so that everyone could see him.

Afterwards, Jesus told Simon, the fisherman, to push the boat out further into the water and let down his nets. "Master," Simon answered, "we were out all night and caught nothing. But if you say so, then we will try again."

He couldn't believe his eyes when he pulled up his nets full of fish! He called to his brother, Andrew, and to his friends James and John to help, and soon the two boats were so full of fish that they were nearly ready to sink!

Simon fell to his knees, but Jesus smiled. "Don't be afraid, Simon. From now on you shall be called Peter* for that is what you will be." Then he turned to all the men. "I want you to leave your nets," he said, "and come with me and fish for men instead, so that we can spread the good news!" The men pulled the boats up on the beach, left everything, and followed Jesus!

The name *Peter* comes from the Greek word for *rock*.

WATER INTO WINE
John 2

Jesus was invited to a marvellous wedding party along with his friends and his mother. Everything was going well until the wine ran out! Mary came to tell Jesus, who asked her, "Why are you telling me this? It is not yet time for me to show myself." But Mary still hoped he would help, and spoke quietly to the servants, telling them to do whatever Jesus told them to.

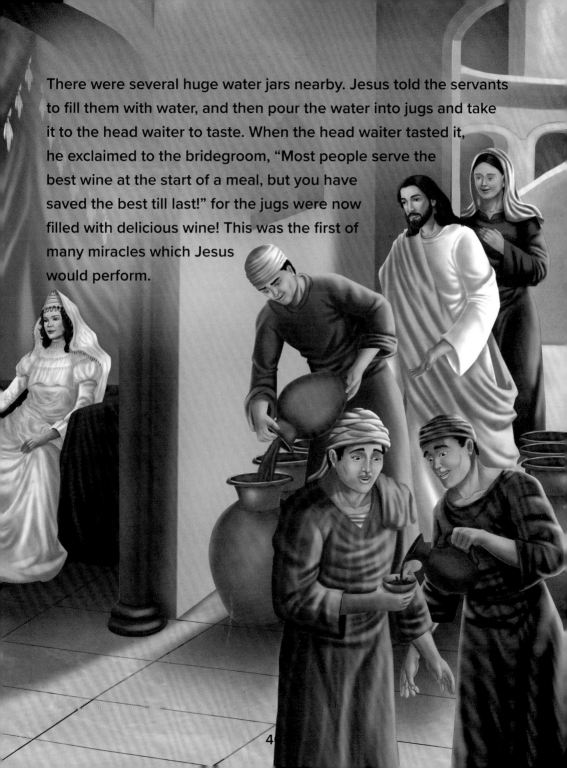

There were several huge water jars nearby. Jesus told the servants to fill them with water, and then pour the water into jugs and take it to the head waiter to taste. When the head waiter tasted it, he exclaimed to the bridegroom, "Most people serve the best wine at the start of a meal, but you have saved the best till last!" for the jugs were now filled with delicious wine! This was the first of many miracles which Jesus would perform.

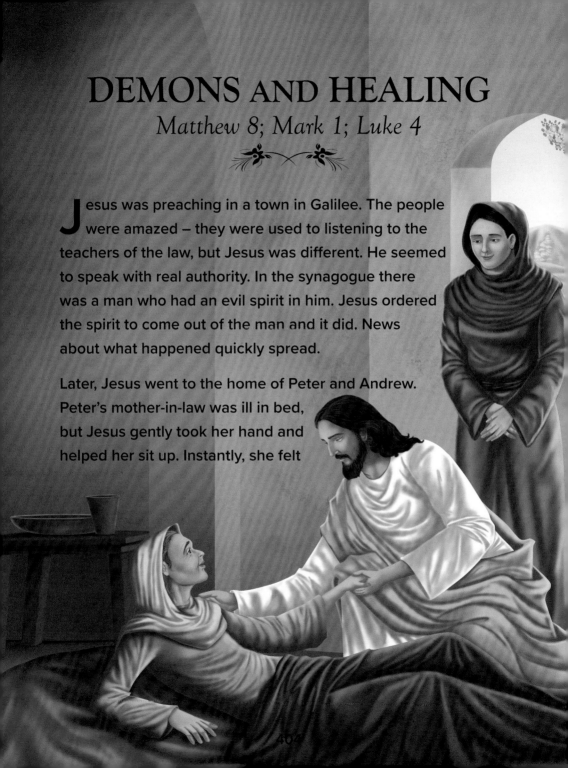

DEMONS AND HEALING
Matthew 8; Mark 1; Luke 4

Jesus was preaching in a town in Galilee. The people were amazed – they were used to listening to the teachers of the law, but Jesus was different. He seemed to speak with real authority. In the synagogue there was a man who had an evil spirit in him. Jesus ordered the spirit to come out of the man and it did. News about what happened quickly spread.

Later, Jesus went to the home of Peter and Andrew. Peter's mother-in-law was ill in bed, but Jesus gently took her hand and helped her sit up. Instantly, she felt

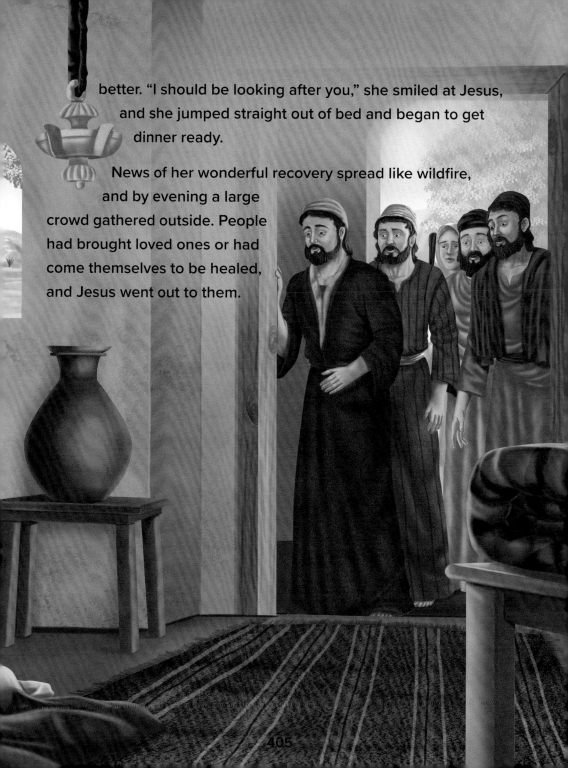

better. "I should be looking after you," she smiled at Jesus, and she jumped straight out of bed and began to get dinner ready.

News of her wonderful recovery spread like wildfire, and by evening a large crowd gathered outside. People had brought loved ones or had come themselves to be healed, and Jesus went out to them.

THROWN OUT!

Mark 6; Luke 4

One day, Jesus was in his home town of Nazareth, reading from Isaiah's scroll foretelling the coming of the Messiah. At first the people were impressed, but when he said, "Today this Scripture has been fulfilled in your hearing," they were taken aback.

Jesus – the son of Mary and Joseph the carpenter – was telling them that he was God's special servant! How could he dare to say such a thing!

Jesus knew that the people would doubt him, that they would expect him to perform some miracle to prove himself, like a showman. He also knew that prophets were never appreciated by the people in their home towns.

The people became angry with Jesus and forced him out of the synagogue. Some were so furious that they wanted to push him off a steep cliff, but when they tried, he simply walked through the crowd and left them standing there in confusion!

JESUS AND THE TAX COLLECTOR
Matthew 9; Mark 2; Luke 5

Matthew had a well-paid job as a tax collector, but when Jesus told him to follow him, he gave up his job on the spot. He wanted all his friends to meet Jesus too. But when the Jewish religious leaders learnt that Jesus was meeting with tax collectors and sinners, they were disgusted. "Why is he mixing with the likes

of them?" they asked one another. "Everyone knows that tax collectors are greedy and dishonest!"

But Jesus told them, "If you go to a doctor's surgery, you don't expect to see healthy people – it is people who are sick who need to see the doctor. I am God's doctor. I have come here to save those people who are sinners and who want to start afresh. Those who have done nothing wrong don't need me."

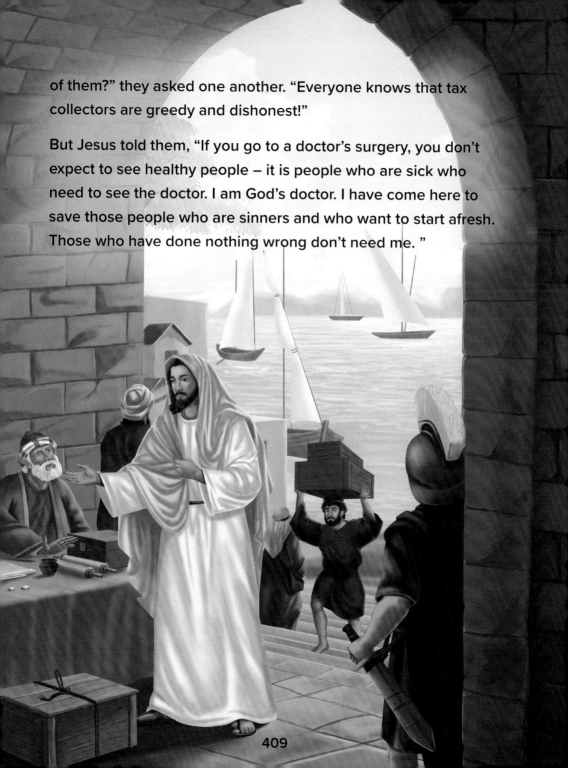

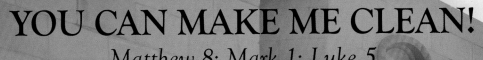

YOU CAN MAKE ME CLEAN!
Matthew 8; Mark 1; Luke 5

One time, a man with leprosy, an awful skin disease, came up to Jesus and fell to his knees on the ground. "Sir, if you want to, you can make me clean," he begged humbly.

Filled with compassion, Jesus reached out to touch the man. "I do want to," he said. "Be clean!" Immediately the man's skin was perfectly smooth and healthy!

The grateful man simply couldn't keep the wonderful event to himself, and before long so many people wanted to come and see Jesus that he could no longer go anywhere without being surrounded by crowds.

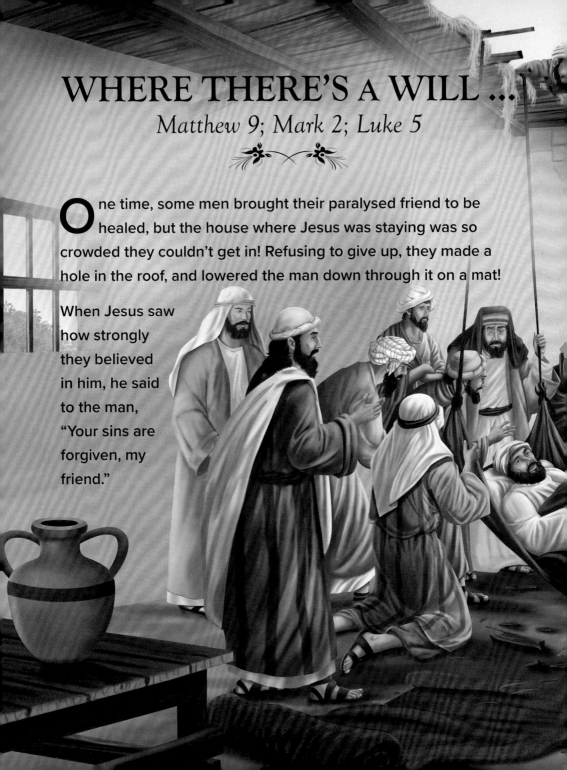

WHERE THERE'S A WILL ...
Matthew 9; Mark 2; Luke 5

One time, some men brought their paralysed friend to be healed, but the house where Jesus was staying was so crowded they couldn't get in! Refusing to give up, they made a hole in the roof, and lowered the man down through it on a mat!

When Jesus saw how strongly they believed in him, he said to the man, "Your sins are forgiven, my friend."

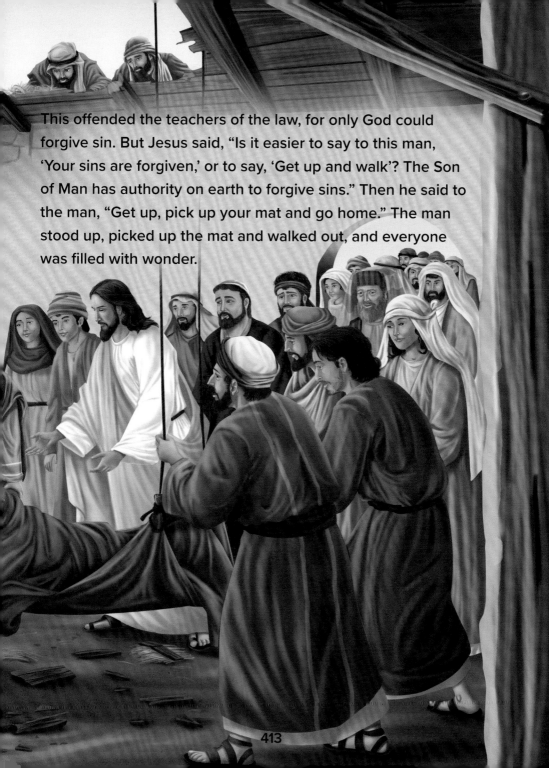

This offended the teachers of the law, for only God could forgive sin. But Jesus said, "Is it easier to say to this man, 'Your sins are forgiven,' or to say, 'Get up and walk'? The Son of Man has authority on earth to forgive sins." Then he said to the man, "Get up, pick up your mat and go home." The man stood up, picked up the mat and walked out, and everyone was filled with wonder.

THE UNHOLY TEMPLE

John 2

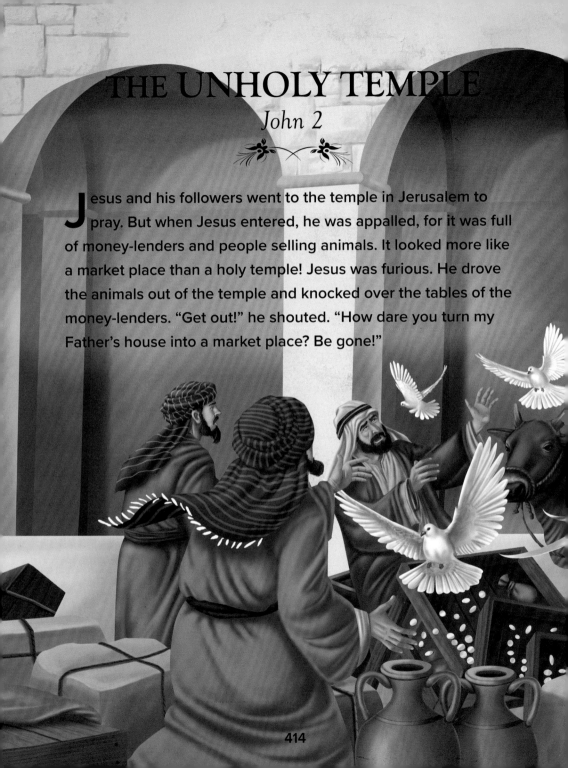

Jesus and his followers went to the temple in Jerusalem to pray. But when Jesus entered, he was appalled, for it was full of money-lenders and people selling animals. It looked more like a market place than a holy temple! Jesus was furious. He drove the animals out of the temple and knocked over the tables of the money-lenders. "Get out!" he shouted. "How dare you turn my Father's house into a market place? Be gone!"

Once the temple was quiet and peaceful once more, Jesus began to teach his followers about God's kindness and mercy. Many of the priests and leaders were jealous of Jesus, and wished to stop him, but they couldn't do anything, because the people paid attention to what Jesus said and listened to him.

THE VISITOR AT NIGHT

John 3

Nicodemus was one of the Jewish leaders. He was impressed by Jesus, but didn't want anyone to know, so he went to speak to Jesus late at night, so he would not be seen. He said he knew Jesus had been sent by God because of the wonderful miracles he had performed.

But Jesus was not impressed with flattery. "No one can see the kingdom of God unless they are born again," was all he said, which confused Nicodemus, who couldn't understand how an old person could be born again.

Then Jesus replied, "Unless you are born of water and the Spirit, you cannot enter the Kingdom of God." And, when Nicodemus still did not understand, Jesus continued, "The Son of Man must be raised up so that whoever believes in him may have eternal life. For God so loved the world that he gave his only

Son, so that those who believe in him should not perish but have eternal life. For God sent his Son into the world, not to condemn it, but so the world might be saved through him."

Jesus was talking about a spiritual birth, not a physical birth – one that would come about by believing in Jesus himself.

THE WOMAN AT THE WELL

John 4

Passing through Samaria, Jesus stopped to rest at a well. When a local woman came to get water, Jesus asked her for a drink. She was taken aback, because normally Jews wouldn't talk to Samaritans. She was even more surprised when he said, "If you knew what God can give you and who it is that asks for a drink, you would have asked and he would have given you living water."

The puzzled woman asked where he could get this special water, to which Jesus replied, "Those who drink this water will get thirsty again, but those who drink the water that I will give them will never be thirsty again."

At this, the Samaritan woman asked eagerly, "Please give me this wonderful water!" — but when Jesus told her to fetch her husband, she blushed and said she didn't have one.

Jesus said to her, "No, you have had five husbands, and you aren't married to the man you are living with now."

The astonished woman ran to tell her friends about the amazing man who knew so much about her. "Do you think he could be God's promised king?" she asked. Many went to see him for themselves, and believed because of that day.

THE OFFICER'S SERVANT

Matthew 8; Luke 7

In Capernaum there lived a Roman officer. Romans did not normally get on well with the Jews, but this officer was a good man, who treated the Jews well. He was also kind to the people in his household, but one of his servants was sick and close to death. When the officer heard that Jesus had come to Capernaum, he came to ask for his help.

Jesus asked him, "Shall I come and heal him?"

Then the officer replied, "Lord, I do not deserve to have you come to my own house, but I know that you don't need to in any case. If you just say the word, I know that my servant will be healed, just in the same way that when I order my soldiers to do something, then they do it!" The officer believed in Jesus so completely that he did not even need him to visit the sick man himself!

Jesus said to the crowd following him, "I tell you all, I have never found faith like this, not even in Israel!"

And when the officer returned to his house, sure enough he found his servant up on his feet and feeling perfectly well again!

THE WIDOW'S SON

Luke 7

One day, when Jesus and his disciples were entering a town, they arrived in time to see a funeral procession coming out through the city gates. The dead man was the only son of a widow, and she was heartbroken.

When Jesus saw her, his heart was filled with pity, and he came up to her and said gently, "Don't cry." Then he walked over and touched the coffin, and the men carrying it stopped.

Jesus said, "Young man! Get up, I tell you!"

At his words, to the astonishment and awe of the mourners, the dead man sat up and began to talk, and Jesus led him to his mother, who was filled with joy and thankfulness.

JUST SLEEPING
Matthew 9; Luke 8

Jairus was desperate! His little girl was dreadfully ill, and he was worried that Jesus wouldn't be able to make his way through the crowds in time to heal her. Then Jesus stopped still and asked who had touched him. "Master, everyone is touching you in this crowd!" said a disciple, but Jesus knew that he had been touched in a special way.

As he looked around, a woman stepped forward and knelt at his feet. "Lord, it was me," she said nervously. For years she had been ill and nobody had been able to help her, but she had known that if she could just get close to Jesus, she would be healed, and sure enough, the moment she had managed to touch the edge of his cloak, she was well!

Jesus wasn't angry. "Woman," he said kindly. "Your faith has healed you. Go home now."

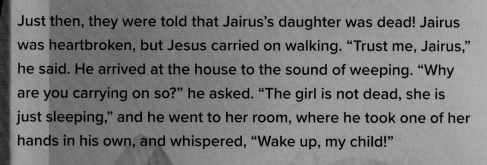

Just then, they were told that Jairus's daughter was dead! Jairus was heartbroken, but Jesus carried on walking. "Trust me, Jairus," he said. He arrived at the house to the sound of weeping. "Why are you carrying on so?" he asked. "The girl is not dead, she is just sleeping," and he went to her room, where he took one of her hands in his own, and whispered, "Wake up, my child!"

In that instant, the child opened her eyes. She smiled at Jesus and hugged her overjoyed parents!

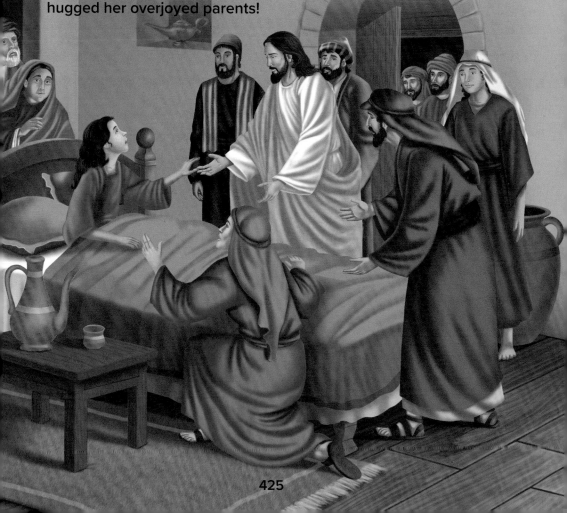

LORD OF THE SABBATH

Matthew 12; Mark 2-3; Luke 6

Jesus and his disciples were walking through a wheat field on a Sabbath. Some Pharisees spotted his disciples picking wheat-heads to eat. They felt this was wrong, for it was like working, and God had commanded them to keep the Sabbath holy. The Pharisees loved their rules – they didn't even think a doctor should work on the Sabbath, unless his patient was about to die!

Jesus reminded them, "When David and his men were hungry he went into the temple and took the bread that was there for the priests to eat. The Son of Man is Lord of the Sabbath."

On another Sabbath, Jesus healed a man with a crippled hand, saying to the angry Pharisees, "What do you think our law really wants us to do on the Sabbath? Does it want us to help people or harm them?" Jesus was trying to explain that the laws God had given them were there to teach them right from wrong, not to be used just to punish and judge. They were supposed to love one another and help one another.

CHOOSING THE TWELVE
Matthew 10; Mark 3, 6

A round this time, Jesus chose twelve men to be his special disciples* to carry on his work after his death. They were a mixed bunch: Peter and his brother Andrew, and brothers James and John, were all fishermen; Matthew (or Levi) was a tax collector, while Simon (not Simon known as Peter) was a patriot who wanted to fight the Romans; and the other six were Bartholomew, Thomas, James son of Alphaeus, Philip, Judas (or Thaddeus) son of James, and Judas Iscariot.

* These men became known as *apostles*, or messengers, for these twelve were chosen by Jesus to pass on his message of good news

Jesus knew they would have a hard task ahead of them. He wanted them to teach the people that God's kingdom is near, and to heal people too. He sent them out to travel from village to village, taking nothing with them except for a staff, because God would provide everything they needed. Everywhere they went they were to rely on the hospitality of the people, and if they were not made welcome, then they were to leave. But those who welcomed them were really welcoming Jesus himself.

THE HEALING AT THE POOL
John 5

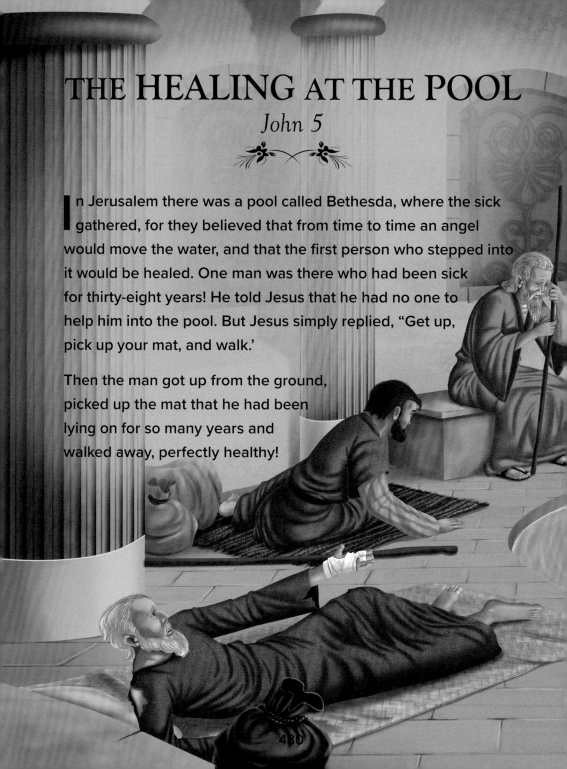

In Jerusalem there was a pool called Bethesda, where the sick gathered, for they believed that from time to time an angel would move the water, and that the first person who stepped into it would be healed. One man was there who had been sick for thirty-eight years! He told Jesus that he had no one to help him into the pool. But Jesus simply replied, "Get up, pick up your mat, and walk.'

Then the man got up from the ground, picked up the mat that he had been lying on for so many years and walked away, perfectly healthy!

Once again, the religious leaders were angry with Jesus for healing on a Sabbath. They were even more offended when he told them, "My Father is always working, and I too must work." Who did he think he was? This was outrageous! But Jesus answered, "I do nothing on my own authority — I am only doing what God wants me to do and has authorised me to do."

SERMON ON THE MOUNT
Matthew 5; Luke 6

Jesus wasn't always welcome in the synagogues, so he would often teach his disciples and the large crowds which gathered outside in the open air. One of the most important talks he gave was on a mountain near Capernaum. It has become known as the Sermon on the Mount. Jesus taught the people about what was truly important in life and gave comfort and advice:

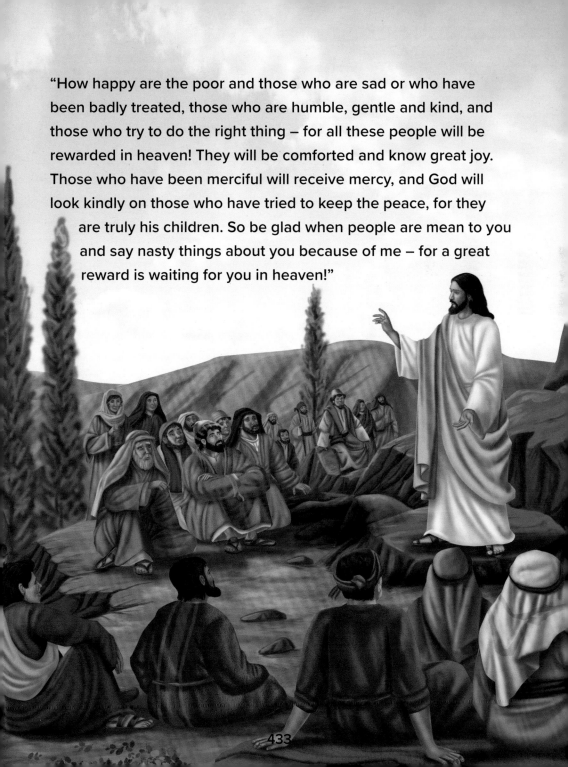

"How happy are the poor and those who are sad or who have been badly treated, those who are humble, gentle and kind, and those who try to do the right thing – for all these people will be rewarded in heaven! They will be comforted and know great joy. Those who have been merciful will receive mercy, and God will look kindly on those who have tried to keep the peace, for they are truly his children. So be glad when people are mean to you and say nasty things about you because of me – for a great reward is waiting for you in heaven!"

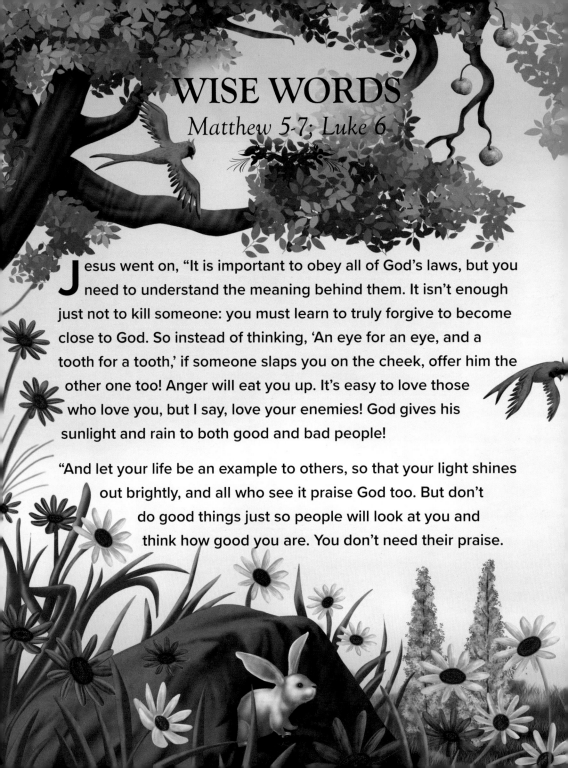

WISE WORDS
Matthew 5-7; Luke 6

Jesus went on, "It is important to obey all of God's laws, but you need to understand the meaning behind them. It isn't enough just not to kill someone: you must learn to truly forgive to become close to God. So instead of thinking, 'An eye for an eye, and a tooth for a tooth,' if someone slaps you on the cheek, offer him the other one too! Anger will eat you up. It's easy to love those who love you, but I say, love your enemies! God gives his sunlight and rain to both good and bad people!

"And let your life be an example to others, so that your light shines out brightly, and all who see it praise God too. But don't do good things just so people will look at you and think how good you are. You don't need their praise.

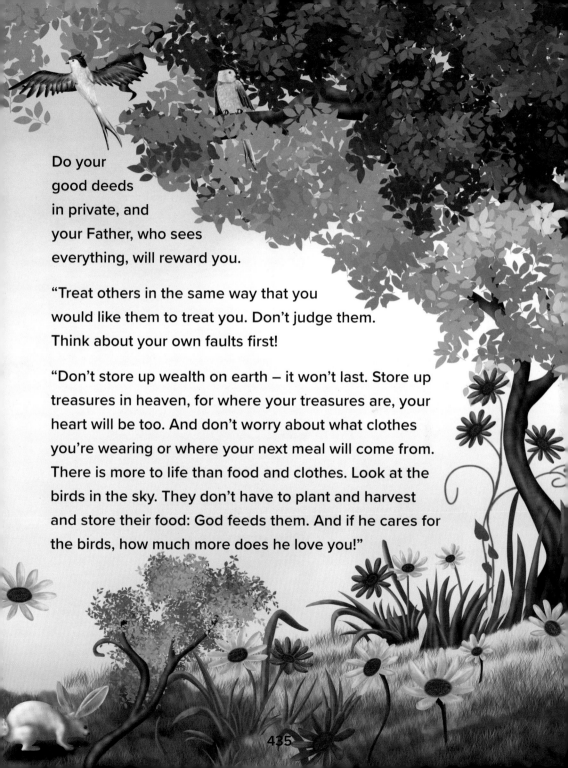

Do your
good deeds
in private, and
your Father, who sees
everything, will reward you.

"Treat others in the same way that you
would like them to treat you. Don't judge them.
Think about your own faults first!

"Don't store up wealth on earth – it won't last. Store up
treasures in heaven, for where your treasures are, your
heart will be too. And don't worry about what clothes
you're wearing or where your next meal will come from.
There is more to life than food and clothes. Look at the
birds in the sky. They don't have to plant and harvest
and store their food: God feeds them. And if he cares for
the birds, how much more does he love you!"

THE RIGHT WAY TO PRAY
Matthew 6-7; Luke 11

Jesus also taught people the right way to pray. They should not try to impress others by praying in public, but should go to a quiet place and pray to God alone. Nor should they keep repeating meaningless words. God knows what is in our hearts, and this is the way Jesus told people to pray to him:

Our Father in heaven,
Hallowed be your name.
Your kingdom come.
Your will be done,
on earth as it is in heaven.
Give us today our daily bread,
and forgive us our sins,
as we forgive those who sin against us.
Lead us not into temptation,
but deliver us from evil.
For yours is the kingdom,
the power and the glory, forever.
  Amen.

"Keep on asking," said Jesus, "and you will receive. Keep on seeking, and you will find. Keep on knocking, and the door will be opened to you."

A FIRM FOUNDATION

Matthew 7; Luke 6

Before Jesus ended his sermon, he said one last thing: "If you listen to my teaching and follow it then you are wise, like the person who builds his house on solid rock. Even if the rain pours down, the rivers flood, and the winds rage, the house won't collapse for it is built on solid rock. But he who listens and doesn't obey is foolish, like a person who builds a house on sand, without any foundations.

The house is quickly built, but when the rains and floods and winds come, the house will not be able to stand against them. It will collapse and be utterly destroyed."

As the crowds slowly dispersed, their heads were filled with all these new ideas. Jesus was nothing like their usual teachers, but what he said made sense. There was much to think about!

THE DEADLY DANCE

Matthew 14; Mark 6; Luke 7

Some time before this, King Herod had given orders to have John the Baptist thrown in prison. He and the queen had been furious with John for telling everyone that Herod had been wrong to divorce his own wife in order to marry his half-brother's wife, Herodias. In fact, Queen Herodias wanted her husband to execute John!

When it was the king's birthday, Herodias arranged for her daughter Salome to dance for him. Her dance was bewitching and exotic, and before he knew it, Herod had promised to grant her anything she wanted, to which the girl (as instructed by her scheming mother) replied, "The head of John the Baptist on a plate!" Herod knew that he had been set up, but he had made a promise. A guard was sent to John's prison, and he cut off John's head.

When John's friends heard the terrible news, they came and took his body and buried it. Then they had to tell Jesus.

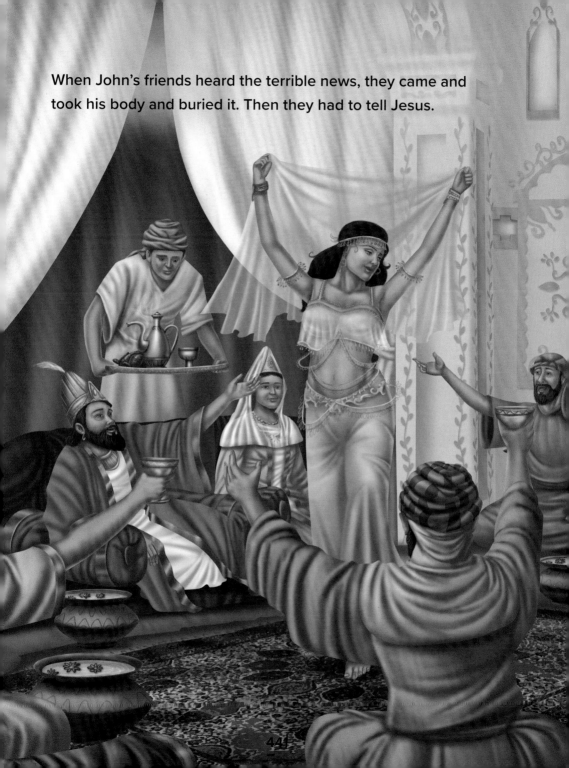

FEEDING FIVE THOUSAND

Matthew 14; Mark 6; Luke 9; John 6

When Jesus heard about John, he tried to go somewhere quiet, but the people followed and he could not bring himself to send them away. When evening came, there was still a huge crowd. Jesus told his disciples to give them something to eat. "But Master," the disciples said, "there are thousands of people and we only have five loaves of bread and two fish!"

Jesus commanded them
to tell the people to sit down, then,
taking the five loaves and the two fish
and looking up to heaven, he gave thanks
to his Father and broke the loaves into pieces.
He gave them to the disciples, who took them

to the people and then came back to Jesus for more bread and fish. He filled up their baskets again . . . and again . . . and again! To their astonishment there was still bread and fish left in the baskets when they came to feed the very last people! More than five thousand people had been fed that day – with five loaves of bread and two fish!

JESUS CALMS THE STORM
Matthew 8; Mark 4; Luke 8

Jesus and his disciples climbed into a boat to travel across to the other side of the lake. Jesus was so tired that he lay down and fell asleep. Suddenly, the skies darkened, rain came pelting down and a fierce storm struck the lake. Huge waves tossed the boat, and the disciples were terrified that they would capsize.

Jesus still lay sleeping. The frightened disciples went over and woke him up, begging him to save them. Jesus opened his eyes and looked up at them. "Why are you afraid? You have so little faith!" he said sadly. Then he stood up calmly, his arms spread wide, and facing into the wind and rain, commanded, "Be still!" At once the wind and waves died down and all was calm.

The disciples were amazed. "Who is this man?" they asked themselves. "Even the winds and waves obey him!"

DEMONS AND PIGS
Matthew 8; Mark 5; Luke 8

Jesus stepped ashore and was met by a man possessed by evil spirits. For a long time this man had lived wild. People were frightened of him and had bound him with chains, but he was so strong that he had torn them apart! When he saw Jesus, he fell to his knees, screaming, "What do you want with me, Son of the Most High God? Please don't torture me!" for he was possessed by many demons which begged Jesus not to banish them.

A herd of pigs was feeding on the nearby hillside. Jesus let the evil spirits go into the pigs, upon which the entire herd rushed down the hillside into the lake and every last pig was drowned!

The people from round about were so shocked when they saw the change in the wild man that they asked Jesus to leave, but the man who had been demon-possessed told his wonderful story far and wide, and everyone who heard was amazed.

PARABLE OF THE SOWER

Matthew 13; Mark 4; Luke 8

Many of the people who came to listen to Jesus were farmers. Jesus tried to pass on his message in a way that they would understand. His stories, often called parables, let people think things through for themselves. To some they would just be stories, but others would understand the real message.

"A farmer went out to sow his seed. As he was scattering it, some fell along the path and was trampled on, or eaten by birds. Some fell on rocky ground where there was no soil, and when they began to grow, the plants withered because their roots could not reach water. Other seeds fell among weeds which choked them. Still others fell on good soil and grew into tall, strong plants and produced a crop far greater than what was sown."

Jesus was telling them that he was like the farmer, and the seeds were like the message he brought from God. The seeds that fell on the path and were eaten by birds are like those people who hear the good news but pay no attention. Those on the rocky ground are like people who receive the word with joy when they hear it, but they have no roots. They believe for a while, but when life gets difficult they give up easily. The seeds among weeds are like those who hear, but let themselves become choked by life's worries, and pleasures. But the seeds that fell on good soil are like those people who hear God's message and hold it tight in their heart. Their faith grows and grows.

PARABLE OF THE WEEDS
Matthew 13

Jesus told another parable: "Once a farmer sowed good seed in his field, but that night, his enemy sowed weeds among the wheat. When the wheat began to grow, weeds grew too. His servants asked if they should pull them up, but the owner said, 'If you pull the weeds up, you may pull some of the wheat up too. We must let both grow until harvest, then we will collect and burn the weeds, and gather the wheat and bring it into my barn.'"

Jesus later explained, "The farmer who sowed the good seed is the Son of Man. The field is the world, and the good seed is the people of the kingdom. The weeds were sown by the devil, and they are his people. The harvest will come at the end of time. Then the Son of Man will send out his angels, and they will weed out of his kingdom everything that causes sin and all who do evil and throw them into the blazing furnace, but the righteous will shine like the sun in the kingdom of their Father."

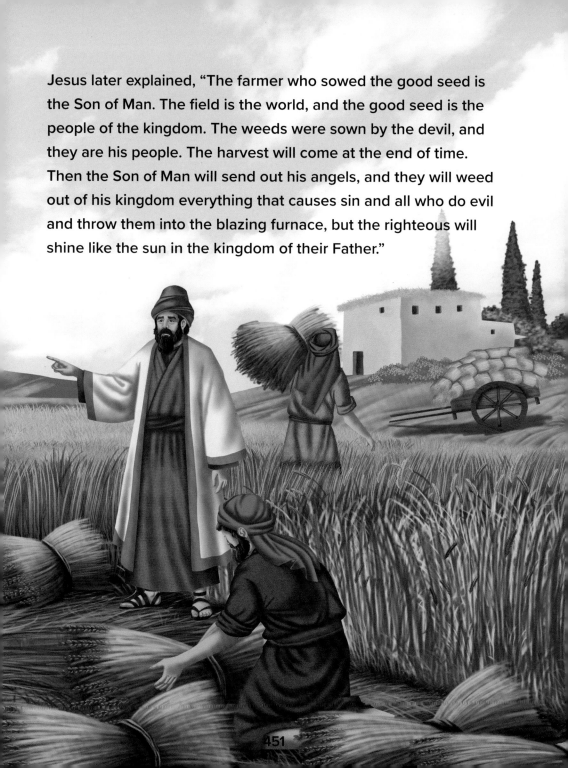

WALKING ON WATER
Matthew 14; Mark 6; John 6

It was late at night and waves tossed the boat violently. Jesus had gone ashore to pray and the disciples were afraid. At the first light of dawn, they saw a figure walking towards them on the water! They thought it was a ghost and were scared until they heard the calm voice of Jesus, "It is I. Do not be afraid."

Peter was the first to speak. "Lord," he said, "if it is you, command me to walk across the water to you," and Jesus did so.

He put one foot gingerly in the water. Then he lowered the other, and bravely stood up, letting go of the boat. He did not sink! But when he looked around at the waves, his courage failed him. As he began to sink, he cried, "Lord, save me!"

Jesus reached out and took his hand. "Oh, Peter," he said sadly, "where is your faith? Why did you doubt?" Then together they walked back to the boat. The wind died down and the water became calm. The disciples bowed low. "Truly you are the Son of God," they said humbly.

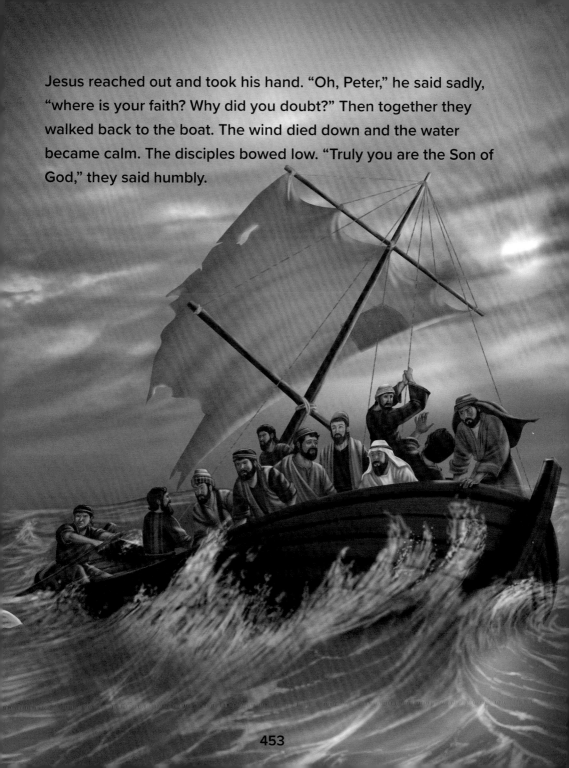

CRUMBS FROM THE TABLE
Matthew 15; Mark 7

One day, a Canaanite woman threw herself at Jesus' feet, crying out in anguish and hope, "Lord, have mercy on me! My daughter is possessed by a demon!" Jesus remained silent, but his disciples urged him to send her away.

Jesus told the woman gently, "I was sent only to the lost sheep of Israel." When she begged him again, he replied, "It is not right to take the children's bread and toss it to the dogs."

"Lord," she replied, "Even the dogs eat the crumbs that fall from their master's table."

Jesus was touched by her faith and said, "Woman, you have great faith! Your request is granted." And when the woman went home she found her beloved child sleeping peacefully, safe and well once more.

THE TRANSFIGURATION

Matthew 17; Mark 9; Luke 9

Jesus climbed up a mountain to pray, taking with him Peter, James and John. All of a sudden, as Jesus prayed, the disciples looked up to see him changed. Light shone from his face and clothes, and as they watched in wonder, Moses, who had led his people out of Egypt, and Elijah, greatest of all the prophets, were suddenly there before their very eyes, talking with Jesus! Then a bright cloud covered them, and a voice said, "This is my Son, whom I love. Listen to what he has to say, for I am very pleased with him!"

The disciples fell to the ground, too frightened to raise their eyes. But Jesus came over and touched them. "Don't be afraid," he said softly, and when they looked up, they saw no one there except Jesus.

457

JESUS AND THE CHILDREN
Matthew 19; Mark 10; Luke 18

Jesus loved little children, for they were good and innocent. He was always surrounded by children, and sometimes his disciples tried to shoo them away. "Do not stop little children from coming to me," he told them sternly. "The kingdom of heaven belongs to them and all those like them."

Once, when the disciples began arguing about which of them was the most important, Jesus beckoned to a little child and put his arm around him. He turned to his disciples, saying, "Whoever welcomes this child in my name welcomes me; and whoever welcomes me, welcomes the one who sent me. For it is the one who is least among you who is the greatest. To enter heaven, you must be like a little child!"

459

THE SECOND CHANCE

John 8

Once, when Jesus was teaching, the Pharisees brought in a woman who had been caught with a man who was not her husband. "According to the laws laid down by Moses, she should be stoned to death," they said. "What do you say?" For they wanted to see what Jesus would do.

Jesus bent over and wrote on the ground. After a long silence he looked them in the eye. "Whoever has committed no sin may throw the first stone." Then he bent over again.

No one said a word. People lowered their eyes uncomfortably, until one of the men turned and walked away. Then another person edged away, and another, and soon only Jesus and the woman remained.

Jesus stood up and said to the woman, "Where has everyone gone? Is there no one left to condemn you?" and she fearfully shook her head. "Well," said Jesus, "I do not condemn you either. Go home, but do not sin again." The woman set off home, filled with gladness and gratitude at being given a second chance.

461

FORGIVENESS

Matthew 18

Jesus tried to make his followers understand how important forgiveness was. Peter asked, "Lord, how many times should I forgive someone who has wronged me? Up to seven times?"

Jesus looked him straight in the eyes. "Don't just forgive him seven times. Forgive him seventy-seven times!" he answered, and he continued, "The kingdom of heaven is like the master whose servant owed him a great deal of money. The man could not pay and he begged his master for more time. The kind master cancelled the debt and sent him home.

"This same servant was owed a small amount of money by another servant, and when he couldn't pay him back, he had the second servant thrown into prison!

"When the master learnt of this, he called the first servant in. 'You've been cruel and unkind,' he said. 'I cancelled your debt because you begged me. Shouldn't you have shown mercy just as I showed you?' He was so furious that he handed him over to the jailers until he could pay back all he owed."

Jesus looked at his followers. "This is how my Father will treat you unless you forgive your brother or sister from your heart."

THE GOOD SHEPHERD

John 10

People asked Jesus who he really was, and he explained that he was like a shepherd. "The good shepherd would do anything for his sheep – even lay down his life to save them. A hired hand would run away if he saw a wolf coming, but the shepherd would never leave them. The sheep will listen to him, and follow where he leads, but will never follow a stranger.

"I am the gate for the sheep. I will let my own sheep through. I know my sheep and they know me. I will lay down my life for them of my own free will, and for this my Father loves me."

When people grumbled that Jesus spoke with people who had done bad things, he said, "Imagine you had a hundred sheep and lost one of them. How would you feel? Wouldn't you leave the other ninety-nine safe, and rush off to look for the lost one? And when you found it, don't you think you would be so thrilled that you would rush home and celebrate? In the same way there will be more rejoicing in heaven over one sinner who repents than over ninety-nine people who don't need to repent."

464

THE LOST SON

Luke 15

Jesus told another story to explain how happy God was when sinners returned to him: "There was once a man with two sons. The younger one asked for his share of the property so he could go out into the world, and soon spent it all on enjoying himself. He ended up working for a farmer and was so hungry that sometimes he wished he could eat the food he was giving to the pigs! But at last he came to his senses and set off home to tell his father how sorry he was. 'I am not worthy of being his son,' he thought, 'but maybe he will let me work on the farm.'

"When his father saw him coming, he rushed out and threw his arms around him. The young man tried to tell him that he was not fit to be called his son, but he told his servants to bring his finest robe for his son to wear and to kill the prize calf for a feast.

"The older son was outraged! He had worked hard for his father all this time, and nobody had ever held a feast for him! Yet here came his brother, having squandered all his money, and his father couldn't wait to kill the fattened calf and welcome him home!

"'My son,' the father said, 'you are always with me, and all I have is yours. But celebrate with me now, for your brother was dead to me and is alive again; he was lost and is found!'"

THE RICH MAN AND THE BEGGAR

Luke 16

Jesus told another story: "There was once a rich man, who lived in a grand house, and whose table was laid every day as if for a feast. At his gate lay a poor, hungry beggar called Lazarus, who used to long for the crumbs which fell from his table! But the rich man was selfish, and never stopped to think about poor Lazarus. At last Lazarus died and the angels carried him to Abraham's side, where he felt no more pain or hunger.

"Some time after, the rich man also died, but no angels came for him. He was sent to the place for wicked people. In torment he begged, 'Father Abraham, have pity and send Lazarus to dip his finger in water and cool my tongue, for I am so thirsty!'

"But Abraham replied, 'Son, remember that you received your good things in your time on earth, while Lazarus suffered greatly, but now he is comforted here and you are in agony.'

"The rich man pleaded that his brothers might be warned, but Abraham told him they already had the writings of Moses and the prophets to warn them. It would be their own fault if they didn't change their ways in time to avoid the same fate as him!"

THE GOOD SAMARITAN
Luke 10

Once someone asked Jesus what the law meant when it said we must love our neighbours as much as ourselves. "But who is my neighbour?" he asked, and Jesus told him a story:

"A man was going from Jerusalem to Jericho, when he was attacked by robbers, who beat him and took everything from him before leaving him by the roadside, half dead. Soon a priest passed by. When he saw the man, he crossed to the other side of the road and carried on his way. Then a Levite came along. He also hurried on his way without stopping.

"The next person to come along was a Samaritan, who are not friends of the Jews. Yet when this traveller saw the man lying bleeding by the roadside, his heart was filled with pity. He knelt beside him and carefully washed and bandaged his wounds, before taking him on his donkey to an inn, where he gave the innkeeper money to look after the man until he was well."

Jesus looked at the man who had posed the question, and asked who he thought had been a good neighbour to the injured man.

The man sheepishly replied, "The one who was kind to him."

Then Jesus told him, "Go, then, and be like him."

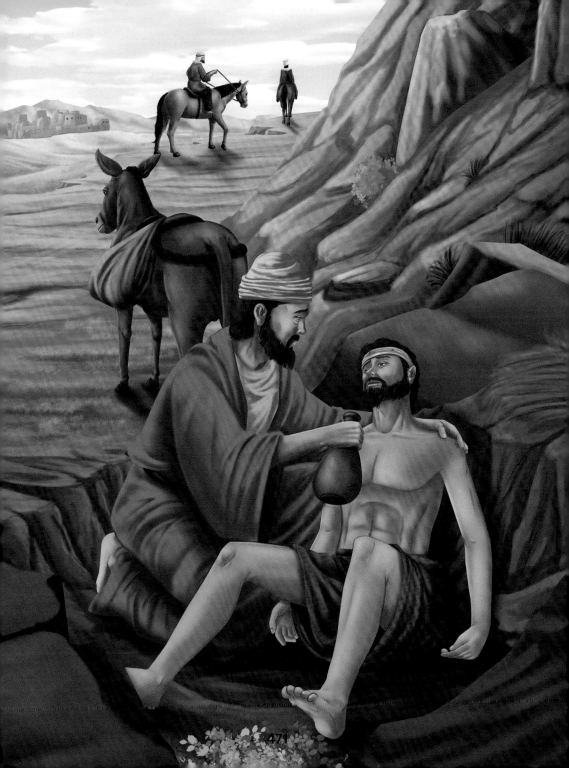

MARTHA AND MARY
Luke 10

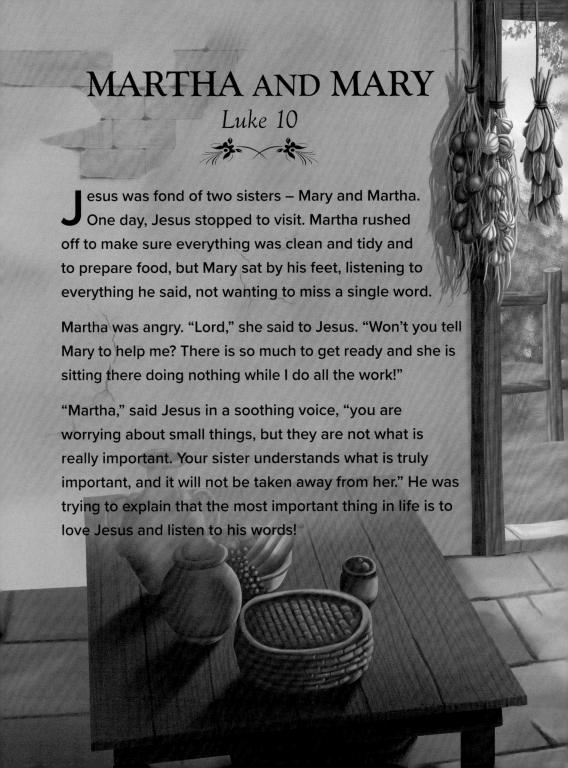

Jesus was fond of two sisters – Mary and Martha. One day, Jesus stopped to visit. Martha rushed off to make sure everything was clean and tidy and to prepare food, but Mary sat by his feet, listening to everything he said, not wanting to miss a single word.

Martha was angry. "Lord," she said to Jesus. "Won't you tell Mary to help me? There is so much to get ready and she is sitting there doing nothing while I do all the work!"

"Martha," said Jesus in a soothing voice, "you are worrying about small things, but they are not what is really important. Your sister understands what is truly important, and it will not be taken away from her." He was trying to explain that the most important thing in life is to love Jesus and listen to his words!

LAZARUS LIVES!

John 11

Jesus received a message from Martha and Mary, telling him that their brother, Lazarus, was very ill, but by the time Jesus arrived at the sisters' house, Lazarus was dead. Martha wept, saying, "Oh Lord, if you had been here, my brother would not have died. But I know that God will give you whatever you ask."

Then Jesus said gently, "He will rise again. Everyone who believes in me will live again, even though he has died."

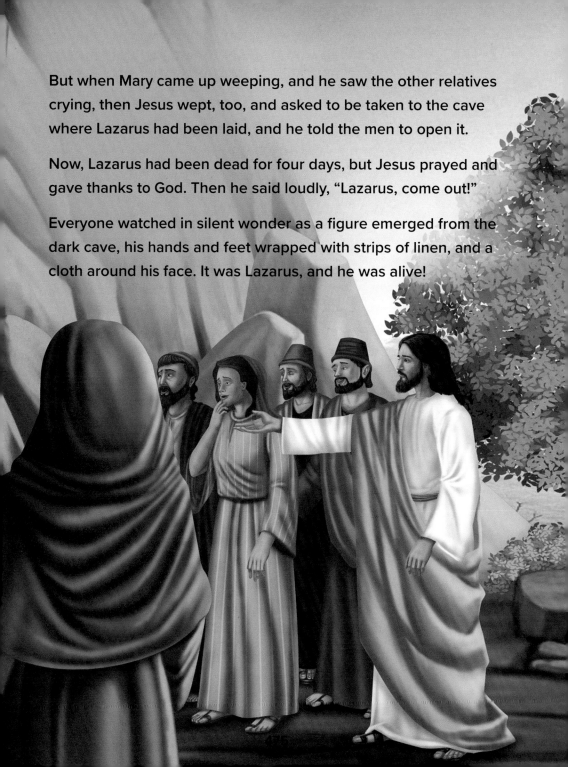

But when Mary came up weeping, and he saw the other relatives crying, then Jesus wept, too, and asked to be taken to the cave where Lazarus had been laid, and he told the men to open it.

Now, Lazarus had been dead for four days, but Jesus prayed and gave thanks to God. Then he said loudly, "Lazarus, come out!"

Everyone watched in silent wonder as a figure emerged from the dark cave, his hands and feet wrapped with strips of linen, and a cloth around his face. It was Lazarus, and he was alive!

THE HUMBLE WILL BECOME IMPORTANT

Luke 18

On another occasion, Jesus looked around at his followers. Some among them thought very well of themselves and so Jesus told this story: "Two men went into the temple to pray. One was a Pharisee, who always paid great attention to the letter of the law, while the other was a despised tax collector. In the temple, the Pharisee stood by himself and prayed: 'God, I thank you that I am not like other people – robbers, criminals, adulterers – or even like this tax collector. I fast twice a week and give a tenth of all I get!' He thought he was very good and far better than everyone else!

"But the tax collector stood humbly at a distance. He would not even look up to heaven, but beat his breast and said, 'God, have mercy on me, for I am nothing but a miserable sinner.'"

Jesus looked around at those who were listening. "It wasn't the self-important Pharisee who earned God's love and forgiveness that day: it was the humble tax collector. For all those who show off and think themselves important will be humbled, and those who humble themselves will become important."

THE RICH RULER

Matthew 19; Mark 10; Luke 18

Once, a rich ruler came to ask Jesus what he must do to inherit eternal life. Jesus told him that he must keep all the commandments that Moses had been given, and the ruler replied, "All these I have kept since I was a boy."

Jesus looked at him. "You still lack one thing. Sell everything you have and give to the poor, and you will have treasure in heaven. Then come and follow me."

When he heard this, the ruler was sad, for he was wealthy. "How hard it is for the rich to enter the kingdom of God!" Jesus said. "In fact, it is easier for a camel to go through the eye of a needle than for someone who is rich to enter God's kingdom."

But he told his disciples who had left all they had to follow him, "You can be sure that everyone who has left behind their home or their loved ones for my sake will be given so much more in return, as well as eternal life."

THE LAST WILL BE FIRST
Matthew 20

Jesus told a parable: "The kingdom of heaven is like the vineyard owner who went out one morning to hire workers. He agreed to pay them a certain sum of money for the day and set them to work. Later on, he went back to the marketplace, and hired more men and told them he'd pay them whatever was right. He did the same thing at lunchtime and in the afternoon, and once more, at about five. When evening came, he told his foreman to pay the workers, beginning with the last ones hired.

"The workers who were hired late received the same amount that had been promised to the first workers. So when those came who were hired first, they expected to receive more, and when they didn't, they began to grumble. 'These worked only one hour,' complained one, 'and you have given them the same as those of us who worked all day long, in the blazing heat!'

"The owner answered, 'I am not being unfair. Didn't you agree to work for this amount? I want to give the one hired last the same as you. Don't I have the right to do what I want with my own money? Or are you annoyed because I am generous?'

"So the last will be first, and the first will be last."

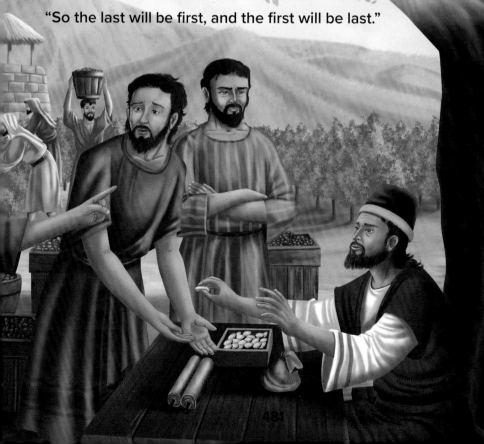

WISE AND FOOLISH GIRLS
Matthew 25

Jesus tried to make his followers understand that they must be ready at all times for his return, for they would never know when it might happen. He told them a story: "Once ten girls were waiting to join a wedding feast. Five were foolish and, while they brought lamps, they had no spare oil. The other five were sensible, and brought extra oil. It was late and the girls fell asleep, for the bridegroom was long in coming.

"Suddenly, at midnight, a cry rang out, for the bridegroom was coming. Excitedly, the girls went to light their lamps, but those of the foolish girls began to flicker, for their oil had run out. They begged for more oil, but the wise girls replied, 'No, for there is not enough for all of us. You will have to go and buy some more!' and they went off to join the bridegroom and went in with him to the feast.

"By the time the foolish girls returned with lighted lamps, the door was shut, and though they knocked loudly, they were told, 'You are too late. I don't know who you are!'"

Jesus told his disciples, "Always be ready, because you do not know the day or the hour of my return!"

BLIND BARTIMAEUS
Matthew 20; Mark 10; Luke 18

Jesus was passing through Jericho on his way to Jerusalem. Blind Bartimaeus was begging by the roadside when he heard a great commotion around him. When he learnt that it was Jesus of Nazareth, of whom he had heard so many wonderful things, he struggled to his feet, and called out, "Jesus, Son of David, have mercy on me!"

People shushed him, but he kept calling. Jesus heard him and stopped by the roadside. "What do you want me to do for you?" he asked gently.

Bartimaeus fell to his knees. "Lord, I want to see!" he begged.

"Receive your sight," said Jesus. "Your faith has healed you." Immediately Bartimaeus' eyes were cleared and he could see everything around him! Instantly, he jumped up and followed Jesus, praising God. When all the people saw it, they also praised God.

ZACCHAEUS IN THE TREE
Luke 19

The streets of Jericho were lined with people eager to catch a glimpse of Jesus. Among them was a tax collector called Zacchaeus. Everyone hated tax collectors and believed that they stole some of the taxes to line their own pockets, so no one would make way for him, and he was too short to see over the crowd. He was feeling frustrated. Then he had a great idea: he would climb a tree! From its branches, he could see the procession as it made its way towards him.

He almost fell off the branch when Jesus stopped right below, and said, "Zacchaeus, come down now. I must stay at your house today." He scrambled down and bowed before Jesus, as the crowd muttered angrily about Jesus visiting a sinner!

But Zacchaeus was already a changed man. He said to Jesus, "Lord! I'm going to give half of everything I have to the poor, and if I have cheated anybody out of anything, I will pay back four times the amount!"

Then Jesus turned to the crowd and said, "It is lost people like Zacchaeus that I came to save. Today he has found salvation!"

THE EXPENSIVE PERFUME
Matthew 26; Mark 14; John 12

One evening, shortly before Passover, Jesus was dining with his disciples and friends in Bethany. Mary came up to him, carrying an expensive jar of perfume. Kneeling before him, she carefully poured the perfume on his feet, using her own hair to wipe them. The whole house was filled with the wonderful fragrance.

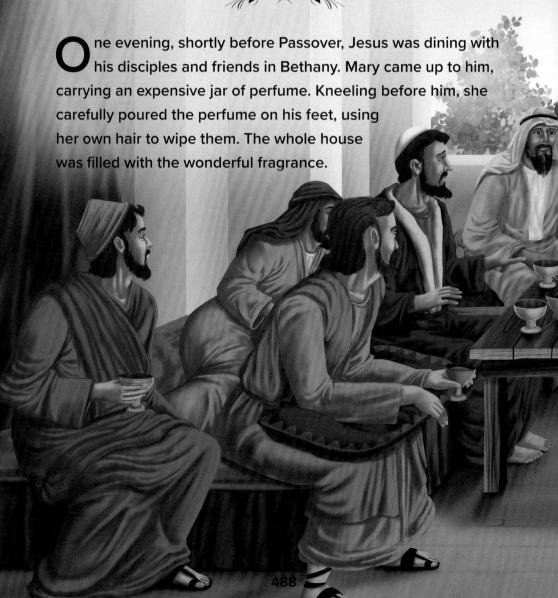

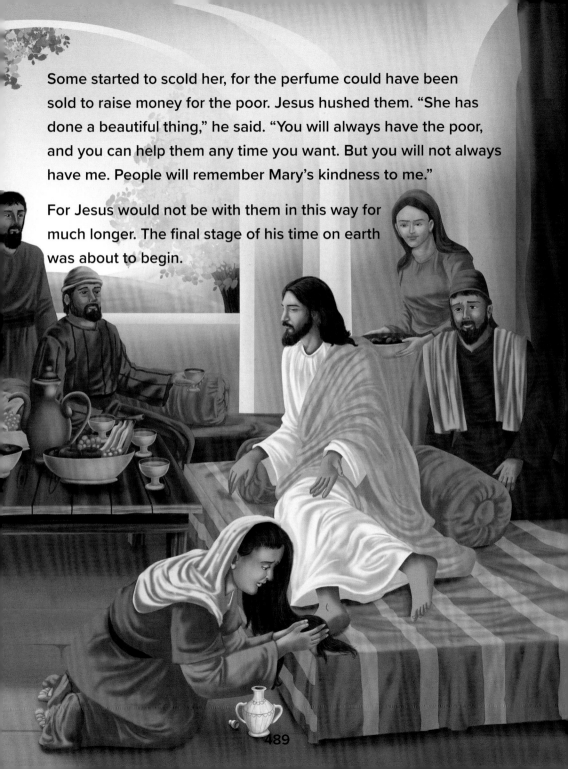

Some started to scold her, for the perfume could have been sold to raise money for the poor. Jesus hushed them. "She has done a beautiful thing," he said. "You will always have the poor, and you can help them any time you want. But you will not always have me. People will remember Mary's kindness to me."

For Jesus would not be with them in this way for much longer. The final stage of his time on earth was about to begin.

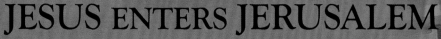

JESUS ENTERS JERUSALEM

Matthew 21; Mark 11; Luke 19; John 12

Jerusalem was packed. It was the week of the Passover festival, and everyone had gathered to celebrate. It was also time for Jesus to start the last stage of his earthly life.

Jesus entered Jerusalem riding a humble donkey. Some of his followers threw their cloaks or large palm leaves on the dusty ground before him, and he was met by an enormous crowd, for many had heard of the miracles he had performed. The religious leaders might fear and hate Jesus, but many of the people truly saw him as their King, and they tried to give him a king's welcome.

His followers cried out, "Hosanna to the Son of David! Blessed is the king who comes in the name of the Lord!"

But Jesus was sad, for he knew that in a very short time these people cheering him would turn against him.

TROUBLE IN THE TEMPLE
Matthew 21; Mark 11; Luke 19

The first thing Jesus did in Jerusalem was to visit his Father's temple. He was appalled to find that all the greedy, cheating people that he had thrown out before, were back again, trying to make money out of the poor people who came to make sacrifices to God. He looked around in anger, shouting, "No! God said that this temple was to be a place where people from all nations could come to pray to him. But you have made it a den of robbers!" and with these words he tore through the temple, throwing everyone out who shouldn't be there.

When he had finished and the temple was once again calm and tranquil, the poor people, the beggars and the sick began to find their way back in, and came to Jesus to be healed and to feel better. Children danced for joy around him, and everyone was happy – apart from the Pharisees, who plotted to get rid of him.

BY WHOSE AUTHORITY?

Matthew 21; Luke 20

Each day Jesus would go to the temple to teach his followers and to offer comfort and healing to those in need of it. The priests, the teachers of the law, and the elders were not happy about this.

"Who gave you authority to do these things?" they asked him, and Jesus replied, "I will ask you one question. If you can answer me, then I will tell you by what authority I am doing these things. Tell me, was John's baptism from heaven, or of human origin?"

The priests and elders didn't know how to answer. If they said it was from heaven, then he would ask why they didn't believe him, but if they said it was of human origin, then the people would be cross with them, for they truly believed that John was a prophet. In the end, they mumbled, "We don't know."

Jesus said, "Then I will not tell you by what authority I am doing these things."

495

THE WICKED TENANTS
Matthew 21; Mark 12; Luke 20

Jesus told a parable: "Once a man planted a vineyard, rented it to some farmers and then went away. At harvest time he sent a servant to collect his share of the fruit. But the tenants beat the servant and sent him away with nothing. He sent another servant, but again they beat him and sent him away empty-handed. He sent a third, and that one was killed!

"In the end, he decided to send his beloved son. 'Surely they will respect *him*,' he said to himself.

"But when the tenants saw him coming, they plotted amongst themselves. 'This is the heir,' they said. 'If we get rid of him then we will become the new owners!' and they threw him out of the vineyard and killed him."

Jesus looked at the priests and Pharisees who were listening. "What do you think the owner of the vineyard will do to the tenants when he finds out?"

"He will kill them and give the vineyard to others who will give him his rightful share," they replied, but when they realised that Jesus had been talking about *them*, they felt tricked and angry!

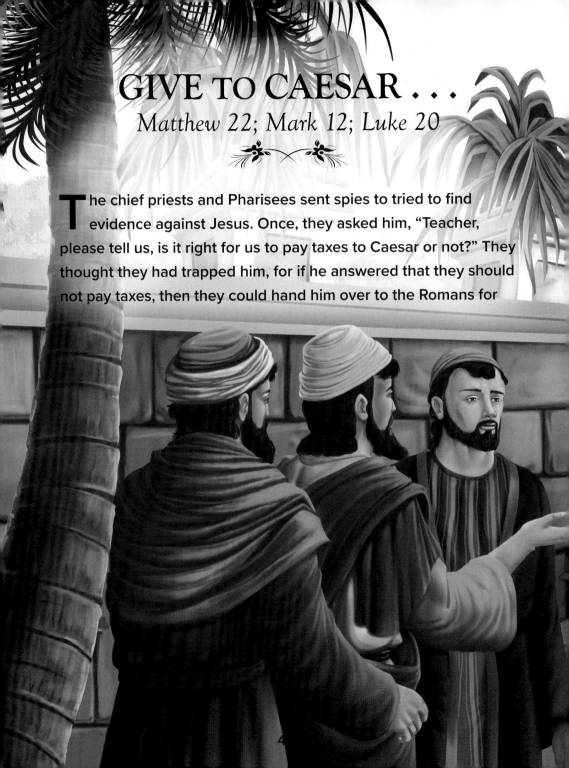

GIVE TO CAESAR . . .
Matthew 22; Mark 12; Luke 20

The chief priests and Pharisees sent spies to tried to find evidence against Jesus. Once, they asked him, "Teacher, please tell us, is it right for us to pay taxes to Caesar or not?" They thought they had trapped him, for if he answered that they should not pay taxes, then they could hand him over to the Romans for rebellion, but if he answered that they should pay taxes, then he would become unpopular with the people.

But Jesus saw through their tricks. "Show me a denarius*," he said, and when someone handed a coin to him, he asked, "Tell me, whose head is on that coin and whose inscription?" and the spies replied that it was Caesar's.

Then he said to them, "Then give back to Caesar what is Caesar's, and to God what is God's." The spies were silent.

* A Roman coin

THE WIDOW'S OFFERING

Mark 12; Luke 21

Jesus was sitting in the temple, watching people put money in the collection boxes as offerings to God. Many rich people put in lots of clinking coins, making sure everybody knew how good they were being! Then along came a poor widow, her young children in threadbare clothes and bare feet. She put in two small copper coins. Together, they were worth less than a penny!

Jesus turned to his disciples. "Do you see that poor widow?" he asked. "The truth is, she gave far more than anyone else here today." The disciples looked puzzled. Surely her coins had been almost worthless!

Jesus tried to make them understand: "All those rich people had so much money that it was easy for them to give huge offerings – they still had plenty left. But that poor widow gave everything she had to give. She clearly loves God with all her heart, and trusts him to look after her, for she gave him everything she had."

501

BE READY!

Matthew 24; Mark 13; Luke 21; John 12

As Jesus was leaving the temple, some of his disciples stopped to admire the building. "These buildings may well look impressive," Jesus told them, "but I tell you that not one stone will be left standing; they will all be thrown down!"

They asked him later when that time would come, and what sign would there be. "You must beware," Jesus answered. "There will be many false prophets trying to deceive you. There will be wars, earthquakes and famines. You must be on your guard.

"The gospel must be preached throughout the world. You will be persecuted and hated, but stand firm to the end and you will be saved. When I do come, you must be ready. Just like the servants who have been left to look after their master's house when he is away, you must keep watch. For you do not know when the master will come back — it could be early in the morning, late at night, or anytime at all. Don't let him find you sleeping when he does return!"

BETRAYAL

Matthew 26; Mark 14; Luke 22

Jesus knew that the Pharisees and those who hated and feared him were waiting for any opportunity to arrest him. He spent the days in Jerusalem in the temple, but each night he returned to Bethany to sleep. Yet even amongst his dearest friends there was one who would be his enemy.

Judas Iscariot, the disciple in charge of the money, was dishonest. He kept some for himself instead of giving it to those who needed it.

His greed made him do a very bad thing. Judas went to the chief priests in secret and asked them how much they would give him if he delivered Jesus into their hands.

The priests couldn't believe their ears! They knew that Judas was one of Jesus' closest, most trusted friends. They offered him thirty pieces of silver . . . and Judas accepted! From then on, Judas was simply waiting for the opportunity to hand Jesus over.

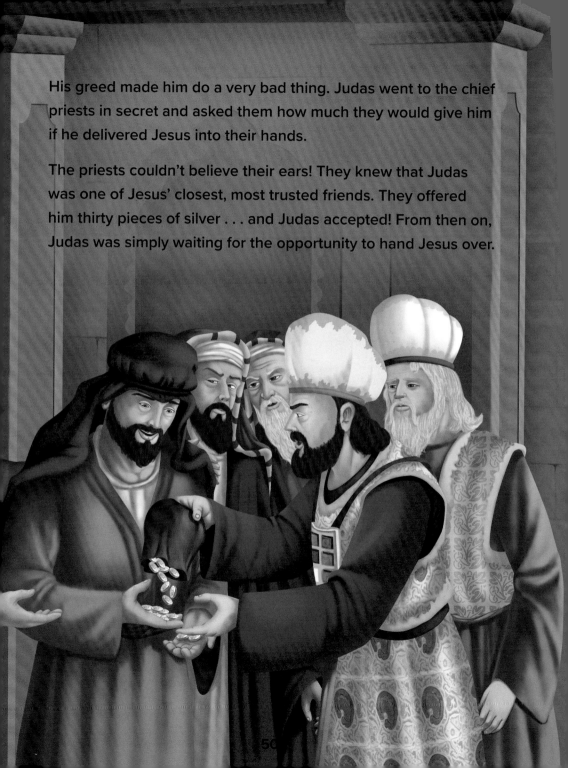

LIKE A SERVANT
John 13

It was nearly time for the Passover feast, and a kind man had set aside a room for the disciples to prepare for it. That night, when they were eating, Jesus left the table, wrapped a towel around his waist, filled a basin with water and then, kneeling on the floor, began to wash and dry the disciples' feet like a servant.

The disciples were speechless, but when he knelt before Peter, the disciple protested, "Lord, you mustn't wash my feet!"

Jesus replied gently, "You do not understand what I am doing, but later it will be clear to you. Unless I wash you, you won't really belong to me," to which Peter begged him to wash his hands and head too! But Jesus answered, "If you have bathed then you only need to wash your feet; your body is clean."

Jesus had washed their feet like a servant, so that they could learn to do the same for one another.

THE LORD'S SUPPER
Matthew 26; Mark 14; Luke 22; John 13

Jesus knew he would soon have to leave his friends. He was sad and troubled. "Soon one of you will betray me," he said sorrowfully. The disciples looked at one another in shock. Who could he possibly mean?

"The one who dips his bread with mine is the one," said Jesus, and when Judas Iscariot dipped his bread into the same bowl, Jesus said softly, "Go and do what you have to do." Judas left then. But the others didn't understand.

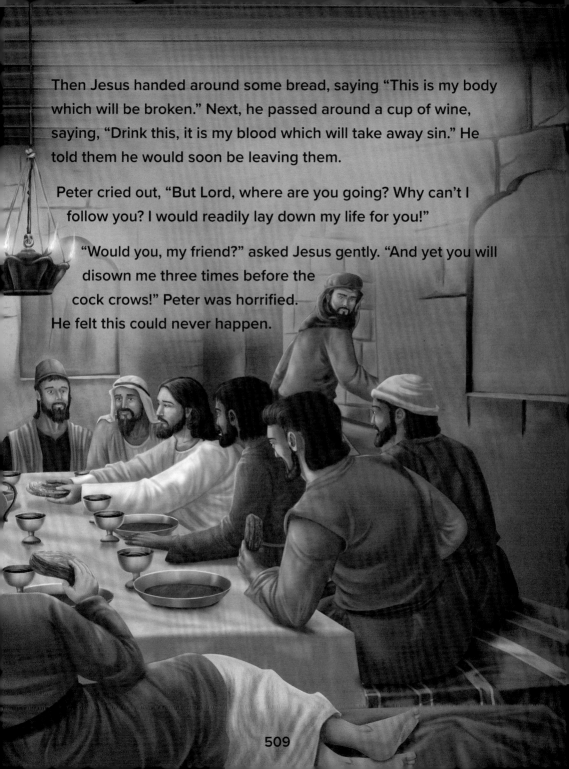

Then Jesus handed around some bread, saying "This is my body which will be broken." Next, he passed around a cup of wine, saying, "Drink this, it is my blood which will take away sin." He told them he would soon be leaving them.

Peter cried out, "But Lord, where are you going? Why can't I follow you? I would readily lay down my life for you!"

"Would you, my friend?" asked Jesus gently. "And yet you will disown me three times before the cock crows!" Peter was horrified. He felt this could never happen.

THE WAY TO THE FATHER

John 14-15

Jesus tried to comfort the disciples, saying that he was going ahead to prepare a place for them in his Father's house, and that they would know how to find their way there. When they asked how, he replied, "I am the way and the truth and the life. The only way to the Father is through believing in me. If you really know me, you will know my Father as well.

"I am the vine, and my Father is the gardener. He will cut off branches that bear no fruit, but look after those that do. You are the branches, and will bear fruit, so long as you remain in me.

"As the Father has loved me, so have I loved you. And I give you this command: love one another, just as I have loved each of you, and everyone will know that you are my disciples. There is no greater love than to lay down one's life for one's friends.

"And remember that if the world seems to hate you, it hated me first. It is because you don't belong to it that it will hate you!"

A NIGHT OF PRAYER
Matthew 26; Mark 14; Luke 22; John 17

Jesus and the disciples left the city to go to a quiet garden called Gethsemane. Jesus prayed to his Father to look after his disciples, and for all those who would come to believe in him because of the message they would spread throughout the world.

Then Jesus went to one side, but he took Peter, James and John with him, asking them to keep him company. He went a little way away from them to pray in private.

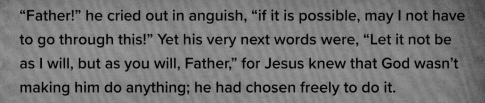

"Father!" he cried out in anguish, "if it is possible, may I not have to go through this!" Yet his very next words were, "Let it not be as I will, but as you will, Father," for Jesus knew that God wasn't making him do anything; he had chosen freely to do it.

When he returned to his friends, they were sleeping. "Couldn't you men keep watch with me for just one hour?" he sighed. He went again to talk to his Father, but when he returned, the disciples were fast asleep again. This happened once more, and this time when he woke them, he said, "The hour has come. You need to get up, for the one who has betrayed me is here!"

BETRAYED WITH A KISS

Matthew 26; Mark 14; Luke 22; John 18

A crowd of people burst into the garden, many armed with weapons. At the head of them was Judas Iscariot. He had told the chief priests that he would kiss Jesus so that they would know whom to arrest, and as Judas approached him, Jesus said sadly, "Oh Judas, would you betray the Son of Man with a kiss?"

Peter struck out with his sword, but Jesus told him to put his sword away, and he allowed the soldiers to arrest him. "I am the one you have come to find," he said quietly. "Let these others go. You had no need to come here with swords and clubs. You could easily have taken me when I was in the temple courts."

When the disciples realised that Jesus was going to allow himself to be taken prisoner, they fled in fear and despair.

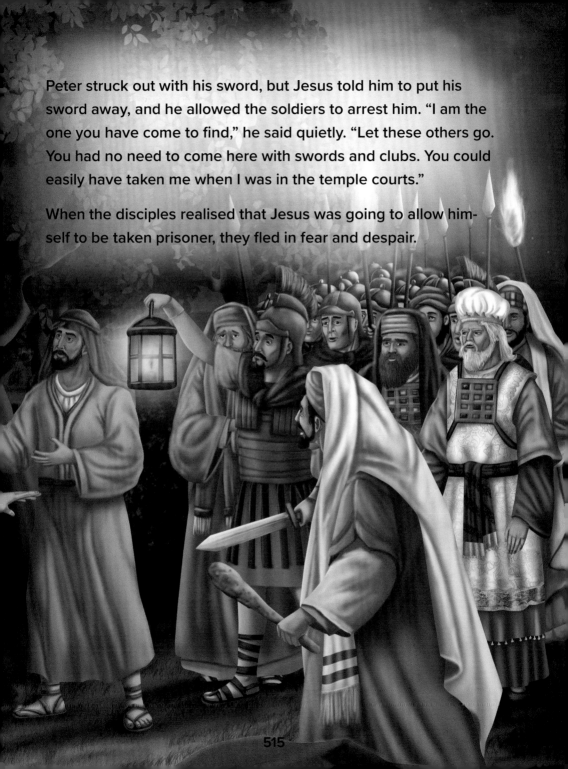

A COCK CROWS

Matthew 26; Mark 14; Luke 22; John 18

When the soldiers took Jesus to be questioned, Peter followed them to the courtyard of the high priest, where he waited outside miserably, along with the guards warming themselves at the fire. As one of the servant girls was walking by, she caught sight of Peter by the fire. "Weren't you with Jesus of Nazareth?" she asked him. "I'm sure I saw you with him."

"No, you've got the wrong man!" Peter hissed quietly, hoping no one else had heard, for he feared what would happen if they believed he was one of Jesus' disciples.

The girl shrugged and walked away, but on her way back, she said to one of the guards, "Don't you think he looks like one of Jesus' followers?"

"I told you, I don't have anything to do with him!" panicked Peter.

Now the other guards were looking at him. "You must be one of them," said one. "I can tell from your accent you're from Galilee."

"I swear I've never even met him!" cried Peter, his heart racing. At that very moment, a cock crowed, and Peter remembered what Jesus had said, and he broke down and wept in dismay.

PASSED AROUND

Matthew 27; Mark 15; Luke 23; John 18

The priests and Pharisees spent the night questioning Jesus. They asked him if he was the Messiah, the Son of God, and Jesus replied, "You have said so. But from now on you will see the Son of Man sitting at the right hand of God."

They were furious, but only the Roman governor, Pontius Pilate, could order his death. So they dragged him before Pilate, but

although Pilate asked Jesus many questions, he could find no reason to put him to death. "But he's a troublemaker!" the priests complained. "He started in Galilee and made his way here!"

When Pilate realised that Jesus came from Galilee, he saw a way of getting rid of the problem, for Herod was in charge of that area. So Jesus was taken before Herod. But however many questions Herod asked, Jesus remained grave and silent. In the end, Herod grew tired of his silence. Then he and his soldiers made fun of Jesus, before sending him back to Pilate.

PILATE WASHES HIS HANDS

Matthew 27; Mark 15; Luke 23; John 18

Pilate was under pressure to order the execution of Jesus, but there was one possible way out. During Passover it was the custom to release one prisoner. At that time, there was a man named Barabbas in prison for rebellion and murder. Pilate called the priests and the people before him and asked who they wanted him to release, and the crowd answered, "Barabbas!" for they had been told to say this.

"What shall I do with the one you call King of the Jews?" Pilate asked them.

"Crucify him!" roared the crowd.

"But why?" continued Pilate. "For what crime?" but the crowd only shouted all the louder.

Pilate did not want to order the execution – but neither did he want a riot! He sent for a bowl of water and washed his hands in it, to show that he took no responsibility for Jesus' death. Then he released Barabbas, and had Jesus handed over to be crucified.

MOCKED

Matthew 27; Mark 15; Luke 23; John 19

Jesus was taken away by the soldiers. "Since you are the King of the Jews, let's dress you for the occasion!" they mocked, and they dressed him in a purple robe, the colour worn by kings, and put a crown of thorny branches upon his head. Then they beat him, and spat in his face, before putting him back in his own clothes and leading him through the streets towards Golgotha, the place where he was to be crucified.

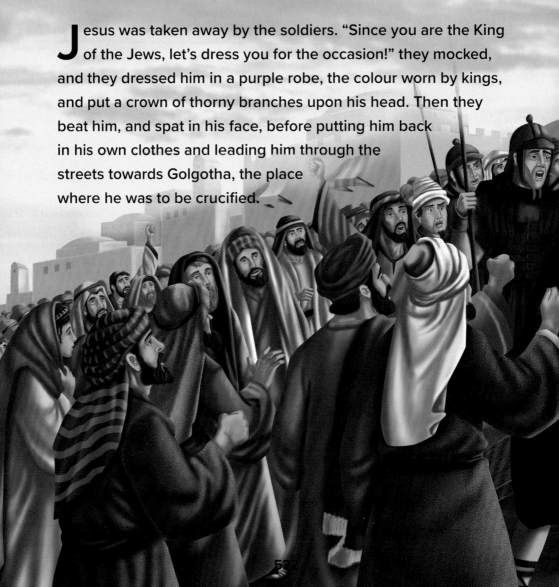

They made him carry the wooden cross on his back, but it was large and heavy, and Jesus had been dreadfully beaten. When he could do it no longer, they snatched someone from out of the crowd to carry it for him. And so the dreadful procession made its way out of the city to the hill of Golgotha.

THE CRUCIFIXION
Matthew 27; Mark 15; Luke 23; John 19

Soldiers nailed his hands and feet to the cross and placed above his head a sign saying, 'JESUS OF NAZARETH, KING OF THE JEWS'. As they raised the cross, Jesus cried, "Father, forgive them. They don't know what they are doing."

Two thieves were crucified beside him. The first sneered at him, but the other said, "Be quiet! We deserve our punishment, but this man has done nothing wrong." Then he turned to Jesus and said, "Please remember me when you come into your kingdom," and Jesus promised he would be with him that day in Paradise.

The guards drew lots to see who would win Jesus' clothes, while the priests and Pharisees taunted him. "If you come down from the cross now, we'll believe in you!" they mocked.

THE DEATH OF JESUS

Matthew 27; Mark 15; Luke 23; John 19

At midday, a shadow passed across the sun and darkness fell over the land for three long hours. At three o'clock in the afternoon, Jesus cried out in a loud voice, "My God, why have you forsaken me?" Then he gave a great cry, "It is finished!" and with these words, he gave up his spirit.

At that moment the earth shook, and the curtain in the holy temple was torn from top to bottom. When the Roman soldiers felt the ground move beneath their feet and saw how Jesus passed away, they were deeply shaken. "Surely he was the Son of God!" whispered one in amazement.

526

527

THE BURIAL

Matthew 27; Mark 15; Luke 23; John 19

Because the next day was to be a special Sabbath, the Jewish leaders did not want the bodies left on the crosses, and so they asked Pilate to have them taken down. A man named Joseph of Arimathea asked permission to take Jesus' body away, and so Jesus' friends carefully wrapped the body in linen and spices, and then placed it in a tomb that Joseph had had built for himself. Then they rolled a large stone in front of the entrance to the tomb, and left sadly.

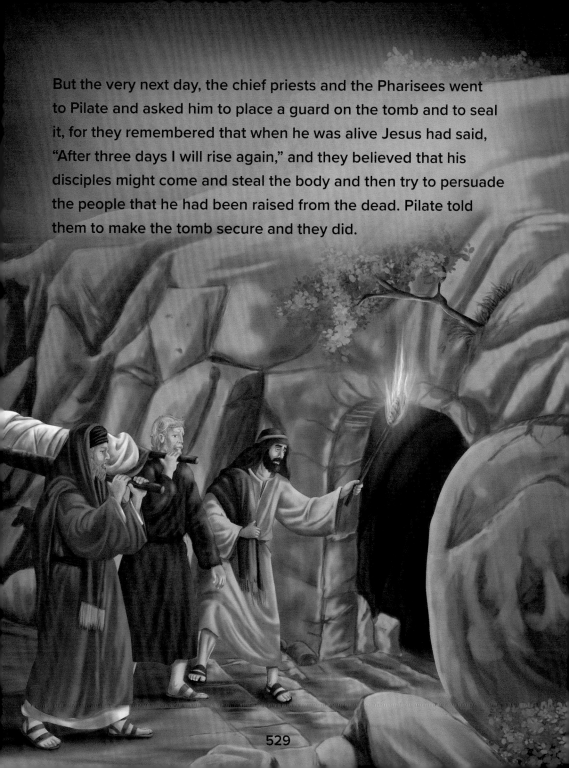

But the very next day, the chief priests and the Pharisees went to Pilate and asked him to place a guard on the tomb and to seal it, for they remembered that when he was alive Jesus had said, "After three days I will rise again," and they believed that his disciples might come and steal the body and then try to persuade the people that he had been raised from the dead. Pilate told them to make the tomb secure and they did.

THE EMPTY TOMB
Matthew 28; Mark 16; Luke 24; John 20

Early on the first day of the week, before the sun had fully risen, Mary Magdalene and some other women went to anoint the body. As they came near to the tomb, the earth shook, the guards were thrown to the ground, and the women saw that the stone had been rolled away from the entrance. And inside the tomb, shining brighter than the sun, was an angel!

The terrified women fell to their knees, but the angel said, "Why are you looking for the living among the dead? He is not here – he has risen! Don't you remember that he told you this would happen? Look and see, then go and tell his disciples that he will meet them in Galilee as he promised."

So the women hurried away to tell the disciples the news, afraid yet filled with joy.

ALIVE!

Matthew 28; Mark 16; John 20

Mary Magdalene stood outside the tomb. Peter and one of the other disciples had come, had seen the strips of linen and had left, in wonder and confusion. Now she was alone. She missed Jesus so much.

Just then she heard steps behind her, and a man asked, "Woman, why are you crying? Who are you looking for?"

Thinking this must be the gardener, she begged, "Sir, if you have moved him, please tell me where he is, and I will get him."

The man only spoke her name, "Mary," but instantly she spun around. She recognised that clear, gentle voice!

"Teacher!" she gasped, and reached out towards Jesus.

Jesus said, "Do not hold on to me, for I have not yet ascended to my Father. Go and tell the others!" So Mary rushed off with the amazing news that she had seen Jesus alive!

A STRANGER ON THE ROAD
Mark 16; Luke 24

That same day, two of Jesus' followers were travelling along the dusty road from Jerusalem to a village. They couldn't stop talking about the last couple of days. Soon another man approached them and asked what they were talking about.

"Where *have* you been?" they asked in amazement, and went on to tell him excitedly all about Jesus, the amazing things he'd taught, and the miracles he'd performed. Then, more sombrely, they told of his death and his disappearance from the tomb.

"How slow you are to believe what the prophets told you!" said the stranger. "Don't you see that the Messiah had to suffer these things and then enter his glory?" and he began to talk to them about everything that had been said in the Scriptures about Jesus. They were enthralled, for he made everything so clear.

At the village, they urged him to dine with them. As they were eating, he took some bread and, giving thanks for it, broke it into pieces and handed it to them. Suddenly, they realised who this stranger really was – Jesus himself! And then he vanished!

The friends hurried back to Jerusalem. They couldn't wait to tell the disciples the good news.

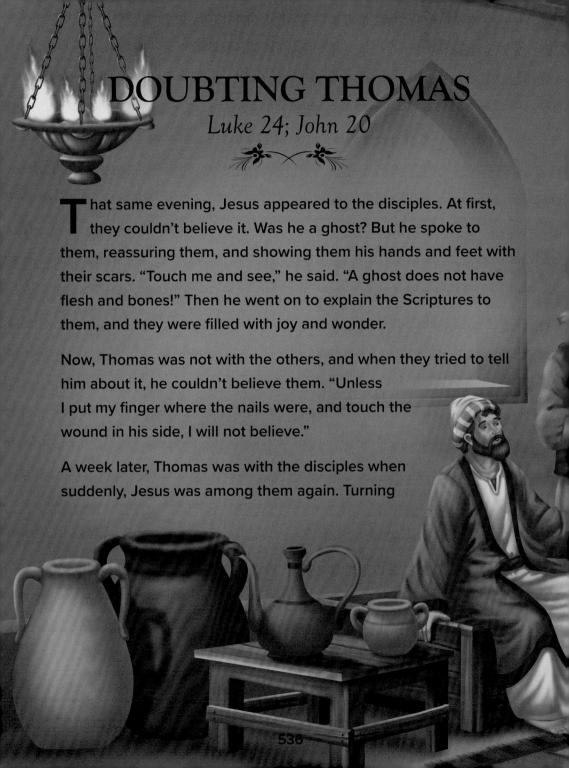

DOUBTING THOMAS

Luke 24; John 20

That same evening, Jesus appeared to the disciples. At first, they couldn't believe it. Was he a ghost? But he spoke to them, reassuring them, and showing them his hands and feet with their scars. "Touch me and see," he said. "A ghost does not have flesh and bones!" Then he went on to explain the Scriptures to them, and they were filled with joy and wonder.

Now, Thomas was not with the others, and when they tried to tell him about it, he couldn't believe them. "Unless I put my finger where the nails were, and touch the wound in his side, I will not believe."

A week later, Thomas was with the disciples when suddenly, Jesus was among them again. Turning to Thomas he said, "Put your finger in the wounds in my hands. Reach out and feel my side. Stop doubting and believe!"

Thomas fell to his knees, overcome with joy. Now he believed!

Jesus said, "You only believed because you saw me yourself. How blessed will people be who believe without even seeing!"

BREAKFAST WITH JESUS
John 21

S oon after this, some of the disciples went fishing, but in the morning came back empty-handed. As they approached the shore, a man called out, "Haven't you caught anything, my friends?" When they shook their heads, he told them to throw their net over the right-hand side of the boat. Shrugging their shoulders, they did so, and were amazed when the net was so full of fish that it was too heavy to haul in!

"It's Jesus!" cried John, and Peter leapt into the water! The others followed in the boat, and by the time

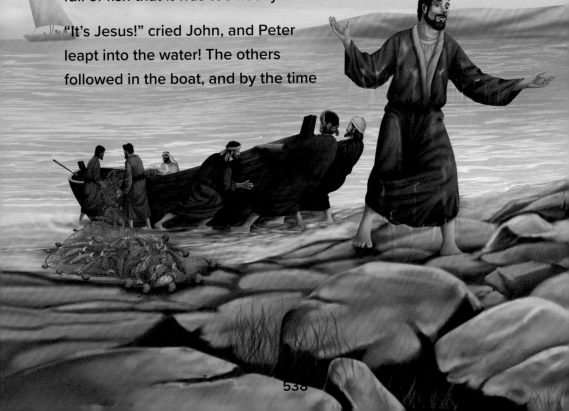

they landed, they saw that Jesus was cooking a meal for them. He told them to bring more fish to cook – they had plenty!

After they had eaten, Jesus turned to Peter and asked him if he loved him most. The disciple replied, "Yes, Lord," but was filled with shame, remembering how he had denied Jesus. Jesus asked the same question two more times. Then Peter said in a hurt voice, "Lord, you know everything; you know I love you."

Jesus said, "Then I have work for you. You will take care of my followers," for Peter would be an important leader in the years to come.

THE ASCENSION
Mark 16; Luke 24; Acts 1

Jesus and his friends were on a hillside outside Jerusalem. The time had come for Jesus to leave the world. In the time since his resurrection, he had made many things clearer to them, and had told them a little about what the future would hold.

Jesus turned to his disciples. "You must stay here in Jerusalem for now, and wait for the gift that my Father has promised you, for soon you will be baptised with the Holy Spirit. Then you must spread my message not only in Jerusalem, and Judah and Samaria, but in every country."

He held up his hands to bless them and then, before their eyes, he was taken up to heaven, and a cloud hid him from sight.

As they stood looking upwards in wonder, suddenly two men dressed in white stood beside them. "Why are you looking at the sky? Jesus has been taken from you into heaven, but he will come back again in the same way that he left!"

THE HOLY SPIRIT
Acts 2

I t was ten days since Jesus had been taken up to heaven. The twelve disciples (for they had chosen a man named Matthias to join them to take the place of Judas Iscariot) were gathered together when suddenly the house was filled with the sound of a mighty wind coming from heaven.

As they watched in wonder, tongues of fire seemed to rest on each person there. They were all filled with the Holy Spirit, and began to speak in different languages – languages they had never spoken before or studied!

Hearing all the commotion, a huge crowd gathered

outside. Great was their amazement when the disciples came out and began talking in different languages! "How can this be?" they exclaimed. "There are people here from Asia and Egypt, from Libya and Crete, from Rome and Arabia – how can we all be hearing them using our own languages to tell us about God?"

Some people only wanted to make fun of what was happening. "They've all been drinking too much wine!" they mocked.

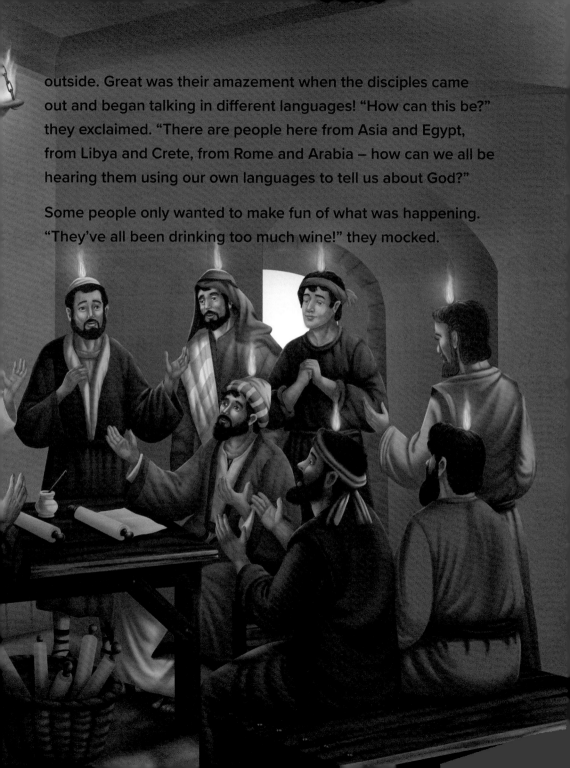

NEW RECRUITS

Acts 2

Then Peter stepped forward. "Listen!" he said loudly. "Of course we are not drunk – we have been filled with the Holy Spirit! Just a few weeks ago Jesus from Nazareth died on a cross. Yet any one of us can tell you that God has raised Jesus to life! This was all part of God's plan. You know that Jesus was sent to you by God, for he worked many miracles and showed you many signs. But God had planned that Jesus would be handed over to you, so you rejected him, and had him killed by evil men. Yet death could not hold him! God made this Jesus, whom you crucified, Lord and Messiah!"

The people looked worried and distraught. What had they done? And how could they make it better?

"If you really are sorry," Peter went on, "then repent. Be baptised in the name of Jesus Christ, and your sins will be forgiven. And you will receive the gift of the Holy Spirit. This promise is not just for you, but for your children, too, and for people who are far away – God's gift is for everyone!"

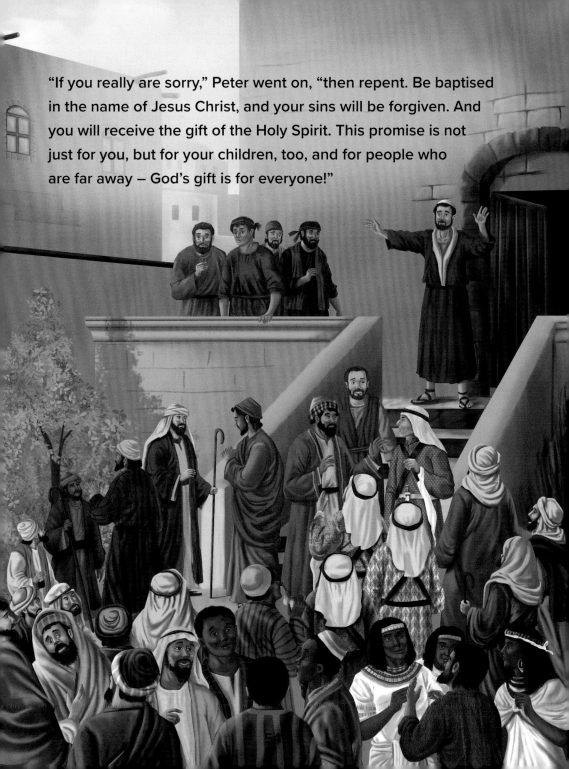

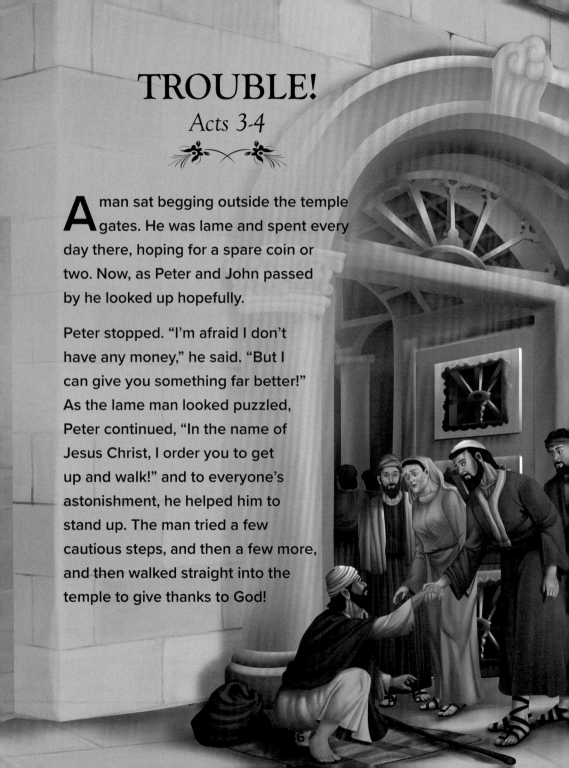

TROUBLE!

Acts 3-4

A man sat begging outside the temple gates. He was lame and spent every day there, hoping for a spare coin or two. Now, as Peter and John passed by he looked up hopefully.

Peter stopped. "I'm afraid I don't have any money," he said. "But I can give you something far better!" As the lame man looked puzzled, Peter continued, "In the name of Jesus Christ, I order you to get up and walk!" and to everyone's astonishment, he helped him to stand up. The man tried a few cautious steps, and then a few more, and then walked straight into the temple to give thanks to God!

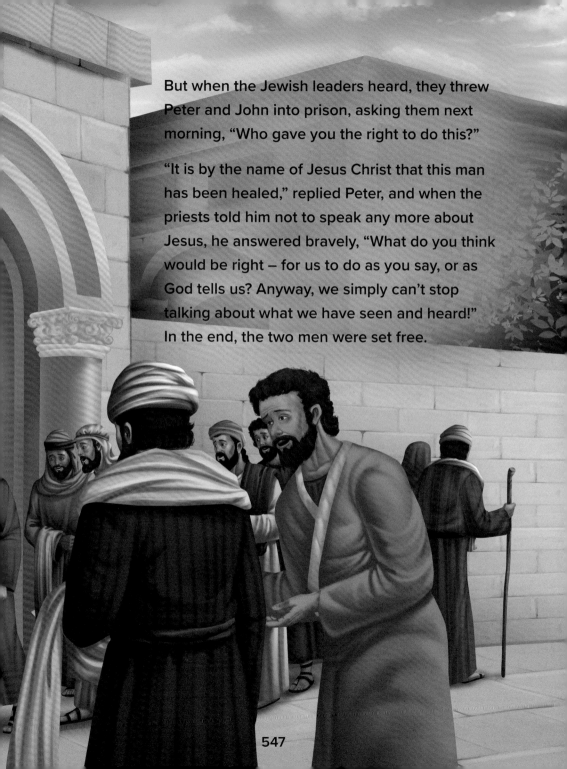

But when the Jewish leaders heard, they threw Peter and John into prison, asking them next morning, "Who gave you the right to do this?"

"It is by the name of Jesus Christ that this man has been healed," replied Peter, and when the priests told him not to speak any more about Jesus, he answered bravely, "What do you think would be right – for us to do as you say, or as God tells us? Anyway, we simply can't stop talking about what we have seen and heard!" In the end, the two men were set free.

FREED BY AN ANGEL
Acts 5

After this, the apostles would meet each day to talk to the people about Jesus and heal people in his name. Many people became Christians, and the Jewish leaders became very angry. They wanted people to listen to *them* – not the apostles!

One day, they threw the apostles in jail. But during the night an angel opened the doors of the jail and brought them out, telling them to go back to the temple courts and spread their message.

The priests sent for them the next morning, only to find the jail locked but the cell empty! When the apostles were found and brought before them, the priests accused them of disobeying their instructions. But Peter and the others bravely replied, "We must obey God rather than human beings!"

Some priests wanted to have them executed, but one said wisely, "If they are just stirring up rebellion, in the end it will all fizzle out. But if they really are from God, then you will not be able to stop them, and will find yourselves fighting against God!" So the apostles were released under strict instructions not to talk about Jesus any more – but of course they did!

LYING TO GOD
Acts 5

Many came to believe in Jesus. They pulled together, sharing what they had: some even sold houses or land so that the money could be used where it was most needed. But not every new believer was honest. Ananias and his wife Sapphira sold part of their land. They decided that they would keep some of the money for themselves, and give the rest to Peter – believing he would never know.

But when Ananias brought the money, Peter looked him in the eye and said, "Why have you lied and kept some back? The land was yours before you sold it, and the money was yours, too. Why lie? You haven't just lied to me, but to God himself!" and Ananias fell down dead on the spot!

When his wife came in unaware a bit later, Peter asked if she had given him all the money, and when she answered 'yes', he sighed. "Oh, Sapphira, how could you lie like that? Can't you hear that sound?" (as footsteps were heard outside the room.) "Those men have just buried your husband – and now they will carry your body away, too!" and at that, Sapphira fell down dead!

The story of the lying couple spread far and wide, and filled everyone with fear and awe.

STONED TO DEATH
Acts 6-7

Stephen was one of seven wise and good men in charge of sharing everything out amongst the new Christians. He was filled with the Holy Spirit and performed such wonders that soon he made enemies amongst those who hated Jesus. He was taken before the Jewish Council, where false witnesses gave evidence against him.

He faced his accusers bravely, his face shining brightly, like an angel's. "Throughout our history you have persecuted our prophets and refused to listen to them. Now you have betrayed and murdered God's greatest messenger. You have been given the law by angels, and yet have not obeyed it!" Filled with the Holy Spirit, he continued, "Look up! I can see heaven and the Son of Man standing at the right hand of God!"

This was too much for the Council. They dragged Stephen out of the city and began to stone him.

But even as they were stoning him, Stephen prayed, "Lord Jesus, receive my spirit." Then he fell on his knees and cried out, "Lord, do not hold this against them." With these words, he died.

PHILIP AND THE ETHIOPIAN

Acts 8

One of the onlookers was a man named Saul who hated the followers of Jesus. He wanted to put a stop to their preaching and believed he was doing God's will. Many Christians had to flee to avoid imprisonment, but they spread the word wherever they went.

Amongst them was Philip. Called by an angel to travel south from Jerusalem, Philip came across a powerful and wealthy man, the treasurer to the queen of Ethiopia, who was reading from the Book of Isaiah as he travelled in his fine carriage.

The Ethiopian was frustrated: he was reading Isaiah's words about how God's servant was led like a sheep to the slaughter, and wanted to know whom the prophet was talking about. Philip explained that it was written about Jesus, and went on to tell him all about God's Son.

The official wanted to become a Christian right away, and so Philip baptised him in a river by the roadside! God took Philip away to preach the gospel in many other places, but the Ethiopian carried on his way, filled with joy and happiness.

THE ROAD TO DAMASCUS
Acts 9

Meanwhile, Saul was still determined to stop Jesus' followers. Knowing that many had fled to the city of Damascus, he set off to arrest them. Suddenly, a blinding light from heaven flashed down. Saul fell to the ground, covering his eyes. Then he heard a voice say, "Saul, why do you keep on persecuting me?"

Saul began trembling. He thought he knew who was speaking, but he had to ask.

"I am Jesus," replied the voice. "Get up and go into the city, and you will be told what you must do."

Saul struggled to his feet, but when he opened his eyes, he couldn't see a thing! His guards had to take him by the hand and lead him into the city. There he stayed for three days without eating or drinking, spending his time in prayer.

A CHANGED MAN
Acts 9

God had great plans for Saul. He sent a Christian named Ananias to the house where he was staying. When he got there, Ananias laid his hands on Saul, saying, "Jesus sent me so that you might see again, and be filled with the Holy Spirit!" Straight away, it was as if scales had fallen from his eyes and Saul could see once more! He arose and was baptised.

Saul (or Paul – for he became known by the Roman version of his name) began to spread the good news about Jesus in Damascus and people were amazed, for he had once been the

greatest enemy of the Christians. But while his enemies became his friends, his old friends soon became his enemies, and he had to escape from the city in a large basket, lowered over the city walls under cover of night. He returned to Jerusalem and went on to become one of the greatest of all the apostles.

PETER AND TABITHA
Acts 9

Kind Tabitha (in Greek her name was Dorcas) lived in Joppa. She spent her days helping others, especially the poor, for whom she made clothes. Sadly, she became ill and passed away. The other Christians mourned her bitterly. They tenderly washed her body and placed it in a room to await burial.

Tabitha's friends sent a message to Peter, begging him to come. When he entered the room in which they had laid her body, Peter was met by a crowd of weeping widows. He soothed them, then

sent them from the room, and once he was alone, he fell to his knees and prayed with all his heart. Then he turned towards the dead woman, saying, "Tabitha, get up!"

At this, Tabitha opened her eyes and sat up! Peter led her down to her friends. Amazed and overjoyed, they could hardly believe their eyes! When the news spread, many more people came to believe in Jesus.

THE SHEET OF ANIMALS
Acts 10

One day, while praying on the roof under the hot sun, Peter fell asleep and had a strange dream. In his dream, there hung before him a huge white sheet being lowered from heaven by its corners. It was filled with all sorts of animals, reptiles and birds. Looking closely, he realised they were all creatures that Jews were forbidden to eat, for they were considered 'unclean.' Then he heard God's voice saying, "Get up, Peter. Kill and eat."

"Surely not, Lord!" Peter replied in horror. "I have never eaten anything unclean!"

The voice spoke again, "Do not call impure what God has made clean."

This happened three times, then the sheet was pulled back up to heaven.

A MESSAGE FOR EVERYONE

Acts 10

Peter awoke to the sound of knocking. Downstairs were three men sent by an officer named Cornelius. Although they were Romans, Cornelius and his family believed in God. God had told him to have Peter brought to his house. The men were Gentiles*, but Peter invited them in, for now he understood his vision, and the very next day he went with them to Cornelius' house, where Cornelius' friends and family had gathered.

* (non-Jews)

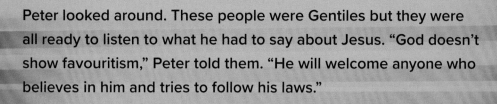

Peter looked around. These people were Gentiles but they were all ready to listen to what he had to say about Jesus. "God doesn't show favouritism," Peter told them. "He will welcome anyone who believes in him and tries to follow his laws."

While he was talking about Jesus, the Holy Spirit came. God had given the Gentiles the same gift that he had given to Jesus' special disciples. God's message is for all the people of the world, not just for Jews. That is what Peter's vision had meant!

ESCAPE FROM PRISON

Acts 12

Not long after this, Peter was thrown into prison. The night before his trial, he was sleeping between two soldiers, bound tightly with chains, while sentries guarded the entrance. Suddenly, light filled the cell and an angel appeared. "Quick, get up!" he said to Peter, and the chains fell from Peter's wrists. Peter followed the angel out of the cell and out of the prison, passing several

guards. Not one seemed to notice him! Soon they were at the gate. It opened, and then Peter found himself outside, walking along a street, and the angel had disappeared!

Peter finally realised he was not dreaming! He made his way to a house where his friends had gathered to pray, and knocked at the door. When the servant heard his voice, she was so excited that she ran to tell the others, without even opening the door! At first they didn't believe her, but Peter kept knocking, and when they finally opened the door, they were astonished and overjoyed.

In the morning, when no one could explain how Peter had escaped, Herod had the unfortunate guards executed.

THE
FIRST MISSIONARY JOURNEY

Acts 13-14

God told Paul and Barnabas to go on a
journey to spread the good news to people
who had not yet heard about Jesus. They went
first to Cyprus, where a false prophet spoke
against them, but Paul, filled with the Holy Spirit,

ASIA

Antioch

Iconium

PISIDIA

Lystra

Perga   PAMPHYLIA

Attalia

LYCIA

*Mediterranean
Sea*

denounced him, saying, "The hand of the Lord is against you and you will be struck blind!" Sure enough, in that instant, the prophet's eyes clouded over and he couldn't see a thing! The island governor was so amazed that he became a Christian.

Next, Paul and Barnabas sailed to the land we know as Turkey, going from town to town, preaching the good news. They went first to the synagogues, but if the Jews wouldn't listen, they taught the Gentiles. They made many friends – and many enemies! Sometimes they were thrown out, and sometimes stones were thrown after them! But each time, they would pick themselves up, and carry on with their mission.

GALATIA

Derbe

Tarsus

CILICIA

Antioch

Seleucia

SYRIA

Salamis

CYPRUS

Paphos

TAKEN FOR GODS

Acts 14

In Lystra, where few people knew of the one true God, Paul healed a lame man. The excited crowd believed that he and Barnabas were gods! The priest of Zeus brought bulls and wreaths to the city gates because he and the crowd wanted to offer sacrifices to the apostles! Barnabas and Paul had a hard job explaining that they were ordinary men and trying to tell them about God!

Soon after this, some Jews turned the people of Lystra against the apostles. They stoned Paul and left him for dead outside the city, but after the disciples had gathered around him, he got up and went back to preach as if nothing had happened.

After that, Paul and Barnabas visited the city of Derbe, before slowly making their way back to Antioch, stopping in towns along the way to encourage those they had already spoken to and to help them as they set up new churches.

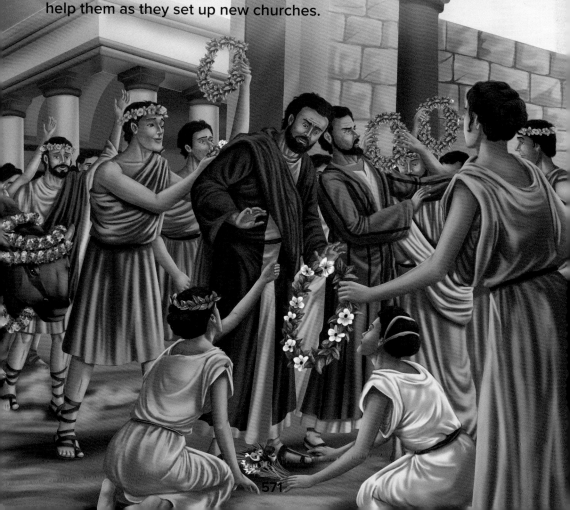

HEALING A SLAVE GIRL

Acts 16

Paul spent some time in Antioch, but was then off on his travels once again. This time, he took a man named Silas with him to Asia Minor. After they had passed through the land, strengthening the new churches, Paul had a strange dream of a man from Macedonia standing and begging him, "Come to Macedonia and help us!"

MACEDONIA

Amphipolis

Philippi

Apollonia

THRACE

Neapolis

Berea

Thessalonica

Troas

ASIA

AEGEAN SEA

LYDIA

ACHAIA

Ephesus

Corinth

Athens

Cenchreae

Mediterranean Sea

The very next day they got ready to leave for Macedonia, in modern Europe, where they were joined by a doctor named Luke. In the city of Philippi, they were followed around by a slave girl who was possessed by a spirit. She ranted and raved so much that, in the end, Paul commanded the spirit to leave her in the name of Jesus Christ.

Instantly the spirit left her, but her owners were angry for she was no longer able to foretell the future – and they had made a lot of money out of her predictions! They had Paul and Silas dragged before the city magistrates. The crowd joined in the attack, and Paul and Silas were whipped and beaten and thrown into prison, with their feet locked in stocks.

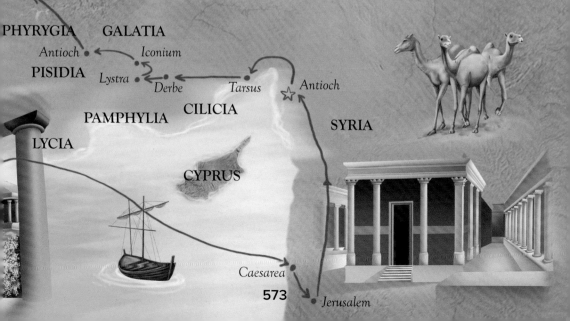

PHYRYGIA GALATIA

Antioch *Iconium*

PISIDIA *Lystra* *Derbe* *Tarsus* *Antioch*

CILICIA

PAMPHYLIA SYRIA

LYCIA

CYPRUS

Caesarea

573

Jerusalem

SINGING IN PRISON

Acts 16

I t was midnight. Paul and Silas were lying in the stocks. The chains were tight and the wood was heavy, but they did not despair. Instead, they were praying and singing hymns. The other prisoners could hardly believe their ears!

Suddenly a violent earthquake shook the prison, the cell doors flew open, and everyone's chains came loose! Fearing punishment

if his prisoners escaped, the jailer was about to kill himself, when Paul called out, "Don't harm yourself! We're still here!" The astonished jailer took Paul and Silas to his own house, where he and his family spent the whole night learning about Jesus. They became Christians that very night!

Paul and Silas returned to the prison and when officials came the next morning, Paul told them they were Roman citizens and had not been given a trial. The worried magistrates came to apologise, but also to ask them to leave.

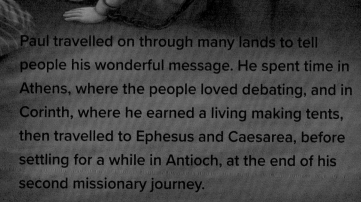

Paul travelled on through many lands to tell people his wonderful message. He spent time in Athens, where the people loved debating, and in Corinth, where he earned a living making tents, then travelled to Ephesus and Caesarea, before settling for a while in Antioch, at the end of his second missionary journey.

RIOT AT EPHESUS

Acts 19

Paul was in Ephesus, on the third of his missionary journeys, when trouble erupted. The people there worshipped the goddess Artemis and had built a wonderful temple in her honour. People came from afar to visit it, and the city was full of silversmiths selling silver images of the goddess.

But when Paul started preaching, many people became Christians and stopped buying the images. The silversmiths were furious and soon the whole city was in an uproar! The angry mob grabbed hold of two of Paul's friends and dragged them to the open-air theatre, where they shouted and argued until a city official managed to calm everybody down.

After this, Paul realised that it would be safer for everyone if he left the city, and so he set off to return to Jerusalem, first heading to Macedonia and then Greece.

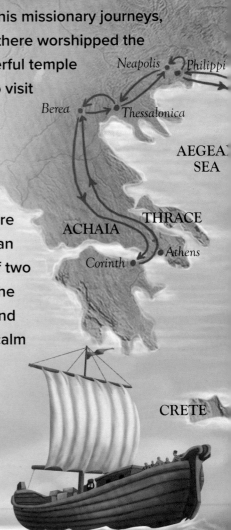

Neapolis

Philippi

Berea

Thessalonica

AEGEAN SEA

THRACE

ACHAIA

Athens

Corinth

CRETE

Troas

Assos

ASIA

Mytilene

PHRYGIA

Antioch

GALATIA

Iconium

Derbe

Tarsus

PISIDIA

Lystra

Ephesus

Trogyllium

Miletus

Perga

CILICIA

Antioch

Miletus

PAMPHYLIA

LYCIA

SYRIA

Patara

CYPRUS

Salamis

Mediterranean
Sea

Paphos

Tyre

Ptolemais

Caesarea

Jerusalem

577

ARABIA

THE GREAT FALL
Acts 20

Paul wanted to return to Jerusalem, to help the Jewish Christians there. On his way, he spent the night in a town called Troas. The Christians there were thrilled that Paul was among them. They crowded into an upstairs room to listen to him, and he talked until late into the night.

One of his listeners was a young man named Eutychus. He wanted to hear everything that Paul was saying, but he was dreadfully sleepy and could hardly stay awake. He was sitting by the window, hoping that the fresh air would keep him awake, but at last he could keep his eyes open no longer and dozed off – plummeting three floors down to the hard ground! When people realised what had happened, they rushed downstairs, only to find him dead. But Paul, coming behind them, knelt by the young man and gathered him in his arms. Turning to the crowd, he smiled, "Don't worry. He's alive!"

People could hardly believe what had happened, and were filled with joy at the miracle. They went back upstairs, and Paul carried on talking to them until daybreak!

"PLEASE DON'T GO!"
Acts 20

Paul's friends did not want him to go to Jerusalem. They all warned him that it would be very dangerous for him – they feared that he would be imprisoned there, and probably killed. "Please don't go!" they begged.

But Paul shook his head sadly. "Please don't try to change my mind with your tears. This is what I have to do. I am ready not only to be put in chains for Jesus, but to die for him."

Even though he knew in his heart that hardship and suffering were ahead of him, Paul would go where God wanted him to go. Before he boarded the ship that would carry him onwards, Paul knelt with his friends and prayed. They all wept as he sailed away. They knew that they would never see him again.

TROUBLE IN JERUSALEM

Acts 21-26

All too soon, trouble flared up in Jerusalem. Some Jews told lies about Paul when he was in the temple, and stirred the crowd up. He would have been killed there and then, had not the Roman governor of the city sent in soldiers. Paul tried to talk to the crowd, but they were too angry to listen, so the commander ordered his soldiers to take Paul to the Roman fort.

The commander sent him before the Jewish council so that they could work out what was going on, but the council only argued amongst themselves and he was sent back.

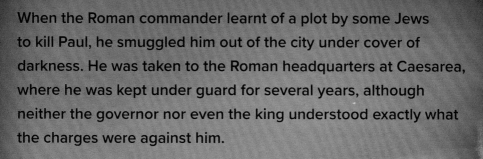

When the Roman commander learnt of a plot by some Jews to kill Paul, he smuggled him out of the city under cover of darkness. He was taken to the Roman headquarters at Caesarea, where he was kept under guard for several years, although neither the governor nor even the king understood exactly what the charges were against him.

In the end, Paul appealed to have his case heard by the Emperor himself, as was his right as a Roman citizen. At last, Paul was on his way to Rome.

SHIPWRECKED!

Acts 27

Paul was travelling to Rome aboard a ship. The Roman centurion Julius, who was in charge, took a liking to Paul and treated him kindly, but their voyage was troubled by bad weather. Paul tried to warn the captain that it would be dangerous to sail onwards, but the captain ignored his advice.

Soon they found themselves in the middle of a dreadful storm. For days the ship was at the mercy of the angry sea. Paul comforted the crew and the other passengers, for God had promised him that they would all reach land alive. Some of the sailors tried

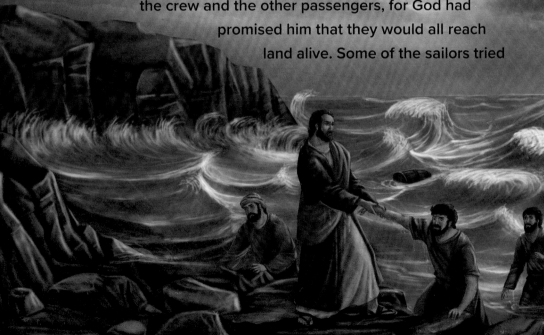

to leave in one of the lifeboats, but Paul told them that they would have to stay with the ship to be saved.

Everyone was excited when the coastline finally came into sight, but suddenly, the ship struck a sandbar. The bow stuck fast and the ship began to be broken to pieces by the surf!

Julius ordered everyone who could swim to make for land, and told those who could not swim to cling to pieces of the wreckage and float ashore. In this way, everyone reached land safely. Every last one of the two hundred and seventy-six people on board was saved, just as God had promised!

ROME AT LAST

Acts 28

Paul and his companions found themselves on the island of Malta. They were cold and wet, but they were alive! Some islanders came to help. They lit a huge fire to warm them. While Paul was putting some extra wood on the fire, a poisonous snake slithered out and fastened itself on his hand. Paul calmly shook

the snake off and carried on as if nothing had happened. The astonished islanders thought he must be a god!

After three months, they set sail once again for Rome. While he waited for his case to be heard, Paul was allowed to live by himself, with a soldier to guard him. Although he was not allowed out, he could have visitors, and so was able to carry on spreading the message to new people. He also wrote letters to the Christians he had met during his travels, to encourage and help them as they set up their churches. It is not known for sure how Paul died, but many people believe that he was executed while in Rome.

THE LOVE OF GOD

Romans 8, 12

Paul wrote to the believers in Rome before he went to the city, to introduce himself and to talk about their faith: "I believe that our present suffering is not worth comparing with the glory that will be revealed in us – and suffering itself produces perseverance, and so character and hope!

"If God is for us, who can be against us? He did not even spare his own Son, but gave him up for us all. If he did this, won't he freely give us all things? There is nothing that will ever be able to separate us from the love of God which is ours through Christ Jesus our Lord – not hardship, or persecution, or hunger, or poverty, or danger, or death."

He encouraged them to live good lives, filled with love and kindness: "Love must be sincere. Hate what is evil; cling to what is good. Love and respect one another, be joyful in hope, patient in suffering, faithful in prayer. Share what you have with those in need. Live in peace and don't think about retribution. Don't be overcome by evil, but overcome evil with good."

THE GREATEST OF THESE
1 Corinthians 12-13

Paul wrote to the people settling in Corinth: "Many of you have been given wonderful gifts by the Holy Spirit. Maybe you can speak in foreign languages, or prophesise, or teach, or heal. None of these is better than the others, so don't get big-headed! Is the eye more important than the ear, or the foot than the hand? No! Each has its part to play. Each is part of the whole body.

"If I could speak every single language in the world and even talk with angels, but didn't love others, I would be no more than a noisy gong. If I had the gift of prophecy, or knowledge, or such great faith that I could move mountains, it would mean nothing if I didn't have love. I could give all I owned to the poor and suffer great hardship, but it would be meaningless if I didn't feel love for the people I was doing it for.

"Love is patient and kind. It isn't jealous, boastful, proud or rude. It doesn't insist on having its own way, or become irritable, or seek revenge, or feel happy when someone else fails. Love protects, and trusts, and hopes. It is steady and true, and it never, ever gives up. Three things will last forever – faith, hope, and love – and the greatest of these is love."

THE THINGS OF HEAVEN
Galatians 2-5; Colossians 3

Paul was worried that many believers were going back to their old ways and thinking too much about rules and rituals, when the true path to God is through belief in Jesus. He wrote to the church in Galatia: "A person is made right with God by faith in Jesus Christ, not by obeying the law. If keeping the law was enough, there wouldn't have been any need for Christ to die!

You didn't receive the Holy Spirit by obeying the law of Moses –
but because you believed the message about Christ! So why are
you now trying to be perfect? Don't you understand? Christ took
upon himself the curse for our wrongdoing. He set us free! Make
sure you stay free, and don't become slaves to the law!"

He sent the same message to the believers in Colossus: "Don't
spend too much time thinking about all the old rules. Think about
the things of heaven, not the things of earth!"

PUT ON GOD'S ARMOUR

Ephesians 6; 2 Corinthians 1, 4-5

Paul told the Ephesians: "Be strong in the Lord. Our enemies aren't made of flesh and blood, so put on every piece of God's armour. Then you can stand firm, with the belt of truth buckled round your waist, and the breastplate of righteousness. Let your feet be shod with the readiness that comes from the gospel of peace, and take up the shield of faith. And take up the helmet of salvation and the sword of the Spirit, which is the word of God."

He told the Corinthians: "God comforts us in our troubles so we can comfort others. The more we suffer for Christ, the more God will comfort us through Christ. We are surrounded by troubles, but are not crushed. We will never give up! The troubles we face now are small, and will not last, for when we leave these earthly bodies, we will have a house in heaven, and an eternal body made for us by God himself!"

A GOOD FIGHT
2 Timothy 2, 4

Towards the end of his life, Paul wrote to one of his special friends, Timothy: "I am suffering and have been chained like a criminal, but the word of God cannot be chained. I am willing to endure for the sake of God's chosen people, so that they, too, may obtain the salvation that comes through Christ Jesus and brings eternal glory. Remind everyone of this saying:

"'If we die with him, we will also live with him.
If we endure hardship, we will reign with him.
If we deny him, he will deny us.
If we are unfaithful, he remains faithful,
for he cannot deny who he is.'

"As for me, my life has been an offering to God. The time of my death is near. I have fought a good fight, I have finished the race, and I have kept the faith. Now I look forward to my reward, which the Lord will give me on the day of his return — a reward not just for me but for all who eagerly await his coming!"

GOD IS LOVE

Hebrews 11-12; James 2; 1 Peter 4; 2 Peter 3; 1 John 4

Other inspiring letters form part of the New Testament. In Hebrews we're told: "Faith is the confidence that what we hope for will actually happen. Our ancestors had faith: Noah built a boat when everyone was laughing at him; Sarah believed she would have a child even though she was old; Moses took his people out of Egypt just because God told him to. Let yourself be filled with faith. Cast off the things that weigh you down, so you have the strength and endurance to run the race set before us!"

The apostle James went on to say, "What good is it to say you have faith but don't show it by your actions? Words are not enough – faith is not enough, unless it produces good deeds."

Peter wrote, "You face hardship and suffering – but don't despair! Instead, be glad, for these trials make you partners with Christ in his suffering. They will test your faith as fire tests and purifies gold, and remember that there is wonderful joy ahead! Don't be disheartened if it seems a long time in coming – God is being patient for he wants everyone to repent. But the day of the Lord will come unexpectedly, so be prepared!

The apostle John wrote, "God is love. He showed how much he loved us by sending his one and only Son into the world so that we might have eternal life through him. Since he loved us that much, let us make sure that we love one another, so that God can live in us and we can live in God. And as we live in God, our love will grow more perfect, and when the day of judgement comes we will not have to fear anything. Perfect love drives out all fear! We love one another because he loved us first."

JOHN'S AMAZING VISION
Revelation 1

The very last book of the Bible is Revelation. Many believe it was written by the disciple John. The author had an amazing vision to pass on: "On the Lord's day the Spirit took control of me, and I heard a loud voice, coming from behind me, saying, 'Write down what you see and send it to the seven churches.'

"When I turned, I saw seven golden lamp stands, and among them I saw a being like the Son of Man, dressed in a long robe, with a golden sash round his chest. His head and hair were white as snow, and his eyes were like blazing fire. In his right hand he held seven stars, and out of his mouth came a sharp double-edged sword. His face shone like the brightest sun.

"I fell at his feet, but he told me not to be afraid. 'I am the First and the Last,' he said. 'I was dead, and behold I am alive for ever and ever! And I hold the keys of death and Hades.'"

In John's vision, the seven lamp stands were the seven churches of Asia Minor, and the Lord wanted John to send a message to those churches, to correct and encourage them. But this was not all. He also sent him a vision of the future . . .

THE THRONE OF GOD
Revelation 4-5

John found himself before the Throne of God. A rainbow resembling an emerald encircled the throne, and it was surrounded by twenty-four other thrones, on which sat twenty-four elders, dressed in white, with crowns of gold.

From the throne came flashes of lightning and peals of thunder, and seven lamps blazed before it. Around it were four living creatures – one like a lion, one like an ox, one with a face like a man, and one like an eagle in flight – all covered with eyes. They each had six wings and chanted incessantly, 'Holy, holy, holy is the Lord God Almighty, who was, and is, and is to come!'

The one on the throne held a scroll covered with writing and sealed with seven seals. At first it seemed that no one could be found who was worthy to open it, but one of the elders declared

602

that the Lion of the tribe of Judah, the great descendant of David, could break the seals and open the scroll. Then John saw a Lamb standing in the centre of the throne, and the four beings and all the elders bowed down in praise, and were joined by a multitude of angels and all the creatures in heaven and earth.

THE END OF DAYS
Revelation 6-20

In John's vision, the seven seals were broken off one by one, and many dreadful things happened to the earth, but those who were faithful to Jesus were protected by the seal of God.

Then seven trumpets were sounded. Hail and fire rained down, the waters were poisoned and the world plunged into darkness. Locusts with thunderous wings covered the earth, tormenting all but those with God's seal. An army of horsemen released dreadful plagues of fire, smoke and brimstone upon the land. Then, when the seventh trumpet was blown, the temple of God opened in heaven, and the ark of his covenant could be seen. There was lightning, thunder, an earthquake and great hail.

John saw that a terrible time was to follow, but finally all that is evil will be destroyed and God's Kingdom will reign. After the Final Judgement, a new heaven and earth will replace the old.

"I AM COMING SOON!"
Revelation 21-22

John wrote: "Then I saw a new heaven and earth, and I saw the Holy City coming down out of heaven like a beautiful bride. I heard a loud voice speaking from the throne: 'Now God's home is with his people! He will live with them. They shall be his people, and he will be their God. There will be no more death, no more grief, or crying, or pain. He will make all things new! For he is the first and the last, the beginning and the end.'

"And I was shown the Holy City, shining with the glory of God. It had a great high wall with twelve gates and twelve angels in charge of them. Its temple is the Lord God Almighty and the Lamb. The city has no need of the sun or the moon, because the glory of God shines on it, and the Lamb is its lamp. The people of the world will walk by its light, and the gates will never be closed, because there will be no night there. But only those whose names are written in the Lamb's Book of Life will enter.

"'Listen!' says Jesus. 'I am coming soon!'"

Let it be so! Come, Lord Jesus, come soon!